IN INDIA

IN INDIA

SKETCHES OF INDIAN LIFE AND TRAVEL FROM LETTERS AND JOURNALS

MRS. MURRAY MITCHELL

GYAN

Published by

Gyan Publishing House
5, Ansari Road
Daryaganj, New Delhi-110002
Phone: 011-47034999, 9811692060
E-mail: books@gyanbooks.com

Distribution Network
gyanbooks.com
India, USA, Canada, UK, Australia

ISBN: 978-93-7133-034-3 (PB)
First Published, 1876

2nd Impression 2025

Printed at: Gyan Press, Delhi.

IN INDIA
Author Mrs. Murray Mitchell

IN INDIA

SKETCHES OF INDIAN LIFE AND TRAVEL FROM LETTERS AND JOURNALS.

IN INDIA

SKETCHES OF INDIAN LIFE AND TRAVEL FROM LETTERS AND JOURNALS.

By

MRS. MURRAY MITCHELL.

LONDON:
T. NELSON AND SONS, PATERNOSTER ROW;
EDINBURGH; AND NEW YORK.

1876.

To

OUR VENERABLE MISSIONARY CHIEF,

THE REV. ALEXANDER DUFF, D.D., LL.D.,

WHOSE LIFE HAS BEEN, AND IS, CONSECRATED TO THE WORK
OF GOD IN INDIA,

These Pages

ARE

AFFECTIONATELY DEDICATED.

PREFATORY NOTE.

HAVING acted as editor of this little work, I comply with my wife's request that I should write a short preface. I shall thus have an opportunity of explaining how much, or rather how little, I have done in my editorial capacity.

The chief merit of the book appears to me to be this,—it is throughout a woman's book about India. Many details are given, especially regarding domestic life among the Hindus, which only a woman could have supplied. We have not many books on India written by ladies; and, if I am not mistaken, there is a considerable amount of information in these pages which will not be found elsewhere.

With regard to the sentiments expressed by the writer, I have, in almost every case, allowed them to stand intact. Very generally I have agreed with them; and if, at any time, I have not done so, I have yet deemed them very natural when the matter was looked at from the writer's point of view. The language is sometimes strong, especially in describing the con-

I.

Outward Bound.

MARSEILLES, *December 12.*

I AM beginning to believe it at last. We are really once more off to India. Now that we are in the ship, and have arranged our cabin, and the sailors are busy hoisting the portmanteaus and mail-boxes on board, and the passengers, with the true Anglo-Indian look, are bustling about the deck, it is easier to believe that it is not all a dream. The direst confusion of course prevails, and the good ship *Poona* will not be ship-shape until we are fairly out. I have deposited myself and my little folding-chair—which my husband got me at the hotel this morning—in a comparatively quiet corner, while I try to make a beginning of "the full, true, and particular" account of everything you enjoined me to send you. But I am not going to describe the "overland route;" you must be familiar with every foot of it, as we have already traversed it six times.

Our journey had a very bleak beginning. We left London a sheet of ice; and from shore to shore *la belle France* was one beautiful expanse of unbroken, unblemished snow. My husband declared that I fairly gave myself up to misery; which I fear was too true. I was nearly annihilated by cold and fatigue, and withered up into a corner of the carriage in a very abject condition. It was rather comforting during that bitter journey to think of the sunshiny land to which we were so rapidly speeding.

As yet, however, there is nothing of the balmy south in the air. In truth, everything is chill and cheerless; and I find it just a little difficult not to "cast one longing, lingering look behind" to you in your pleasant homes, and to what was our own most pleasant home a few brief weeks ago, with no thought but that it would be ours for many a day and year to come. But God's thoughts are not as ours. Good soldiers of their queen and country are ever ready to go where duty calls; and shall not the soldiers of the King of kings be equally ready when their Lord has need of them?

We are getting under way. The *Poona* steams gallantly out, and the noble city is being left behind. But how unsteady we feel! The blue water already is crested with white, and breaks into showers of spray. Both sea and sky look ominous, and as if they meant mischief. The wind *soughs* and wails in fitful gusts, as if gathering its strength. The passengers disappear one by one. Surely the demon of the sea is not going to claim his prey already; but certain sensations do warn one that a hasty retreat below may be needful. The good old salt at the wheel looks skyward rather grimly, and shakes his head as he is interrogated by a very anxious-looking passenger. The only acquaintance we have yet made on board is Sir James Anderson, who commanded the *Great Eastern* when she carried the cable which was laid to America; on that occasion we had the good fortune to be of the company who went round in her to Bantry Bay, and it is pleasant to meet again. He and my husband have been pacing the deck together, but they begin to reel in a very unsteady way. And now we lurch and roll heavily, and the good ship shivers as if she feared the coming strife.

II.

Our Voyage.

GULF OF SUEZ.
On board the "Mongolia," December 24.

HERE we are in a new world. Sunny skies, glassy seas, gentle winds, hot days and hotter nights, instead of the ice, and wind, and cold, and tempest we have left behind. The change is magical. All now is serenest beauty. The sky is a wonderful cloudless blue; the sea dances and sparkles in the slanting sunlight as if it never did anything but play; the brown serried sides of the rocks, and the distant mountain-peaks which looked down on the Israelites of old, and the solemn desert stretching away to its awful solitudes, are all aglow in the beauteous amber light of an Eastern evening. It is like the morning of joy after the night of weeping.

There is no doubt that the weather has been dreadful; it was the wildest passage we ever made in all our many journeyings. I suppose I must have slept sometimes, and yet the impression was that I never slept. Some of the gentlemen hardly undressed. It was a task to hold on to one's berth; but the wearing thing was the indescribable everlasting noise—the angry roar of the sea, the furious thud with which it assailed the ship, the mournful wail of the wind, and the never-ceasing creak and crash of the poor distressed vessel as she bravely contended with the storm. You can fancy, then, what a moment of thankful relief it was when we sighted the low flat Alexandrian shore, and the windmills and shipping, and found that most unexpectedly we had got over the dreaded "bar," and were arrived. We seemed to have a new comprehension of the Psalmist's meaning when he says, "Then are they glad because they be quiet; so He bringeth them unto their desired haven."

Now that it was over, it was something to have seen a real storm at sea. One day, when the gale was at its height, I cajoled the captain into letting me go on deck to see the waves; for we women were banished below out of harm's way. The kind man lashed me firmly to a mast, to prevent my being tossed about the deck, like our portmanteaus in the cabin; and then I saw some of "Jehovah's wonders in the deep." It is no figure of speech to say that the sea "ran mountains high;" it was exactly as if a vast stretch of mountain-tops, by some wild convulsion of nature, had been thrown into violent commotion, the giant heads now tossed wildly to the clouds and then tumbled down again to the lowest depths, while the savage wind caught the summits and broke them into sheets of boiling foam. It was indeed a spectacle of awful grandeur, the sublimest I ever looked on, and I felt that it was well worth encountering the gale to have witnessed it.

We have made the pleasant discovery that our new ship, the *Mongolia*, one of the floating palaces of the P. and O. Company, is commanded by an old friend, Captain Stewart, under whose kindly banner we have sailed before. He has given us seats at table beside himself, which secures to us sundry privileges; not the least of these being that we sit opposite to the venerable Lady Franklin and Miss Cracroft, her niece. Our intercourse with these ladies is delightful. Lady Franklin's energy and enterprise are wonderful; and she talks readily, not only of her heroic husband, but also of her own surprising feats of travel, which have extended over many lands.

We have one hundred and nineteen first-class passengers on board; and among them are many delightful people, whom it is a privilege to know. Indeed, we have never sailed with a pleasanter company; and, better than this, we have never found so many before who seem to prize Christian fellowship, and who are not afraid, in any circumstances, to live and act as if they really loved and followed Christ. We have a most refreshing little service each forenoon in the saloon, which is very well attended—the bell being rung by the captain's orders to call us together. We make great friends too with the tars, and Dr. M. has little services in the evenings for them between decks. They are such fine fellows, though they look rough; and have soft bits in their hearts to those who can find them out. They give me a grim smile sometimes when I say, "What *shall* we do to keep you from those dreadful grog-shops in the bazaars when you get into port?"

There is a nice little piano on deck. At first everybody was shy; no one could play or sing, until a brave little woman, with a magnificent voice, showed the example, and then all discovered their gifts,—and now we have a charming little concert every evening.

Of course we have our grievances. The most perfect of steamers is not elysian. It certainly *is* very hot, now that we are off Mocha; and people growl and grumble, and make a great deal more fuss than when there were real troubles, if not dangers to face. An experienced old Indian once gave his daughter this excellent advice, when she wanted to know *how* she could bear the heat: "Keep your seat, my dear, and keep your temper." I don't think there could be a better recipe for life at sea than just this,—especially the latter part.

ADEN.

We have had a delightful day at Aden. We got into harbour during the night, rose with the day, and landed. We formed parties; went first to the hotel and ordered breakfast, secured some carriages, horses, and donkeys, and set out to see the famous tanks, *said* to be built by Solomon, and the cantonment, which is four miles from the point at which we land. One of the syces rather astonished us at starting. He was a small half-naked Somāli urchin, with tangled locks dyed a bright orange. He disputed our start in the most determined way, gesticulating and shouting, "Pay me moony! pay me moony!" My husband tried to pass him and make him get out of the way. But no, the little imp clung on to the bridle, vociferating, "Pay me moony!" At length, provoked beyond endurance, Dr. M. jumped from his horse, to try the effect of something else than words; when, to his amazement, his tormentor suddenly disappeared. With a single bound he cleared the parapet and jumped into the sea below! Presently he rose to the surface, paddled about, as these half-aquatic creatures do, and grinned up to us, enjoying his triumph and our discomfiture. After a good laugh we proceeded; and soon the precocious youth appeared behind, keeping at a safe distance from the riding-whip. We soon became great friends, however, and at the end some bakshish was added to the "moony."

But the conduct of the boy, which looked so eccentric, tells a tale. Our countrymen often treat these poor little "niggers," as they call them, very shamefully. They use their horses and donkeys, and don't always pay for them—except, perhaps, with cuffs and kicks. I am afraid the Englishman abroad is not always the sort of person the Englishman at home would care to recognize.

We had a most entertaining day on shore; and soon after five were steaming away into the Indian Ocean, having been saluted in every way possible by the ships in the harbour. The jagged brown peaks of Aden were lit up with glory, and transformed into unearthly beauty by the sun, which was now sinking in marvellous majesty behind a bank of clouds gorgeous with crimson and gold.

GALLE, CEYLON.

We have spent another charming day on shore. We entered the harbour of Galle at daybreak on Tuesday; and what a lovely scene it was! Mountains and hills in every variety of shape; groves of palm-trees, and the beautiful jack-fruit, mango, and plantain; the houses, the fort, and town-wall, stretching down to the water-edge; and the pure water itself, as calm as a mirror, with islands and shipping and boats,—all glowing in the morning sunlight. The whole country looked as green and dewy and fresh as an English scene in the early summer. It was beautiful!

A Wesleyan missionary—Mr. Nicolson—played the part of good Samaritan to us. He heard we were on board; came down and picked us out of the verandah of the hotel, which swarmed with natives oppressively intent on selling rings and ornaments of tortoise-shell; drove us up through the most beautiful woods to Richmond Hill, where his house is, and where we received a most kindly welcome from his very agreeable wife. This is the friendly sort of thing that Indian people do. I shall not easily forget the pleasant day we spent with these kind missionaries, nor all they told us of the island and the people, and their work among them. Their bungalow is most charmingly situated, and the views from it gave us an idea of the beauty of the island. The luxuriance of the vegetation is beyond description. You can imagine it when I tell you that people say there are twenty millions of palm-trees in Ceylon, and other wood in proportion; while the whole place seems a garden of wild flowers and creepers and the richest foliage.

Tho natives are as troublesome with their begging propensities as the Arabs are at the Pyramids. One young savage pertinaciously ran after us for miles as we drove back to the hotel, demanding bakshish. We took no notice; and in revenge, I suppose, he watched his opportunity, made a dart at Dr. M.'s umbrella, which he held in his hand, wrenched it away, and fled with it like a deer up the hill. But in a twinkling Dr. M. had leaped from the carriage and sped after him like the wind, while we all held our breath to see who should win. The wayfarers stood open-mouthed, and looked on; no one joined in the pursuit. It was a fair match; he was gradually gained upon, and fearing what might follow if he were caught, he threw the umbrella with all his might in one direction and fled himself in the opposite. It rather marred, to us, the pleasure of the recapture, that the rogue escaped the punishment he richly deserved. As it was, Dr. M. was sufficiently out of breath as he slowly returned. We received him with plaudits for his victory; but he answered, rather apologetically, "You know, I could not afford to lose my good umbrella."

One peculiarity of the Singalese is, that you can hardly distinguish the sexes, the men and women look so much alike. Their costume is exceedingly similar; the only difference I noticed was that the men wear high combs in their long hair, while the women have no such decoration.

MADRAS.

We are now lying off Madras. It is a scorching day, and the powers that be have ruled that I am not to land; though I long to try one of those funny catamarans which crowd round the ship, and cut through the surf we can hear and see boiling about the beach. Dr. M. has had a glimpse—hardly more—of our missionary friends, and the Free Church Institution and Girls' Boarding-school. The Mission buildings lie there in imposing array along the shore; and it is very tantalizing that they seem so near, and are yet so far.

We are taking some notabilities on board. One of these, whose face is unmistakable, has just come up to my husband. This is Sir Richard Temple, one of the ablest men and most distinguished civilians in India. There are three young-looking lords, who are "doing" the East, they say; India, China, and Japan being now quite included in the "grand tour."

But the event of the day is the arrival on board of Drs. Macleod and Watson, who have penetrated thus far on their semi-official journey as deputies from the Established Church of Scotland to her missions in India. There was quite a little excitement as they stepped on deck, disguised after the fashion of Anglo-Indian travellers. Dr. Macleod's massive head has disappeared into the capacious depths of a *sola topee*, or sun-cap. I am afraid your sense of propriety would be shocked, could you see the transformations as to attire which the exigencies of climate necessitate.

OFF THE SANHEADS.

Our voyage draws to a close. We have stopped beside the Pilot-Brig, and have taken the pilot and a new passenger on board. The latter is General Norman *—a name well known

* Now the Hon. Sir H. W. Norman.

in Britain as well as India. He was Lord Clyde's adjutant-general before Delhi in 1857.

I have had three days of salutary solitude in my cabin. Old maladies began to show themselves as soon as we got within the tropics; and the sickness and quiet are a very useful and needed preparation for the work before us. Patience and faith must have their *perfect* work.

It has been very pleasant to us to meet and exchange greetings with the Scotch deputation, who are "separated" to much the same errand and work as we are. Dr. Macleod is delightful—genial and hearty, and overflowing with humour. He thirsts for information, and picks it out of everybody who has any to give; or, as he himself expresses it, he "has a crap for a' corn" of this description. Above all, his big heart is thoroughly roused in the great cause of missions, and he is sure to stir you all up on his return.

We are now entering the Hooghly. There is a general excitement over the ship. We are all packing up, and everywhere you see the bustle of preparation to land.

There is nothing to strike one much as you approach the mouth of the river. First, there is a long, low, indistinct margin of sand; then, as the channel narrows, a dense jungle, with clumps of the picturesque cocoa and other palms, which seem to wave us a welcome to their tropical domain; then an occasional native hamlet of very poor little huts; now we proceed onwards between two flat shores of the brightest and most luxuriant green. You may fancy with what an intensity of interest and expectation we watch it all. The river itself is as yellow nearly as the "yellow Tiber;" and people tell us of hidden dangers beneath the smooth waters, and we hear the initiated congratulate each other as some quicksand or some hidden bank and shoal are safely passed. The Hooghly is a very difficult piece of navigation; and yet, as we slowly steam on, the busy scene on its surface becomes busier and more animated every moment. Crowds of native craft of the most varied description continually pass us by. There are fleets of fishing-boats, and some queer-looking cargo-boats, with thatched roofs from bow to stern. Now and then a magnificent ship on its way to the ocean is towed past by a tiny tug-steamer; and now further up, as we approach Calcutta, there comes a perfect forest of masts. Ships of all nations lie thickly moored in the stream; and we see that we have reached one of the great commercial centres of the world.

It was now late in the evening. The sun had set, and the quick darkness was setting in, when we stopped in mid-stream and dropped anchor. The authorities said we were too late for safety in this treacherous river; but if so, we were blissfully ignorant. On one hand was an imposing building, which we were told is Bishop's College; and on the other, the King of Oude's palace; and stretching upward, the handsome line of houses called Garden Reach. Then the boats came alongside, and there was a rush of people on deck; and there followed the usual meetings and greetings of friends, and all the excitement of arrival.

We were very soon welcomed by Mr. Duff, Mr. M'Donald, Mr. Bruce, and other kind friends. Mr. Duff took possession of us and our effects in the most hearty, delightful, restful way. He put us into his wife's carriage on the shore, where she and other lady friends waited to receive us; and with hearts filled with inexpressible thankfulness to Him who had so graciously watched over our going out and coming in, we were soon beneath our friend's hospitable roof. And all I can say is, we are thoroughly at home.

III.

In Calcutta.

CALCUTTA, *January*.

WE have been about a week in Calcutta, and have seen so much and done so much, it looks a year. I am charmed with the place and people, and everything; and as for the climate, it feels almost perfection. The cold is as great, I think, as anything I have felt in the plains before. Last night, when driving home over the Esplanade, the wind felt so keen, I was glad of my shepherd's-plaid; and at night, two good blankets and a quilt are quite needful for comfort. If I were only strong and well, how I should enjoy this new and yet familiar life!

Dr. M. is very much in his element, making rapid acquaintance with "young Bengal," who come to him in great numbers, talking, discussing, and making friends. He is likewise busy gaining acquaintance with Bengali. It is of the same family as Marathi and Hindi, and therefore easy of acquisition to one knowing these or Sanscrit, which is the root of all the cultivated northern dialects. To me Bengali sounds very different from Marathi, but many of the names of things are similar; and Hindustani, which is almost the *lingua franca* of India, is spoken by the servants, so I get on delightfully. There is far less English spoken by the servants here than in Bombay and Madras; though, from the intelligent looks and listening attitudes of the dark forms behind our chairs at table, I strongly suspect more is understood than is allowed. Among educated Bengalis, English is spoken extremely well; even gray-headed men converse in it fluently, though the expressions are sometimes stilted and bookish.

Dr. M. has something like a levee every morning after chota-hāzari (or preliminary breakfast), in a pleasant little verandah-room opening to the garden, which Mrs. Duff has most kindly given him as a sitting-room and study. A great many old Bengali friends of Dr. Duff have called, besides the youth of our own Institution and Mission, and many others. The older Babus come in generally attired in clouds of white muslin, with broad turbans on their heads. The young men wear surtouts of broadcloth, like clerical coats, buttoned to their chin; with trousers and English boots, and no turban. Their hair is closely cut, like that of our own countrymen; and the surprising fashion seems to prevail of wearing nothing on the head in the streets. The most respectable men walk about bareheaded; and what their brains can be made of, to stand this flaming sun, is a lasting wonder to me. But it is etiquette to wear the turban when on ceremony, and on all grand occasions. This head-gear is all of the same pattern,—a broad, round, flat thing, like a bread-platter; the crown white, and the brim highly ornamented with cross rolls, made of coloured chintz, or shawl-like device,—which has altogether a pretty effect, but is not nearly so picturesque as the turbans of every hue and shape and size which crown the heads in the west of India. While on this subject, I may say that the servants wear white turbans, white coats, and *cummerbunds*, or yards of thin calico rolled round their waists. This looks a clean and pretty livery; and the domestic law is, that no servant shall venture into the august presence of his master or mistress divested of any one of these articles of attire.

It is too soon for me to speak of the religious state of Calcutta, though one cannot be here for a day without hearing of the extraordinary and interesting movement among the comparatively new sect calling itself the Brahmo-Samaj. One of the earliest visitors we had was the new leader of this movement—Babu Keshub Chunder Sen. I had heard so much of this singular man, that I felt quite a little flutter of excitement as his card was handed in; and I acknowledge to having met him with a deeper feeling of interest than anybody else I have seen since our arrival. Some people say he is conceited. On the contrary, he seems to me quiet, calm, not self-conscious, and even a little shy. He is a follower of the great Rammohun Roy, the founder of the Samaj; which, however, has taken a fresh start under this new and earnest chief. Of his creed I cannot speak much as yet: it seems to be a kind of pure Theism. But listening, with the deepest interest, to his conversation with Dr. M., I was surprised to find how much of his doctrine he takes from Christianity. He spoke with loving reverence of the Fatherhood of God, and with the most profound admiration of the character and teaching of Christ. Of course, he has got all these ideas from the Bible; and I believe he would acknowledge this. It is *not* Christianity, however. Christ is to him only a wise and holy teacher. Yet may we not hope that it will develop into life; that the dry bones will live; and that this most interesting man will, ere long, see Christ to be divine, and receive him as his Saviour? I am sure he is a true man, and an earnest and sincere seeker after truth. At least, this was how he impressed me.

We have had a most interesting meeting in the Town Hall—a "Pan-Missionary Meeting," as it was called,—all Churches and Societies having been represented in the speakers and in the audience. The Bishop, who is a nephew of Dean Milman, presided; and the tone of the whole was thoroughly large-hearted and catholic.

One speaker—Mr. Lewis of the Baptist Mission—alluded very interestingly to Carey and his coadjutors, and told us of their Bible translations, and how eight editions of the whole Bible, and twenty-six editions of the New Testament, had been sent forth by these devoted men from Serampore. My husband, in his address, told us how Carey had visited our Institution when quite in its infancy, and at the sight of the assembled lads studying in a Christian school he had exclaimed to Dr. Duff, "What has God wrought! When I began my missionary career, I could not have induced these youths to come to be taught if I had bribed them with all Bengal." The last speaker was Dr. Macleod, whose speech was very telling.

What I want to describe is the scene which the Town Hall presented, as being so different from anything of the kind you can see at home. The platform was at one extremity of the noble room, well raised from the floor, and filled with a distinguished assemblage, including the Viceroy, the Lieutenant-Governor, the Commander-in-Chief, Sir William Muir, Sir Henry Durand, Sir Richard Temple, General Norman, and many others gathered from all classes of the community. Of course, the clerical element was strong. Below the platform, in the foreground, sofas, covered with red, were arranged, on which sat rows of well-dressed ladies—indeed, all the fair society of Calcutta. Round them little crowds of men were grouped, mostly standing, or leaning against the massive pillars; some in plain English dress, and others in the handsome uniforms of the civil, military, and naval services. Here and there a native celebrity, in gorgeous and picturesque costume, stood talking to somebody; or a Bengali Babu in plain dark robe, relieved by a white scarf or sash, like a University hood, or enveloped in a beautiful Indian shawl of brilliant colour and priceless value. One or two of my old friends the Parsees I noticed, with the high dark turban; and several thoughtful-looking men in the semi-European dress of the Bengali Christian,—among whom Mr. L. B. Day was conspicuous, Mr. Tagore, and others. The venerable countenance of the Rev. Krishna Mohun Banerjee was distinguishable on the platform. Indeed, he spoke, and spoke exceedingly well. Then backward, all down the columned aisle of the beautiful room, there stretched row on row of dark intelligent faces, surmounted by the flat variegated turban or embroidered cap; or, here and there, the higher head-gear of some stranger from the Upper Provinces or the West. It was a most impressive sight; and it gained much in significance when one thought that this was a *missionary* meeting, and that all these men, of so many opinions and nationalities, had merged their differences in the grand question, What can be done for the elevation and enlightenment of India? It showed the widespread interest there is in mission work, and that there are many who believe that the faith of Christ only can raise India in the scale of nations. I could not help wondering what Carey would have said could he have seen this meeting, indicative of so great a change since the intolerant day when he was driven to settle under a foreign flag.

IV.

The City of Palaces.

CALCUTTA, *January* 7.

I MUST now try and obey your injunction to give you a description of this great capital of our Eastern Empire. I will give you my own impressions, and this will answer your question whether Calcutta deserves its name of "City of Palaces."

On the whole, I think it *is* worthy of its flattering appellation; only, I should be disposed to give it the added title of a "city of hovels." It is a strange medley of grandeur and squalor, and is made up of two cities, quite distinct, and greatly differing. One is European, and the other native. The European part is quite as handsome as it has been described to be, and well deserves its fame; but it does greatly interfere with the pleasure and gratification one naturally feels in contemplating all the magnificence, that the native town should present so grievous a contrast. As soon as you get away from the streets and squares inhabited by the English and the richer natives, you find the bazaars mean, dirty, irregular, and breathing odours certainly *not* "Sabæan," nor drawn from any part of "Araby the blest."

The houses of the English are large, square, stately edifices with flat roofs, not beautiful in construction, and yet redeemed from plainness by their pillars, porticoes, verandahs, and venetian windows. They stand in rows, or squares, with beautiful little sheets of water in the centre. Each dwelling has its own compound or garden, and separate entrance-gate, within which stands the porter's lodge—the cell of that important functionary, the "durwān," or gate-keeper. The bungalow of the mofussil, with its pretty bowery porch, deep cool overhanging roof, and verandah gay with creepers and evergreens, is a far more picturesque abode than the lofty mansion of Calcutta; but the latter is undoubtedly much more comfortable to live in.

After all, what Calcutta has to boast of more than even her "palaces," and what make her the beautiful city she really is, are her magnificent Esplanade and her glorious sea-like river.

The Esplanade, or Maidān, as it is called, is a noble expanse. In Clive's time, about a hundred years ago, it was a wild jungly swamp, famous only for snipe-shooting. Wonderful to say, it is not burned up and brown, like every other Indian plain I have seen, but, from the frequent showers, and being on the margin of the river, it is as fresh and green as any English park. It has a few fine tanks; and it is dotted over with some pretty trees—which, however, were much more numerous before the cyclones of 1864 and 1867, which did such terrible havoc, and swept away its chief beauties. It is intersected by plenty of wide, well-kept drives, and is ornamented by some pretty gardens and a few handsome memorial columns and statues. The Ochterlony Monument is a beautiful towering shaft, from the top of which you have one of the finest views which is to be had of Calcutta. Indeed, the Maidān is the centre of all that is grand or imposing: what is shabby and unsightly creeps behind out of view. Facing it, along its eastern margin, stand the beautiful pillared "palaces" of Chowringhee. At one end there is the new court-house, a very handsome building, which is in course of completion; the town hall also, and other buildings of less pretence; and further on, the noble pile of Government House, with four handsome entrance-gates, and surrounded by grounds and shrubbery. The Eden Gardens lie in front, and are a very charming addition to the beauties both of Government House and the Esplanade. From this point the business town stretches northwards; including Dalhousie Square, with its many buildings, among which the domed post-office stands conspicuous, and a beautiful wide street lined with offices and shops; the vista being beautifully closed by St. Andrew's Kirk with its graceful spire. Then at the further extremity, nearly two miles across the green expanse, you see the cathedral, with its noble spire, the general hospital, and jail; and further on still, the beautifully wooded suburbs, Kidderpore and Alipore. Fort William stands toward the river, and with its ramparts and buildings forms a striking object in the scene; while the whole is bordered and beautified by the Hooghly, a branch of the grand old Ganges, with its crowd of masts and flags, its barges and yachts and green boats, and landing ghāts, and all its busy life.

Along the river-bank lies the "course," or drive, where all the fashionables go every evening as soon as the sun is low enough. Here you meet every sort of vehicle, from the grand equipage of the Governor-General, with the attendant body-guards in scarlet and gold, down to the funny machines called "ticca gharrees" (the cabs of Calcutta)—which are generally drawn by two little rats of ponies harnessed with rope. The carriages, two or three deep, go slowly up and down the road; everybody bows to everybody else; you "eat the air," as Orientals say; you hear the band play; and then you drive quickly home. This always appears to me the most monotonous and wearisome of pleasure-drives. Outside there are some lovely country roads and lanes, which seem to present endless points of attraction. They are fringed with feathery bamboos and beautiful flowering shrubs; their margins are carpeted with verdure and wild flowers; the very ditches are beds of loveliness, where you find a wealth of jungle treasure: but then these drives lack the gaiety and the fashion and the fun.

The sunsets, however, are often very beautiful; and the scene on the Maidān, as it grows quickly dark, is most striking. The lamps are lit, and the whole wide plain becomes completely encircled with glittering lights, just as the stars "rush out," and the dome above becomes resplendent with its brilliant host.

But, as I said, behind all this there lies a very different picture. A few of the native bazaars are wide enough, though the buildings which line them form a series of the most extraordinary contrasts. Here is a Babu's palace; and next to it, the meanest hut. Most of the streets are simply narrow lanes, which have deep odoriferous drains on either side full of stagnant water (though this is being altered now), with a plank across to every door. It is sometimes difficult, in threading these labyrinths, for two conveyances to pass abreast. The houses in these poorer bazaars are mere huts, rudely constructed of bamboos and mud, or sometimes only date-matting with bamboo posts, roofed with red tiles, and not even picturesque in their poverty and squalor. The shops are ranges of queer, open, low stalls—piled round with merchandise, if they contain cloths; or if sweetmeats or grain, then the goods are arranged on shelves like steps. The bazaars of Bombay and Delhi, and some of the other cities I have seen, are clean and tidy, and picturesquely Eastern. Not so those of this comparatively modern capital. Dilapidation seems written on most things; for which, however, the cyclones may largely account.

It is all strangely, deeply interesting; and I never weary of watching the quaint scenes, and all the fantastic novelties, with which pure native life abounds. You are surprised to find that some of the lanes are skirted by high blank walls, instead of houses, as you imagine, presenting here and there a small closed door to the street. Within these walls, however, are some of the finest houses of the rich native gentlemen; with their zenanas, the prison-like homes of the higher-born women of Bengal. These houses face inward to a court, paved generally with marble, and ornamented with pillars and balconies, and perhaps a fountain. This may lead onward to another court, or half-garden, with a few plantain, pomegranate, and other trees, and a small tank in the centre. There is sometimes a low column with a flower-pot upon it, containing a sacred plant, which is watered and cherished, and has offerings made to it. But I hope afterwards to describe the insides of the houses to you, especially the zenana part of them; so at present we shall remain without.

A fine, broad, handsome road sweeps almost entirely round Calcutta, except on the river-side. This is appropriately called the Circular Road; and what is interesting about it is, that it covers the site of the old "Maratha Ditch." This ditch was made by the citizens as a protection when the plundering hordes of Maratha horse were scouring the plains from Bombay to the Ganges, and from the Himalayas down to the far South. All India stood in terror of these fierce, gallant little freebooters. But after they were subdued, about half a century ago, and there was no further cause for dread, the ditch was very sensibly filled up again with the rubbish which had been dug out at its formation; and out of it sprung this good and useful road. The nickname "Ditcher," which clings to the denizen of Calcutta, had its origin from the Maratha Ditch.

The Black Hole, of dreadful memory, disappeared some fifty years ago. It was only eighteen feet wide and fourteen deep, with a very small door, and window with iron grating. It is just as well, I think, that this place of torture should have been swept away, leaving nothing behind but a terrible tradition.

In the population which crowds the bazaars, you miss the remarkable mixture of race and the picturesque Orientalism which are so striking in some other cities. In Bombay, for example, besides all the different tribes of Hindustan in their varying garbs and head-gear, you find the tall Arab in his flowing burnoose, the Persian in his cone-like cap of sheep-skin, the Parsee, the Jew, and the Israelite,* the fat Banyan or cotton-merchant of Guzerat, the Chinaman with his tail, men from Eastern Africa, and from Central Asia,—representatives, I suppose, of almost every nationality under heaven congregate in the busy streets of the capital of Western India, each in his own costume, and speaking his own tongue. Perhaps only in ancient Alexandria, or in Constantinople and Cairo of our own day, would you find such a motley assemblage of race, with their different manners, costumes, tongues, and creeds. But Calcutta presents little beyond Bengali life; even the Musulman element, which is large, does not alter this, for nearly all the Mohammadans of this province were originally Hindus.

The Bengali, as a race, are rather slight in physique, with lithe active figures, dark complexion, keen eye, bright intelligent expression, and features often finely cut. The Babu of the period, or "young Bengal," is dressed in white trousers, shiny

* The Beni-Israel of Bombay do not intermingle with the Jews of Cochin, Arabia, or Europe.—*Edit.*

boots, a long coat of broadcloth picked out in red or yellow at the seams, and a scarf of delicate white muslin becomingly arranged to cross on the breast and hang down the back, something like a Highlander's plaid. To this is added, in full dress, the flat, round turban, fashioned in rolls of shawl-pattern and white, with the shirt-collar and gold studs and albert chain of any English dandy. The orthodox Hindu gentleman, on the contrary, wears his simple white "chapkan," or cotton coat, and usually has a splendid Cashmere shawl thrown over his shoulders.

Very few women are to be seen in the Calcutta bazaars, and these only coolies, or of the lowest castes. The whole female community of the upper and middle classes are shut up in their zenanas, and never, on any pretext, go abroad except in closed-up gharrees or palanquins. You sometimes meet one of these conveyances with a sheet tied closely round over window and door; and you know that a woman is within, who not only must not be seen, but must not *see*. The lady of the Turkish harem may see what she can through the veil which completely conceals her face. Not so the poor zenana lady. She must not have so much as a passing glimpse of anything going on in the outer world. Even if she goes to the river to bathe in the sacred waters, and do pooja, or worship—and this is almost the only thing which takes her abroad—she must go in a palkee with a perforated bottom, that the water may enter and make her pure without her requiring to leave her asylum.

Let us rejoice and give thanks to God that now these poor prisoners, by reason of our zenana missions, are becoming "prisoners of hope," and are daily (some of them, at least) hearing of the pure river of the water of life, and are being invited to come and share in the glorious liberty with which Christ makes his people free.

You do not see here, in everyday life, much of the religion of the people. Idolatrous observances, except at pooja times, or festivals, do not obtrude themselves publicly. Temples are not numerous, and the daily worship goes on principally within the homes of the people; for in every house of the higher orders there is a "gods' house,"—a low room fitted up as a temple, and dedicated to the household deities,—where the idols are enshrined and offerings made. In Benares, "the sacred city," your heart is sickened at every turn by the sight of its awful idolatry; and in Western India you come continually on a temple, or an idol, by the wayside; or it may be simply a stone, rudely daubed over with red paint, before which some poor woman may be prostrating herself, with her head in the dust. Here it is simply that the customs are different, not that image-worship is a thing of the past, or even rapidly passing away, as some sanguine people would persuade you. The gods and goddesses are not those of a bygone idolatry, like those of Madagascar and many islands of the South Seas. Heathenism is still an existing, appalling fact. The Indian systems have taken long ages to grow up, and they will die hard. The worship of the monstrous ten-armed Kāli is in daily practice within her own temple at Kāli-ghāt; and festival processions are sorrowfully frequent, when the deities are carried through the streets amid shouts and plaudits, and the horrible din of tom-toms, cymbals, and shrill wind instruments.

It will take much hard self-denying work, much prayer and much self-sacrifice on our part, and the part of India's own sons, before we shall be able to speak of the religious systems of Hindustan as an extinct heathenism. But, thank God, that day will come; for it is written that "all the ends of the world shall see the salvation of our God."

Speaking of the sights in the streets, I must tell you of a very gay affair we witnessed as we returned through the native town last evening. This was a marriage procession. Such exhibitions take place very frequently in the wedding "season,"—the auspicious day having been determined by the family guru, or priest, and the astrologer. The sound reached us of wild music and tom-toms, accompanied by a wretched European brass band. The glare of many lights shone in the distance, and presently a dense crowd of people came up, some bearing huge torches, others banners and umbrellas. Some carried small forests of painted trees and flowers made of tinsel and coloured paper; others trays of sweetmeats, fruits, cakes, pān-supāri, garlands, and rose-water. Next came one or two fantastically-shaped things on wheels, like boats—filled, I believe, with the bridegroom's relations; and next the bridegroom himself, bedizened with jewels and garlanded all over with sweet-smelling flowers, enthroned beneath a gorgeous canopy of silk and gold, and borne aloft on the shoulders of four men. Attendants waved punkahs over him, and offered him sweetmeats. Then came more people, and paper trees, and flaming torches; guns were fired; rockets thrown into the air; red and blue lights were displayed; the people were hilarious; laughter and fun and jokes abounded;—and altogether it was a very pretty sight. I should think, however, the cynosure of all eyes, the poor little bridegroom,—for he was a mere boy,—will be tired enough of the grand ceremonial, and be glad when it is over, and he has arrived at the house of his bride. Here the shout will be heard, "The bridegroom comes!" and the little girls of the house, with torches in their hands, will go forth to meet him and bring him in; and then the marriage ceremony will proceed. This seems to me such a pretty custom—the young, unmarried girls of the house, who are still free, going out to meet the bridegroom. They also do as the Jews of old did at their celebrations,—"send portions one to another, and gifts to the poor."

How true to Eastern life, even at this day, are the beautiful narratives and parables of Holy Scripture!

V.

In the Streets.

CALCUTTA, *January.*

A MORNING or two after our arrival, a fine tall elderly native gentleman, in a loose, embroidered coat, and with a remarkably pleasing countenance, was shown in just as we were beginning breakfast. You may imagine how pleased we were when he was introduced to us as the Rev. Jagadishwar Bhattacharja of Mahanad, one of the excellent Bengali ministers of our own Church, whose name you will at once recognize.

He, with Messrs. Lal Behari Day, Prosunno Koomar Chatterjee, and others, were among the first converts of the Mission; also poor Koilas and Mahendra, who died early. It was so pleasant to see one of the men whose names have been as household words with us, and with all who have watched the earlier progress of the Scottish Bengal Mission under Dr. Duff and his noble first associates, Dr. Mackay, Dr. Ewart, Mr. John M'Donald, Dr. Thomas Smith, and Mr. Fyfe.

Mahanad is one of the Mofussil stations of the Free Church Mission, and has been for several years under the superintendence and ministry of Mr. Bhattacharja. He came down on purpose to see us and bid us welcome to Calcutta; and his hearty shake and warm greeting made a delightful impression, for he was the first Bengali Christian we had seen, and therefore his visit was a notable one. We have since seen several of these friends, and I hope our acquaintance with them will make rapid progress. It will not be my fault if it does not.

After breakfast, Mr. Bhattacharja very kindly agreed to escort me on an expedition I was longing to make—namely, to explore the *locale* of our Mission in Cornwallis Square, as well as make the acquaintance of Mrs. Fyfe and the other ladies and families with whom we shall soon be so closely associated in our work. Mr. Fyfe had carried off my husband, to introduce him to everything and everybody; but this did not do for me.

If you will now accompany us on our expedition, we shall carry our investigations a little further into the native town, and also see the outside of some of the chief educational establishments of Calcutta. Of these there are not few. I scarcely think I have ever seen a place where there are so many colleges and schools of every sort. You are at once impressed with education as a great fact. Happily, Christian education is also a fact, and has been so especially since that memorable day when Dr. Duff founded the first Christian "Institution," for giving a thorough English education, with God's Word for its basis, to the youth of this great heathen country. Now "the little one is becoming a thousand," and sister institutions have sprung up on every side. Better still, the work is no longer the imperfect, one-sided thing it necessarily was for long years, when half the community,—the women,—were excluded from participating in the boon the men accepted for themselves; when, as Dr. Duff expressed it, it was as impossible to reach the females of the higher classes and castes as to "scale a wall of brass fifty cubits high."

Now, thanks be to God, all is changed; or, I ought to say, is beginning to change. The ban is removed, and the women are allowed to share in the blessing of this moral and religious training, which is making its sure way, and is even now filling the land with a new life.

It is not, however, as you pass through these crowded bazaars that you note the progress. On the contrary, one sorrowful thought will take possession of you and weigh you down: How little is done; these masses seem hardly touched!

They say that when Carey first conceived the project of carrying the gospel to India, he used to sit on his stool with a map of the world hung up before him. His eye would thus "affect his heart," like that of the sorrowful prophet of old; for Christendom would seem as a speck beside the great overspreading mass of Heathendom.

So it is when you look abroad over India, and tread its teeming bazaars; heathenism still seems to present such an unbroken front, that you ask, with a kind of despair at your heart, "Who hath believed our report?" And yet afterwards, when you have seen further, and have talked with intelligent Hindus, and have come in contact with the earnest mind of the youth of the land, full of the great struggle caused by the opposing forces of truth and error, and are comforted because you recognize the sure triumph which truth is gaining, then you must take care not to lose the first impression in the thankful joy of the second, nor forget how your spirit now is stirred within you as we pass slowly through the native town, and realize that India still seems almost wholly given to idolatry.

Our progress in our strange little equipage is leisurely enough to admit of abundant observation. This is the "ticca gharree" of which I spoke,—which, though rickety and certainly very peculiar, is a most useful article to those who have not yet been able to supply themselves with a "machine" of their own. Our course from European Calcutta is through a long stretch of street, which might well be called "straight," as for several miles it holds on the even tenor of its way, and carries us through a series of those strange contrasts for which I said Calcutta bazaars seemed to me remarkable. Now we go through a square with good houses, a pretty little lakelet in the middle, and some trees and greenery about; and next a picturesque bit of squalor in wretched little huts, inhabited by the poorest of the poor. Then we come to a Babu's palace, with stately gateway, and gardens and courts within; and just opposite, a tumble-down unsightly ruin,—what once was a stately house reduced to a mass of ugly bricks, clambered over by nettles and jungle. Next we come on a row of those strange little booth-like shops, open in front, in which are little piles of different sorts of grain for sale, or sweetmeats, or oil, or servant's turbans, or anything; within which the proprietor sits on the floor—not in cross-legged dignity, as you would expect if you had been among the Turks, but on his heels, nursing his knees, and doing nothing in particular, unless gossiping with his neighbour. The liquor-shops, I am sorry to say, are much the most numerous, as well as the most gaily ornamented. Then there is a line of venerable buildings, with nothing to notice but their age, which they say were the offices and godowns (or storehouses) of the first "factory," in the early days of the old Company. Then again a line of low sheds, filled with old iron and broken-down gharrees; and similar sheds which do for stables, in which stand poor little broken-backed ponies, with their dirty half-naked syces squatting about. The only good thing you notice about all these miserable erections, whether huts or sheds, is that they are tiled, not thatched. This is by the order of Government, Mr. Bhattacharja told me; a most needful precaution against those dangerous fires which, in the time of thatched roofs, used to be of very frequent occurrence. The number of medicine-shops, or "apothecary's halls," as they are grandly called, which line this road is truly wonderful. Not that the healing art is so popular, but that so few professions are open (they think) to educated Bengalis. For this reason, those of law and medicine are much overcrowded. A Hindu gentleman considers it quite beneath his dignity to be a farmer,—"to *dig* he is ashamed,"—which looks strange to our more healthy English notions.

One of the buildings in our route, which we ought by no means to pass without particular notice, is where the new water-works are in operation for giving a supply of good water to the city. The waters of the Hooghly are now good for something else, even in the eyes of the people, than cleansing away their sins. These are now carried into every quarter, native and European; and the great filtering process by which they are rendered pure and wholesome, brings a most blessed change from the old condition of things, when there was no help but to use the standing water gathered in tanks from the periodic outpouring of the skies. This water-system, along with the no less important drainage-system, is going to do more than anything else for the physical well-being of the "city of palaces."

Early in our drive, our attention is attracted by a pretty little church which stands at a corner of Wellesley Square. This is the Free Church; which has been said by good judges to be, architecturally, the prettiest in Calcutta, though now it looks somewhat weather-beaten from the late cyclone, and has one of its turrets laid prostrate in the compound. Inside and out, I am charmed with this dear little church. At right angles to it, facing the pretty gardens of the square, stands the "Madrissa,"—the Government college for the Mohammadan portion of the community. In the matter of English education, the Mohammadans are much behind the Hindus; and all the zeal of the able and learned Principal of the "Madrissa" fails to inspire them with the love of European learning. Their own Arabic and Persian lore, of which they are so proud, is certainly very insufficient for the requirements of this age.

I forgot to point out St. Xavier's College. It is a Roman Catholic Institution, where the Jesuits conduct both a day and a boarding school. That handsome dome, towering a little distance away, marks the position of "La Martiniere," a great institute for the education chiefly of the children of European parents, and named after its founder, General La Martine, who also endowed a similar institute at Lucknow. These handsome buildings, standing in the spacious compound ornamented with some fine trees on our left, where you see a number of East Indian lads busy at play, belong to the "Doveton College." This is a noble institution. It provides high-class education for the large and important East Indian community; and though not exactly founded by Captain Doveton, yet has benefited so much by his liberality in its endowment that it now bears his name. It has been from time to time presided over by such able men as the Rev. Andrew Morgan, who was early taken from his noble work, Dr. George Smith, and others. It comprises an infant-school, a boys' boarding-school and college, and also a young ladies' boarding-school.

Next we come to the "Cathedral Mission College," the chief educational establishment of the Church Missionary Society. It was founded a few years ago by the excellent Bishop Cotton, whose death was a grievous loss, not only to Bengal, but to all India. This institution is simply a college, having no school department attached to it, as the establishments of the Scotch Churches have, and also that of the London Missionary Society. The hundred and fifty young men who at present attend its classes are all undergraduates of the University; and it does seem very important that so many youths, who are advanced so far, should thus be brought under direct Christian training. It will give you an added interest, in looking at this building, to know that it was the first residence in India of Dr. Duff. It was in this very house that he delivered that memorable course of lectures which so startled the Hindus, awakening them from their long death-like sleep, and giving a great shock to the stronghold of their orthodoxy.

Next, as we hold on our way, we come to the famous Government institution called the Presidency College, which year by year pours forth its flood of purely secular learning, to produce mighty results for either good or evil. It is a very large building, rather low, and occupies a great part of a square to itself. All these vehicles which stand about are waiting to receive the *alumni* who now stream from its halls. These white-robed, bareheaded, swarthy lads do not look like the turbulent outpouring of a school in Britain. They do not jostle, and push, and turn somersaults. Wrapped in their white muslin scarfs, their books under their arms, and a very earnest look on their bent faces, they come quietly on. I wonder if they are busy calculating, poor fellows, what their probable *marks* will be in the approaching terrible University examinations, so big with the fate of many young Bengalis! If they pass, they have some chance of employment, especially under Government: if they don't, then despair fills them; for, unfortunately, they have learned to look more to Government than to their own energies and resources to help them up the ladder of life. Across the road from the Presidency College, a new handsome University hall is in process of erection, where the annual Convocation will be held, at which degrees are granted in arts, medicine, and law: of course, not in theology. Still further on, an imposing and massive structure rises in extensive grounds of its own, with shrubs, and trees, and plenty of fresh grass. This is the Medical College and Hospital. The College is the largest medical school in the British dominions. The Hospital is a great boon, bestowed on Calcutta through the generosity chiefly of a native Rajah, who, after the outbreak of a deadly fever, supplied most of the funds for its erection. Some convalescent soldiers are now busy playing at bowls on the grass, and seem very happy, while other patients are sunning themselves in the verandahs. The present Principal is our friend Dr. Norman Chevers, who came out in the same steamer with us,—a very able physician and variously accomplished man. His house stands in a corner, prettily embowered, not a stone's cast from the College.

At length we turn off into Cornwallis Square, certainly the handsomest we have passed through. In the centre there is a fine large tank, which looks quite a lake, with a pathway round it, and some grass within a railing; and a broad, good road outside, off which the gateways open. At one end a native mansion faces the water, with a handsome pillared front; but here the usual incongruity strikes one at once—the surroundings are so odd, being those queer little tiled booths I spoke of. On one side there is a pretty little church and parsonage, embowered in trees, like those of an English village. They belong to the Church Missionary Society; and a Bengali congregation worships here statedly. Further on, on the same side, stands the beautiful building known so well as the Bethune School. This is an institution for the education of the female children of the higher castes and classes, which was founded by the Hon. Drinkwater Bethune in 1850, and, during his life, supported by him. It now belongs to Government, and is largely attended. The instruction, however, is purely secular. As in other Indian girls' schools, the children only remain until the age of seven or eight, when they are married, and disappear for life into the recesses of the zenana.

On the other side of the tank there is in one corner the building belonging to the Normal Female School and Instruction Society, a large three-storied house; and at the other a large compound, with a handsome gateway, in which stand the Institution and Mission-house of the Established Church of Scotland. This Mission is now presided over by Dr. Ogilvie, an old class-fellow and a valued friend of my husband, who was one of the first to give us a hearty welcome when we arrived.

Between the "General Assembly's Institution," as it is called, and the Normal School, stand what I had come chiefly to see—namely, the Mission-house and compound, and other buildings, belonging to the Free Church Mission. I need not tell you with what interest and emotion I entered these.

The compound and garden are beautiful, with plenty of grass, which looked green and fresh, as if there had been no fierce sun to scorch its colour out. The house is large, airy, and comfortable. Mr. Fyfe afterwards took us all over it, and showed us every corner; including a funny little bungalow-attic, which was built on the flat roof of the house by Dr. Mackay, who, among his other scientific tastes, was fond of star-gazing, and made this little chamber on the house-top his observatory.

A second large compound adjoining the Mission-house grounds contains the neat little chapel and manse belonging to the Free Church Bengali congregation. There is also a lecture-room facing the street, which is used as a preaching-place, in which the native Christians who work as evangelists have a service every evening. And, finally, there is a long barrack-like building in the same compound, in which several young men connected with the Mission reside

I called at the Bengali manse, as well as the Mission-house, and made the acquaintance of Mrs. Shib Chunder Banerjee and her family. Her excellent husband, though busy at his office all the week, yet preaches in the native church, and acts as pastor,—"and all for love, and nothing for reward."

But I must speak afterwards of the operations of our Mission, when I shall have become better acquainted with them. I have by no means exhausted the catalogue of schools in Calcutta; but I have said enough to show the immense facilities there are for high education, especially in English, and how eagerly all classes—except, indeed, the Mohammadans—have availed themselves of their great privileges in this respect.

VI.

Calcutta Life.

CALCUTTA, *February*.

I ACCOMPANIED Mr. and Mrs. Duff this morning to hear Dr. Macleod preach. The "Kirk" (St. Andrew's Church) was fairly crammed in every corner, and with the *élite* of Calcutta society. There was also a considerable sprinkling of native gentlemen. The sermon was a feast, though it was less a sermon than an address. He preached for fully an hour and a half, and yet it seemed short. It was impossible to help listening; he spoke, or rather talked, with such conversational ease and telling naturalness, that, as the saying is, you might have heard a pin drop. His subject was taken from the first chapter of the First Epistle of John. A Hindu had put the question to him, a day or two before, "*Why* Christ should have suffered?" and the drift of his argument was to answer this, and to show *how* as well as *why* the Lord Jesus had suffered. He had no written sermon before him, not even notes. He stood calm and erect in the pulpit, his massive form and noble head making him look the embodiment of intellectual power. He gave us first a striking analysis of the character of Christ, and then went on to show that the holier and purer the nature, the deeper its comprehension of the sinfulness of sin, and the greater its capacity to suffer in view of the desolation and woe which sin had wrought; and as he spoke of this part of our Lord's sufferings, and of the life-long agony it must have been to a holy, divine being, who could not look upon iniquity, merely to live in a world like this, he rose to a lofty eloquence, mingled with pathos, which brought tears from many eyes. He spoke also, of course, of the reason *why* Christ should have borne all this—finishing the life-long tragedy with His death on the cross. He set forth the gospel in its simplicity, using apt and striking illustrations; but the former was the more powerful part of the discourse.

Soon after Dr. Macleod began, my attention was attracted by a figure standing a little way off in the gallery where we sat, robed in black, with his arms crossed on his breast, and leaning against a pillar. This was Babu Keshub Chunder Sen. His thoughtful gaze was fixed intently on the speaker; and during the whole of the address he never stirred, seeming to drink in every word.

I could not help a little prayer running in my heart all the time for this most interesting man, that he might be led step by step to a knowledge and experience of that "fellowship with the Father and with His Son Jesus Christ" of which we were hearing, so that, his own joy being "full," he might be able with yet fuller purpose to work for the deliverance of his beloved country. May the Father of Lights give him and *it* new and ever increasing light, even that of the glorious and blessed gospel of His dear Son!

I have been so ill that the doctor has told me I must go home again. This is a terrible trial of faith. The sentence is so far mitigated that I am to be allowed to wait until the dear old

Mongolia, with our good kind captain, comes back from a cruise China-ward; and in a month there are many possibilities.

Both Mr. and Mrs. Duff are quite untiring in their kindness. There is nothing which could give us pleasure that they do not think of; and everybody they fancy we should like to meet they invite to the house. We have thus seen some very interesting people. Miss F. dined here last night, and sat with me afterwards in my room, Mrs. Duff having gone out to an evening party. I had some delightful talk with this lady, who gave me much information about the good work which goes on in Calcutta. There seems to be considerable life, and much earnest activity, in doing good. She told me of her own labours, chiefly in the hospitals and jails, and interested me exceedingly in individual cases which she related. The people she spoke of are Europeans and East Indians—not Hindus or Mohammadans.

Another person whom I think it quite a privilege to know, and who is a mine of information in all matters connected with native female work, is Miss Brittain, an American lady, and head of the "Home" for zenana teachers, in connection with the "Women's Union Missionary Society" of America. I have spent a day with her, and her energy is quite catching. She has organized a most efficient woman's mission, and her teachers go out into the houses of the native gentry all over the city. Her account of the manner in which the ladies receive her instructions is most touching. She says she has often seen the tears roll over their faces, as she has spoken of the love which made Jesus come down from His home above to seek and save and comfort the poor and heavy-laden ones of earth. The tenderness and lovingness of the gospel touch these tried and weary hearts.

It is all so different from the harsh utterances of their own sacred books, which pronounce woman to be false, cruel, impure, and everything that is bad. I remember hearing of one woman who said, "Ah! I know who wrote your Bible! It must have been a woman; no one but a woman would say such kind things about women. Yes, I know who wrote your Bible!"

Another notability—to whom I have lost my heart—is the Rev. Mr. Long, missionary of the Church Missionary Society. He is a remarkable man, and most interesting, though perhaps a little apt to soar above the conventionalities of society. The cause of the common people is dear to his heart, and he does more for them and for the lower castes than almost anybody else. He has schools for them in the villages and rural districts, and spends and is spent, like his Master, in befriending the downtrodden and helpless. Once upon a time Mr. Long was quite the hero of Calcutta. A fierce quarrel arose between the indigo planters and the ryots, or Bengali cultivators. True to himself, Mr. Long espoused what he believed to be the cause of the oppressed. Some clever Bengali wrote a play, in which there was considerable dramatic power, called the "Nil Darpan," or "Indigo Mirror;" the object of which was to expose the abuses of indigo planting. Mr. Long had the work translated and published, whereupon the planters were furious, and instituted proceedings against him in the High Court. Feeling ran very high in Calcutta; the planters had many Europeans to back them, while the Government and the missionaries (with exceedingly few exceptions) were on the side of the ryots. The court gave it against the missionary, who was heavily fined, and sentenced to a month's imprisonment. A native gentleman came forward and paid the fine down there and then, but Mr. Long had to go to prison. He was at once raised into the position of a martyr, and was visited and "interviewed" by nearly all Calcutta. The imprisonment was a thing to be proud of; but his friends say the anxiety and confinement broke him down very much. Something else has also broken him down,—the recent loss of a most loving and beloved wife.

One great good, they say, has resulted from this little episode in Mr. Long's career—the natives trust the missionaries more than ever, and look upon them as their true friends. In rural districts, among the wilder people and cultivators, the missionary is quite the father of the people; they come to him with their wrongs and grievances, and thus he often forms a most useful link between them and Government.

Soon after our arrival, my husband presented his letters of introduction at Government House, and was received by the Viceroy with the utmost kindness and cordiality. We had an invitation to dinner at once; and the party was very pleasant and not at all stiff, although, when we entered the grand drawing-room,—which, by the way, was a beautiful sight,—there was no one in it we had ever seen before but our kind friends Sir William and Lady Muir.

Sir John Lawrence* is a plain man, most unpretending in manner, but with a noble massive head, indicative of great power, and with a singular benignity of countenance. I waited with true feminine impatience and curiosity until, after all the guests were assembled, he came into the room, accompanied by an aide-de-camp. I need not say what a pleasure it was to meet and converse with this distinguished man. Nor need I enlarge on his invaluable services during his long official career. In

* Now the Right Hon. Lord Lawrence.

the time of the mutiny, when he was Lieutenant-Governor of the Punjab, he may be said to have been, through God's blessing on his promptitude and firmness, the saviour of India.

This dinner at Government House gave us our first peep into Calcutta society, which seems to be very pleasant and refined —as indeed Indian society usually is.

I dislike great dinners, they are so long, and hot, and wearisome. Evening parties and "at homes" are much better. We go at any time, stay an hour or two, walk about the spacious rooms which most Calcutta houses possess, speak to our friends, and come home when we are tired. There is no crushing or crowding as at home, the verandahs give so much room; and altogether these are the most sensible and pleasant of our social gatherings. We were at a most enjoyable party of this kind at the bishop's. Miss Milman did the honours. The Palace is a very handsome house, and the rooms and verandahs were lovely with lights and evergreens. Some very beautiful plants and flowering shrubs in large pots and tubs were grouped about the handsome pillars, and filled the ends of the wide verandah, Chinese lanterns twinkling through the greenery very prettily. The band played in the garden below; and altogether it was a gay and pretty scene. We had dined at Sir Richard Temple's, and he drove us to the Palace, and told me who the people were. One of the most notable of the personages present was Prince Golām Mohammad, a grandson of the celebrated Tippoo Sahib; a quaint little fantastic old man,—his mouth red with beetul-nut, which he kept munching diligently,—dressed in cloth of gold, with a strangely-fashioned but handsome dark turban on his head, and his whole small person blazing with diamonds and jewels. Can this be the descendant of the grand old chief, the lion of Mysore, I thought, whom Cornwallis and Wellesley found not unworthy of their steel? The prince has been in England; he dined with the Queen, a circumstance in his history which he makes a point of relating to every one he meets. Her Majesty has since sent him a gift of her portrait, accompanied by a letter; an honour of which he is quite as proud as of the dinner. Both picture and letter are framed and hung up together, and are his very proudest possessions.

The feature in Miss Milman's party which pleased me most was the presence of some native Christians. This is the only time we have met any of them in society. At a similar entertainment at Government House there were some native gentlemen present, but no native *Christian* gentlemen. Here there were a good many, and ladies also. One or two of these latter spoilt themselves by over-dressing, which was as imitative of the English style as possible. Such a mistake! Those in the pretty modest white veil over a simple gown looked infinitely nicer.

We have had a very pleasant visit from the Rev. Lal Behari Day.* You remember he is the husband of your friend B. I was so glad to see him again. He is now a professor in the Government College at Berhampore; and he has come down partly to meet Dr. Macleod, who wished to have some talk with him, and partly to welcome us to Bengal. He is evidently a very superior man. He expresses himself in faultless English; and his conversation gives evidence both of much reading and much thought. There are younger men, too, connected with our Mission, for whom I have conceived a very high regard, both on account of their character and their attainments. The Free Church College may well be proud of such *alumni*.

* Mr. Day is the author of "Govinda Samanta; or, The History of a Bengal Rayat"—a most interesting and instructive story, written in a graphic and easy style, exhibiting the lights and shades of Hindu village life

February 18th.

One of the grand problems which always presents itself for solution to the new-comer in Calcutta is, *Where shall we live?* Our experience forms no exception to the rule. Houses are scarce, and rents exorbitant. For the last month my energies have been concentrated on the quest for a house with a rent at all within our means......Our present difficulty is now happily arranged: we are to remain as the guests of our kind friends here until they sail for England a week or two hence, and then we retain this house until the end of the year. Mr. Don, the minister of the Free Church, whose wife is now at home in quest of health, is to live with us.

"Chumming" is quite an institution in Calcutta; and a very sensible one, the cost of living being so great. Two or three people unite and form a "chummery," as they call it. They live together, and share all household expenditure; and thus checkmate the landlords, who have so little conscience in the matter of rents. I dare say you would be prejudiced in favour of a house to yourselves; but here, as everywhere else, "necessity has no law." I am quite certain we shall enjoy our "chummery" very much.

VII.

Glimpses of Native Life.

CALCUTTA, *February*.

MY heart has been strangely stirred and touched to-day. I have had my first glimpse into zenana life and zenana work. You know that one of the great desires of my heart in returning to India was to see and, as far as I could, to help in this most interesting and to me comparatively new phase of mission work. Of course, in Western India we tried to get access to the women, and in a few isolated cases were admitted into families to teach the ladies; but the zenana (or Hindu harem) is not an institution in the other presidencies in the same sense it is in Bengal. The women lead much less secluded lives, and therefore, though their need of instruction may be as great, one seems to commiserate them less; at least, one's heart does not ache over them so painfully as mine did today. I had often heard of the "prison-homes" of Bengal, of their "caged" inmates, and so forth; and now I know that these are no figures of speech, no fiction, no exaggeration. It is a terrible reality that the gentle creatures I saw, and more than thirty millions like them, are in virtual imprisonment—and, in the solemn language of the Apostle, are living without God and without hope in the world. It is an appalling truth, and one's very soul is burdened with the thought of it. We think we are doing a great missionary work; the Churches think so, and our nation, I dare say, thinks so, with so many Societies engaged. Whatever is doing for the men, here are the women, half the community, shut up and utterly helpless—what is doing for them? One is told that female education is advancing, and it may be so, inasmuch as it is now possible to get access to the women; but the truth is, that while there are about thirty-three millions of women in Bengal alone, only about fifteen hundred of these are receiving instruction.

Let us pray without ceasing, and work without ceasing, for the women of India. O day of days, when the Light of Life and Healer of the nations shall be revealed to this unhappy land!

I am not going to describe what I saw to-day until I have seen more. Mrs. R. kindly took me round and introduced me to several families, each one more interesting than the other. One was the family of Babu Keshub Chunder Sen; and I was particularly pleased to know his wife, a sweet, refined-looking person, with a pensive look on her gentle face. His mother, whom we also saw, is a woman of much intelligence, with a sprightliness of manner very unlike the generality of Hindu ladies. Her belief and pride in her remarkable son were very manifest, and very pleasant to see. He himself received us in the kindest way, but he did not accompany us into the ladies' apartments; and I confess to having been rather sorry to find in his house just as much *a zenana* as in any of the other houses we had visited. Of course, I should not have expected anything else; for it cannot be possible, even with the desire and will, to set aside all at once the usages and laws of ages.

How many mysterious points of etiquette there are in a Hindu family! A younger brother may see an elder brother's wife, and enter her apartments, and talk to her; but an elder brother may not see the wife of any younger brother. Hence, I suppose, it was that Mr. Sen did not come with us into the inner little chamber where the ladies of his family waited to receive us. His younger brother came in soon after; and I was much amused to see a pretty young girl instantly veil herself closely, and turn away, covered with confusion. This was her husband; and it is quite improper to see or be seen by one's husband in the presence of other people!

My heart yearned to some of those gentle, timid, clinging creatures, who welcomed us with so much grace and shy cordiality. Mrs. R. spoke to them quite glibly in Bengali. My Marathi tongue, alas! is of no use here; and these ladies don't know even Hindi. I was therefore obliged to let smiles and loving looks, and a sympathy which I knew came straight from my heart, take the place of words. I hardly know with whom the grand idea of zenana missions originated, but I think I am right in saying that the honour of starting this work really belongs to Dr. Thomas Smith, the Rev. Mr. Fordyce, and Mrs. Mullens. I think I could show that it really lies at the root of all work for India.

How much intellectual life there seems to be among the Bengalis! Here is another deputation of some six nice-looking young Babus, who have gone into the little room to wait for Dr. M.; their errand being to ask him if he would "do them the honour" to preside at another lecture.

Of lectures, meetings, conversaziones, and such like, there is no end. My husband is in for countless lectures on all subjects. A sleek Bengali gentleman who called on Saturday made quite a set little oration. "Sir," said he, "the Hindu people are very thankful for your advent." I wish I could remember all the pretty speeches which are made to us; they would amuse you much.

Dr. M. says there are very few among the educated men of "young Bengal" he has met who profess belief in Hinduism. The older men are orthodox, and sometimes very prejudiced. Not so the younger men: most of the students frankly call themselves "theists," even though they do not belong to the Brahmos. In talking to these interesting lads, how often one is reminded of the rich young man in the Gospel, who so earnestly sought an interview with Christ, yet went away sorrowful because he could not give up *all* for Him!

A Babu has just been telling us that the future of India is to be a grand struggle between the Brahmo-Samaj and Christianity; and, of course, the Samaj is to come off victorious. Mr. K. C. Sen gave an address the other evening in the Town Hall to celebrate the anniversary of the Samaj. All Calcutta crowded to hear him, including the Viceroy, the Chief, and all the great people. The immense hall was so crammed that Dr. Macleod, Dr. Mitchell, who went late, and many others, had to stand. The lecture, or discourse, or whatever it was, was deeply impressive—calm, persuasive, even eloquent, and wonderfully well expressed.

How *is* this strange movement to end? What relation is it to hold to the Christian Church? Is this man, who has done so much to break down idolatry and reform the abuses of ages among his people, to go so far, and no further? Is he to stop short on the threshold—to be so near the kingdom, and yet fail to enter in through Him who alone is "the way, the truth, and the life"?

A man of much note in the Christian community has just

called—the Rev. Krishna Mohan Banerjee, a venerable-looking and highly intelligent Bengali gentleman. His hair, which is fast becoming gray, was well brushed off his forehead, and hung long down behind; and the dress he wore was a sort of Anglicised Indian—a long, black coat, buttoned to his throat, with white tie, and English trousers and boots. He and his brother, who lives at Bishop's College, are the patriarchs of the Native Christian Church, and are greatly respected both by Natives and Europeans. The Rev. K. M. Banerjee is profound in Sanskrit lore. He was much indebted to Dr. Duff in the earlier part of his career.

Two Bengalis, enveloped in webs of lovely white muslin, have just been in. I often take my work and sit by my husband as he talks to these men; it is so interesting to hear the varied opinions and strange notions they give utterance to. The conversation is generally brought round very quickly to the subject of religion: so he asked these two rather elderly, comfortable-looking gentlemen what they professed in the matter of belief.

"I, sir," answered one very pompously, "am a Quaker."

A Quaker! This was a startling and very unexpected reply. All sorts of fantastic opinions seem to be absorbed by this seething, restless Calcutta mind; but who could have expected to find Quakerism among them?

"Are you also of this society, my friend?" Dr. M. inquired, turning to the other.

"No, sir," said he delightedly; "I am an enlightened Hindu."

This one seemed so pleased with himself! However, we privately thought "the Friend" perhaps the more "enlightened" of the two.

The explanation is, that the Society of Friends had at one time a mission in Bengal; and one of their tenets being that baptism was not needful, they of course found a good many followers. Baptism seems to be the great obstacle in the way of many of these young men, who believe in Christianity and yet shrink from professing it. They know that as soon as they are touched by the waters of baptism they are thenceforth expelled from caste and from their father's house. Not that the water breaks their caste: it is the public declaration of themselves as Christians that cannot be tolerated, and that opens the gulf which immediately yawns between them and every former association and tie. Their fathers constantly say to them—and, harder still, their mothers plead with them till their hearts are breaking—"Believe anything; hold any doctrine you please; but do not be baptized." This is the sorest temptation, I believe, with which the enemy of souls can assail them. Just think of it! My heart often feels breaking for them. How many among us could stand such a fiery ordeal, and yet be faithful to our Lord?

In joining the Brahmos far less sacrifice is involved: they have no rite corresponding to baptism. The difference in joining the Brahmos and joining the Christians is simply this, that in the former case a man seldom loses worldly status or possessions; in the latter he generally loses all and everything. Thank God, however, that so many have been found faithful to Christ; and for them the promise is sure, "Every one that hath forsaken houses, or brethren, or fathers, or mothers, or wife, or lands, for my sake and the gospel's, shall receive an hundredfold more, and shall inherit everlasting life."

VIII.

A Day at Serampore.

CALCUTTA, *February.*

THE dream of many days has been fulfilled, and we have seen Serampore!

Who does not remember the thrill with which, from the time we stood at our mother's knee, we heard stories of Carey and his cobbler's stool and his missionary map, and his heroic resolve to go forth and "convert the heathen;" and this, too, at a time when such resolves were looked upon, even by Christian men at home, as wild and Utopian? It was here, in Serampore, as every one knows, that Carey and his associates, Marshman and Ward, commenced their glorious enterprise, and planted the first mission in Bengal. I ought to except, however, what the excellent John Kiernander was enabled to do. He arrived in Calcutta just one year after Plassey was fought; but his work, which was both evangelistic and educational, was carried on chiefly among the East Indian and Indo-Portuguese communities. Carey and his coadjutors worked directly for Hindus; and the goodly vine which God helped them to plant has taken deep root and flourished. It has sent its boughs forth in many directions, and will, we believe, at no distant day fill the whole of India. It was not that they chose this spot as the best whereon to found their mission. British intolerance forced them to work under a foreign flag; and Serampore being then a Danish settlement, they came here, and found at least toleration and a shelter, and liberty to obey their Master's last command, "Go into all the world, and preach the gospel to every creature."

We made our little excursion a few days ago, and spent a charming day with Dr. and Mrs. Smith, whose residence is the very house which was occupied by the missionaries. Our short journey up was made in the fresh cool of the early morning, so as to avoid the heat and glare of the day. Mrs. Duff accompanied us, and we got there to breakfast. We went by train, on the Calcutta side of the Hooghly, to Barrackpore; and returned on the opposite side by the Great Indian line to Howrah, a large suburb which lies opposite to Calcutta, and is the terminus of the railway; from which we crossed in a steamer ferry-boat, and so got home late in the evening.

This was our first glimpse at the country outside Calcutta; and both in going and returning we were lost in admiration at the rich beauty and luxuriance of the vegetation. Nature has indeed scattered her bounty with lavish hand in this gorgeous country. Never was seen greater wealth of jungle loveliness than we sped through on the banks of this Queen of Rivers. The profusion and variety of wild plants and grasses and low shrubbery, as well as beautiful trees in full foliage, are indescribable. In many places the trees were festooned and garlanded all over with lovely climbing-plants, covered with resplendent flowers; and the very huts in the little hamlets we passed were clambered over and embowered with the most beautiful creepers and gourds and water-melons, as if the teeming Earth did not know what to do with the wealth of her treasures. What surprised me much—having a vivid memory of the brown, sunburned plains of the Deccan—was the wonderfully brilliant green and dewy freshness of the grass.

Would that this land were spiritually a garden of the Lord, with trees of righteousness, and the sweet fragrance and fruitfulness of all heavenly things, in something of the measure in which it possesses this natural loveliness! What a goodly land would it be—a very "Hephzibah," in which God and man might "delight!"

The villages are quaint and pretty and picturesque, being a group of a few curiously-shaped little huts, generally circular, with overhanging, deeply-thâtched roofs, standing on little mounds, to raise them above the swamps which too often surround them. They nestle daintily among the rich jungle; and are often shaded by the beautiful plantain, with its broad satiny leaf of lovely pale sea-green, or dark mango-groves, or the graceful willow and feathery bamboo. But fever and malaria must ever have their sure victims here, one would think.

Barrackpore is charming. It is a large military station, and the headquarters of several regiments. We walked from the railway-station through an English-looking park of noble expanse, with some very fine trees standing singly, or in avenues and clumps, some of them covered with gorgeous scarlet and yellow blossoms. The houses are mostly one-storied bungalows, sweet and bowery with flowers and evergreens and trailing plants. Most stood in gardens, in which were huge beds of roses in full bloom, which sent us delicious whiffs of fragrance through the clear morning air. Here again the wonderful green of the grass surprised us, so different to the burnt, brown plains we have been used to see in India. The park was as emerald as the Emerald Isle itself.

There is a Government House in the park, with small bungalows about for the staff, which is usually a favourite residence with the Viceroy; who can take refuge here, not so much from the cares of government, which I suppose he carries about with him, as from the toils and claims of Calcutta society, which often must be worrying enough. Here also is a beautiful monument to the lamented Lady Canning, erected by her husband.

When we came to the river-bank, we got into a pretty little green boat, and were rowed swiftly across and set down close to the habitation of our friends, which stood in a large green compound across the road.

We had never seen Mrs. S. before; but the welcome she gave us might have come from an old friend, it was so hearty; and an old friend she seemed, before a few minutes were over.

There is still a mission in Serampore connected with the Baptist Society; and the mission-houses, little chapel, and printing-press all stand in the spacious grounds which surround the original mission-house where the great missionary trio dwelt. This is now the headquarters of the *Friend of India*, and the residence of our hospitable entertainers. A large, handsome, upper-storied building, which stands in a green compound of its own further down the river-bank, is the college; which is doing a great work in giving a good English Christian education to the youth of all this district.

I need not say that our hearts beat a little faster as we entered the house. It is thoroughly and delightfully Indian in construction and arrangement. The rooms open one from another, and are divided by pillars, and arches, and purdahs; giving one a sense of expansion and cool breathing-space, which makes the perfection of a house in the tropics. The whole finishes off with a wide verandah,—the centre of attraction to every one,—which stretches along the river-front of the house, and on which the sitting-rooms open. This is made shady by cool green blinds; and here we sat and talked, listening to the gentle lap of the water, or watched the pretty boats glide swiftly by, while the joyous breeze came to us, sweet and cool, across the broad expanse of the river.

In the centre room we found a substantial breakfast laid out—a very welcome sight after our early travel. Our Indian breakfasts are quite as excellent as the famous Scotch ones, and much prettier, regaling the eye along with other senses. We always decorate the table daintily with fresh-gathered flowers, and all the year round have some sort of fruit,—plantains, guavas, oranges, limes, Cape gooseberries, and in some higher parts of the country ripe luscious figs and piles of grapes, and sometimes even strawberries.

Our first feast, however, was on the lovely view from the verandah, which is exceedingly beautiful, especially in the morning and at sunset. The glorious river lay close below, now still and soft, like a sheet of molten silver, reflecting the pure blue of the heavens, which still gleamed with the tender light of the morning. Lovely cloudlets, with delicate tints of gray tipped with rose, were pencilled in exquisite lines along the horizon, and had not yet been out-dazzled by the full blaze of day; little boats darted about, "floating double" on the glassy calm of the water; and the life they threw into the deep repose of the scene added a fresh charm to its ideal beauty. Across the river the noble park of Barrackpore, with its dazzling green and beautiful trees, gleamed in the sunny light; pretty white bungalows were dotted about, half hidden in foliage, with here and there a monument and handsome building. Wood and tangled jungle fringed the water-edge; and altogether it was a vision of loveliness I shall not soon forget. If there had only been a background of mountains, it would have been perfect; but though rich and beautiful, Lower Bengal is not endowed with this crowning charm of hills—it cannot boast of even a hillock.

On the other side of the house, across the compound, lies a space "where once a garden smiled." This was Carey's garden, some remains of which are still to be seen. He was devoted to botany and the cultivation of flowers; and it is consoling to think that this great man had so much that was human about him as so to love his garden. This taste has now its full development and perfected enjoyment in the paradise of God above, in the midst of which is the tree of life, whose leaves are for the healing of the nations, and doubtless also

> "Flowers of all hue, and without thorn the rose."

It touches one to hear that the good man's death-bed was somewhat troubled by fears as to the possible fate of this cherished spot. "Dear brother Marshman," he said pathetically, "I am afraid, when I am dead and gone, that you will let the cows get into my garden." One is thankful to know that this desecration has not been permitted; but what is nearly as bad has really happened—part of the hallowed place is now the site of a jute-factory!

Carey, as I have said, was an accomplished botanist, and in the compound there still stand some magnificent old trees—mahogany, teak, mango, tamarind, and other fine specimens of Indian wood—which were planted by him. They have been thinned, however, in a most melancholy way by the cruel cyclones.

The whole place is clustered over thick with memories, and,

I think, especially touching are those which hang round the little chapel. It is a plain, unpretending, low, white-washed building; its only embellishments being some pretty columns which support the entrance-porch in front, and a cool gray marble floor inside; but it is the very old chapel they built, and contains the quaint round little box of a pulpit where they preached. It is a hallowed place, where your heart gets strangely touched. You tread softly, and speak in hushed tones, as if it were an abode of the dead. The walls have some marble tablets *in memoriam*, commemorating the missionaries, their "beloved associate," Mr. Mack, and Dr. Marshman's wife, who herself was a devoted missionary.

The most important part of the great work which these early missionaries were permitted to accomplish was undoubtedly in connection with their numerous Bible translations. Eight editions of the complete Bible, and twenty-six editions of the New Testament, in the leading languages of India, were sent forth from Serampore,—the direct fruit of the labours of these devoted men.

On the occasion of Dr. Duff's last visit to Carey, the final sheet of his Bengali Bible was brought in from the printer. He burst into tears; uttered the most fervent thanksgiving to God that he had been permitted to finish this work; and said, "Now, Lord, lettest Thou thy servant depart in peace!" He prescribed the text from which his "dear brother Marshman" should preach his funeral sermon; and the choice was very characteristic of the humble believer, trusting to nothing he had been able to do himself, but simply to the blood of Christ. He said: "You will preach my funeral sermon; and let the text be, '*By grace are ye saved.*'"

Toward evening we were favoured with a sunset of the most

wonderful and enchanting beauty. The heavens and the earth were lighted with a glory which no painter—not even Turner, I think—could delineate, and certainly no pen could describe; and when we strolled out by the river-bank as it grew cool, the calm surface of the water seemed turned into burnished gold.

Our friends took us to see another of those touching memorials of the past with which Serampore abounds. This is the picturesque ruin of a small deserted temple, which stands on a wooded knoll at a pretty bend of the river, called "Henry Martyn's Pagoda." Here the saintly Martyn loved to spend his quiet hours in meditation and communion with God and prayer. He was usually alone as to human companionship; though sometimes the Rev. David Brown—an excellent chaplain of the good old Company, like Martyn himself—joined him, and broke in on his solitary musings.

Fellowship with the Father and with the Son are needful to spiritual vigour everywhere, but doubly needful in India, where there are comparatively few privileges, few means of grace, and an atmosphere of blighting heathenism on every side. One must go the oftener to the fountain, if there are few streams flowing from it to drink at by the way. Henry Martyn knew this, and often sought this lonely spot to have his soul "restored" by direct and living intercourse with his God; when this tiny poor bare room, once an idol-shrine, would become to him as the presence-chamber of the King, whence he would come forth comforted and refreshed, and fitted anew for the sore battle he had to fight for his Lord in this land, darker then than even now. It is almost a relief to think that this sorrowful man was early taken to his rest, and that the weary fight was not long protracted. It takes stern stuff and iron wills, as well as souls on fire and hearts full of enthusiasm, to meet the terrible foe of this many-sided heathenism; and Martyn, and Carey, and the rest must often have had sore need in their still harder times.

I lingered some time beside the poor little pagoda, and I was very sorry to see it so fast falling to decay. Pretty climbing-plants, with delicate tendrils and luxuriant blossoms, are busy clambering over it, and cling lovingly to the fissures and crannies; a peepul-tree has struck its roots deep into the ruin; everything seems to do its best to clothe the old walls, and make the decay beautiful,—just as the graces of the Spirit seem to flourish peculiarly and with the brightest perfection round the ripened and departing Christian.

But, after all, the little spot is best garlanded by its own hallowed memories, and I wish that something could be done to arrest the progress of decay. As we sauntered home through the tangled path, a lovely radiance from the "after-glow" of the sun just set lingered in the western sky, shedding its soft light on the quiet river at our feet; and I could not but think of the "after-glow" from such lives as these great missionaries had lived in this place for their Master. Not a transient gleam like this, which even now was passing into darkness, as the shadows of the evening fell rapidly round us, but one which "will live, and spread, and kindle," as the religion of Christ makes its sure way over the land.

The hallowed past, and the bright cheery cultured present, combined to make our day at once a singularly pleasant and profitable one.

IX.

Housekeeping.

March 10.

WE have had a very busy fortnight and general upturn: our friends the Duffs have sailed for England, and we and our "chums" are now fairly established.

These home-goings are certainly great drawbacks to Indian life. We were up before daylight to get the party for the steamer under way. The luggage had been sent on before; and we all drove down in the carriage to the ghaut, or landing-place on the river—I carrying my little pet, Mabel. She would have nothing to say to her new nurse, an Englishwoman, as her beloved ayah had to be left behind. It was a bitter parting for both; and the poor old woman has been breaking her heart for her *baba* ever since. I am nearly as bad as the ayah; and the last look I got of the wee darling, as she sat on the new woman's lap, holding up her little arms to me with a wail and such a beseeching look, still haunts me. It is specially hard to pass the nursery-door.

The scenes on board a homeward-bound ship would need hard hearts to be able to stand them......

When we returned from the ship, everything looked so changed and desolate. We found our new khansāmạn, or head-servant, installed, and waiting for orders. He is a fine old man, with a venerable beard down to his waist, and a singularly mild and pleasing expression of countenance. He was clad in cool white; a fresh-starched calico coat, loose trousers, which looked like a petticoat, a flat turban, and a bright scarlet shawl wound round his waist in numerous folds. This garment is called a cummerbund, and the bright bit of colour had the happiest effect. As we entered he made a profound salaam—the very picture of a servant! I am sure I shall like him; and I don't think he will cheat me more than he considers absolutely necessary to keep up the credit of the profession.

The bearer was also in attendance, head over another department. He is a great contrast to the dignified Musulman. All table-servants must be Musulmans, as no Hindu of any caste would come in contact with your food for the world. The bearer is a Christian, and an old servant of Mr. D.; a small, keen-eyed, dark Madrassi, with a towering mass of white turban, and full of springy activity. It is nice to have a Christian servant; but this man looks perhaps rather too clever.

Mr. D. has come to his quarters, and we are all very happy; but the great drawback is that the accounts of his dear wife's health are not very reassuring. The separation this cruel climate often necessitates from wife and bairns, is the grand sorrow and darkening to many an Indian life.

One of the Sunday services in which my husband takes part, along with the missionaries, is of the deepest interest and importance. It is held in the Institution every Sunday morning at six o'clock, and is attended by many of the educated young men of Calcutta,—not Christians, but Hindus; and it is delightful to think that so many of these young men are induced to come thus steadily and systematically to hear the simple gospel preached. Some of them are from Government colleges, and have not the opportunity which those in our missionary colleges have of receiving Christian instruction during the week. But for this, and similar missionary services, these men would hardly hear the glad tidings of salvation.

My husband fancied he would feel tongue-tied here, not knowing Bengali, and would miss the power of preaching "in the other language" (as we say in the Highlands), which he enjoyed in the Marathi-speaking country; but he finds more than an ample sphere opened to him through English. Many are kept from coming to India by the belief that a difficult native language must be acquired before the missionary can preach to the heathen. It is not so here, however. Any man, straight from home, with the love of Christ burning in his heart, need not lose a moment now before his usefulness begins. If he comes to Calcutta, or any of the great cities of India, he will find many who will understand him in English; among whom, I believe, there are some who are hungering and thirsting for the bread and water of life.

We have begun a Bible-reading on Saturday evenings at eight. Last time the drawing-room was quite full; and we had a most interesting and refreshing meeting.

We have been getting into a whirl rather, but shall relapse into quiet, I hope, when the people go off to Simla. Society here is cultivated and exceedingly agreeable. It has the charm which Indian society often possesses over that of our own colder country; it is more sociable and friendly. There is no stiffness, and not much exclusiveness; indeed, there is hardly room for exclusiveness when everybody is either "in" or "out of" society. In short, we fraternize as only those people can who are fellow-exiles from the dear old fatherland. Most people entertain; hence there are constant dinner-parties. We consider it quite needful to keep some reserved evenings in the week, which are sacred to home and home-engagements; otherwise, "dining out" would soon be a distressing consumption of time. Government House is pre-eminently a centre of hospitality, and there is a free friendliness combined with the state which befits the receptions of Her Majesty's representative, which makes the reunions there the pleasure they are. There is much that is pretty and graceful about our social gatherings. There are many young ladies in Calcutta; and their cool, light costumes, and especially their sweet, bright faces, make the parties much more charming. The variegated dresses of the men, too, add to the effect,—there are so many red coats, and the handsome uniforms of so many services. Two points of difference between Indian and home society strike the eye at once; here there are hardly any old people, and very few boys and girls. These go home as children.

The annual exodus to Simla is now taking place. The different public offices, with all the families of the great and small who constitute their following, emigrate to the far-off, delicious hills; and government will be administered from that serene vantage-ground for the next seven or eight months. Some of the unhappy mortals who must dree their weird in the sweltering plains, object to this yearly flight; but to neutral people, like myself, it does seem a sensible plan to go where the work which has to be done can be done best, as well as most comfortably.

The number of servants one requires is appalling. Indeed, servants and house-rent are the most formidable items in Indian expenditure; and you *must* have what is considered the proper number. It is not a matter of choice, but of necessity. The man who cleans the rooms won't touch a plate off which you have eaten, to be made Emperor of Hindustan. It would break his caste. The man who drives your horse won't groom him or cut grass for him.

The list is pretty much as follows:—You must have the headman of whom I have spoken (the khansāman), who is responsible for all the others. He goes to bazaar and buys your food; another man (the cooly) carries it home; a third cooks it; a fourth (the khitmutgar) brings it to table, and waits on you while you eat it; and a fifth washes the plates. Then you must have a "bearer" to dust the furniture, and a "sweeper" to sweep the rooms. You must have a man to supply the house with water (the bheestee), and another (the dhobee) to take away your clothes and wash them. Then a durwān is necessary to keep your gate; and a gardener, or two if you cultivate flowers. The size of your stable must regulate the number of men required for it, as one man will not look after two horses. You must have a syce for each horse, and a coachman besides, if you own "a machine." Then if you have children, you must have ayahs corresponding with their number, and bearers as well. A durzee, or tailor, to counteract the mischief your dhobee does, who washes your clothes by thumping them on not always very smooth stones; and a peon, to go with chits, or notes, are certainly desirable, if not indispensable; besides the race of day and night punkah-walas,—who are quite indispensable in the hot season,—who have nothing else to do but to pull your punkah when they choose to keep awake. As to *cheating*, a certain amount always goes on, and you must just give in to it if you want a quiet life. A very nice friend of mine is always in a state of chronic indignation with her servants,—changing, turning off, cutting pay, and scolding, until hardly a respectable servant will stay with her: but she punishes herself, for they do not care. She thinks I am too easy-minded, and encourage immorality in this cheating form. But there seems no use in setting out to make the native world come up to our standard of propriety, and so servants have always stayed with us: they get interested, and serve us well; and I think we are perhaps as little cheated as our neighbours are. What I cannot stand is cheating the dumb creatures. When our clever coachman uses the horse's gram (a sort of pea) for himself, then, I confess, I do get angry. This coachman is a Mohammadan, and a most religious man. Unfortunately, he has also a very bad temper. I find him saying his prayers in the most public, ostentatious way, and at the most unseasonable times. For instance, the other day, when I stopped at the door of a house to pay a visit, on my return I found him kneeling on the roof of the gharree instead of sitting on the box; and when we got home he half-killed the syce, an inoffensive lad, in a fit of savage passion. He punishes the horse, too, I am afraid, in more ways than defrauding him of his gram; for the creature turns his ears back and looks askance at him whenever he comes near.

X.

The Free Church Institution.

I VISIT the Institution sometimes, and always with new pleasure. It is intensely interesting to sit by my husband, as he is surrounded by a circle of some score of fine intelligent lads, with thoughtful faces and searching looks, all intently fixed on his face, as he talks, and questions, and lectures, and explains. He encourages them to question him in return, a liberty they avail themselves of largely. It amuses me much to hear them put the most difficult and sometimes far-fetched questions,—generally on some point in English literature, or some abstruse question in philosophy, and always with the apparent expectation that they shall be answered off-hand. I am afraid their belief in their teachers would be very rudely shaken if they were at any time found to fail in their reply. I accompanied him yesterday; and to introduce you thoroughly to this noble college, I will tell you what I saw.

We started soon after nine, and drove through the narrow streets as fast as the numerous obstructions would allow. The strange and novel scenes in native life one constantly comes upon in these bazaars have always a fresh interest for me. The streets are sometimes ludicrously narrow, and in one of the narrowest we came to a dead halt behind a long train of bullock-carts laden with jute. The one in front having unluckily lost its wheel, it was capsized right across the road, and formed an impassable barrier to everything that followed. Here was a dilemma, and no doubt a salutary lesson of patience, if Dr. M. could just have spared the time, and was not so particular about being punctual. It was very droll to watch the apathetic movements of the bullock-men, and to see how coolly they took the whole affair, as they leisurely tied up the broken machine, utterly regardless of our shouts of "juldi, juldi" (quick, quick). At length our syce managed to induce the weary little beasts to drag their loads to the side, and we got past, but with the loss of nearly half an hour.

The native town presents very different aspects at different parts of the day. In the early morning there is the busy buying and selling, and working at the different trades. In the evening there are the gossiping groups you see seated on their heels everywhere outside the houses and shops, enjoying the cool air and talk together; but at noon, on every door-step, before every shop, wherever there is a scrap of shade, on every available spot, lies a sleeping man. The faculty of sleep which the natives possess is wonderful and most enviable. I often notice the punkah-walas sitting on the floor pull-pulling with a monotonous, rather mesmeric motion of the hand, while the head lies on the breast fast asleep. I have sometimes seen a long train of bullock-carts drawn to a side, the patient little beasts never proposing to stir, while their drivers lay, each under his cart, in the dust or mud, calmly taking his siesta. I might have helped myself to a bag of rice, or bale of jute, and no one been a bit the wiser. The noontide sleep, after he has bathed and eaten, seems to be as needful to a native as his night's rest or daily bread.

Having at length overcome all difficulties, and steered our way through a lane—called by some "Dr. Duff's Strait," because he always drove through it to school—so narrow that our gharree had no more than room to pass, and with the usual deep ditch at either side, we arrived at "Duff-iscool" (Duff's school), as the Free Church Institution is popularly called.

You may imagine with what interest one looks on this noble missionary college, where the higher Christian education, which is carrying such a tide of blessing over India, may be said to have originated; and where, day by day, fully a thousand of the youth of this great heathen city receive at least as thorough a Christian training as it has been the glory of Scotland, since the days of John Knox, to give to her sons. The general training is as thorough and good as any Government college provides, with the grand added advantage of religious instruction.

The Institution is situated quite in the native town, in a very populous district, and is an exceedingly handsome and massive structure. It cost about a lakh and a half of rupees (£15,000), collected by Dr. Duff in Britain, America, and India. It is surrounded by a pretty green compound, and the drive takes you round the pillared front to the portico, where, on the one hand, there is the large lecture-hall, and on the other a flight of steps which lead at once to the middle floor; while underneath there are low, vault-like chambers, some of which are used as class-rooms for beginners. Facing the entrance, at the top of the steps, there is a large room seated for gallery exercises; and beyond this, on either hand, stretch long, wide corridors, with rows of open windows, off which the class-rooms for the school division range. On the upper floor, similar class-rooms are arranged for the college and higher school; and over the gallery stands the library, a noble, lofty room, lined with books, and ornamented by a few pictures, the chief being portraits of the missionaries who formerly taught here. It is spacious and airy, and wonderfully cool, though the indispensable punkah is nowhere to be seen except in the library. All the pupils are dressed in white, the young men generally being wrapped in fine soft muslin. There are no turbans or head-gear, as in the other presidencies. All have bare heads and close-cropped hair, like English lads; and most wear shoes and stockings. One thing very observable is the entire absence of all idolatrous marks on the foreheads or persons of the pupils. Orthodox Hindus, as a rule, when they perform their morning ablutions, put on some mark on the forehead, arm, or breast in white paint or red, in lines or in dots, according to the ceremony they have been performing, or the god they worship. But not one of the lads I saw in the Institution showed any such idolatrous sign; a most significant and encouraging fact.

The first part of the work of every day is the opening religious exercises. These are conducted in two different rooms—in Bengali for the junior, and in English for the more advanced. A short passage of Scripture is read and briefly and pointedly explained, and then a short prayer is offered up. The whole only occupies about ten minutes, and all are expected to attend. The non-Christian lads sat during the prayer, but all were very quiet and attentive. After this the work begins. The first class was composed of about fifty mere beginners, who were occupied in learning to pronounce English words. In the lowest classes, great attention to pronunciation is needful, or the boys would never learn to speak accurately. It was very droll to see the frantic endeavours the little fellows made to get their tongues about the unaccustomed sounds. The word "sash" was given; it seemed very hard, and indeed impossible, to some of the taller boys, who were beginning their English education rather late, and who could not get beyond "sass" or "shash." The bright, keen-eyed younger ones did much better; and all seemed to think it great fun, and tried new words and combinations with an appreciation of the mirth which would hardly have been possible to shy English boys. Nothing delights a sharp little fellow more, whose tongue is glib, than to be allowed to give the rest of the class difficult words to pronounce.

From this there were classes in every different stage of advancement; there were lessons on objects, geography, history, grammar, and indeed every branch taught in schools at home. One thing which strikes every visitor is the eagerness and intelligence of these boys, who learn with a pleasure and a will not often seen among schoolboys in Europe. The proficiency in mental arithmetic was something wonderful; and the readiness with which the boys cast up long sums in their heads was so surprising to the slower processes of my own brain, that I thought they must be answering by chance. But no. I took my pencil ignominiously, and calculated, and they were correct in every instance I tried.

All this was very interesting; but much more so were the classes for Scripture knowledge, which are taught by native Christians and the missionaries. With the more important historical parts of the Old Testament and the Gospels, even the younger classes seem quite familiar; and they are able to repeat a good deal by heart, especially the narratives of the parables and miracles. A great delight of the younger boys is to be allowed to repeat poetry. Their memories seem filled with it,—pretty pieces on the goodness of God, love and respect to parents, truthfulness, forgiveness, and all the deepest lessons in morality and religion; though a very good rule obtains, that no piece is to be committed to memory which the boy cannot translate into his mother tongue. In short, the training these boys receive fills their minds from the outset with the good seed of moral and religious truth. The other studies of the college department are determined by the University regulations; which, of course, are binding on the Missionary as well as Government colleges, the University fixing the subjects of examination, and giving academical degrees to those who pass. English literature, Bengali, Sanskrit, mathematics, and mental philosophy, are the subjects chiefly prescribed.

It was a deeply interesting morning, and all the gentlemen were very good showing me the work. I sat beside the native professors, Messrs. Chatterjee and K. Banerjee, for some time, and enjoyed their classes and teaching exceedingly. It stirs one's heart to think of all the good this great Institution has done for India; how many men it has sent forth from its halls and class-rooms, who are now scattered over the length and breadth of the land, at least of all Northern India, as missionaries, evangelists, and teachers, besides many useful, enlightened men who now hold posts of trust and influence everywhere. We have met numbers of such wherever we have travelled over India.

XI.

Our Homes.

CALCUTTA, *March 23.*

YOU put me in mind of a promise I made in a rash moment always to remember "the bairns' bit" in my letters; and you say you want to be told some of our "manners and customs," and what our house is like, "especially auntie's own room." Well, to begin with our room, where I am now sitting at my writing-table in my favourite window. Yet, what is to come forth from a brain reeling with quinine; and what sort of tale is a fevered head likely to tell? But it is mail-day, and the head must do its work whether able or not.

Our Indian rooms, then, do not enter from corridors and narrow passages, as at home: they usually open off wide cool verandahs, or from one to another; for every arrangement here is made on one principle, and with one object, to secure as much air and free ventilation as possible. Two large doors at the foot of our pretty drawing-room, which always stand open, but for privacy are hung across with green damask curtains, give entrance to this apartment, which is on the upper floor, and delightfully big. I am afraid you would think it looked bare and uninhabited, for the walls are unpapered, and the floor is covered with only a simple cool matting. Most Calcutta houses would certainly strike you as lacking the aspect of cozy comfort our dear old home apartments wear. But the numerous doors and windows, with their green venetians, are suited to our climate, and have a cool and cheery effect. Opposite to where I sit, an open door leads into a pleasant little room for Dr. M.; at one corner another great door opens on to a wide verandah which stretches along the whole side of the house, looking on to the garden, whence comes a delicious breeze, which at this moment is coquetting rather freely with my paper. From another corner I have access to what is almost the chief necessary of life in this grilling land, a charming bath-room, which is almost as big as one of your ordinary bed-rooms. On a low platform made of cool chunām, or plaster, stand rows of *chatties*,—round globe like little utensils made of coarse red pottery filled with water, ready to dash over you at any minute,—and a huge, deep *gurra*, a reservoir of the same unpretending character, into which you can plunge bodily when driven desperate by mosquitoes or heat. But the chief charm to me in my room is this window at which I sit, though to most people the charm I mean would be a decided drawback. Just below there is a *bustee*, or native village, composed of miserable little huts, filled with the poorest of the people, swarming with children who are innocent of any garb but what nature has given them, always dreadfully noisy, and often offensive in worse ways. But here I see the life of the common people; and my window affords me many an interesting study, which I should like to picture to you if I had time.

But before we look abroad, I must finish the picture within. The first thing that would attract your attention, could you enter just now, would certainly be a novel erection in the middle of the room, and which looks like a little room in itself, only the walls are of net, and the roof of white calico. This is suspended from the ceiling; and inside there is a large, wide, low cot or bed, a small table, and chair. This is our citadel, in which we are safe from the attacks of our mortal enemies, the mosquitoes. There is another mysterious arrangement within the mosquito walls which would puzzle you. A deep frill of thick calico, gathered on to a narrow strip of wood, is hung from the top of the bed, and stretches right across. A string is attached to this, which is carried out through a tube in the wall, and is pulled from without. This is the night punkah, which is one of the necessary evils attending the strange, and in some respects unnatural, life we of northern latitudes must lead in this tropical land. This queer little machine waves over us all night; and without it we should not be able to close an eye, the heat is so dreadful now. But all that can be said for it is, that it is the least of two evils. The punkah-walas, as the men are called who do the pulling work, are very aggravating. Whenever they think we are fairly asleep they stop, and deliberately take a little nap to themselves; whereupon we wake up in soaking heat and terrible wrath, and by the time we have roused the man and cooled down in every sense, sleep has fled and is not to be wooed back. Among the many delusions which obtain among you folks at home regarding this wonderful land, a favourite one is that it abounds in luxury. Now the greatest luxuries I know are this rather doubtful one of a night punkah, and a glass of really cold water; which of course means that it is iced.

The other night one of our gentlemen, anxious to rouse, but most unwilling to strike, the slumberer, threw some water on the face of one of the punkah-walas, who, instead of pulling, was laid comfortably on his back, sound asleep; when instantly the man took to his heels, and was no more seen. He would not have minded a thrashing much; but I fancy he thought the water endangered his caste.

Our drawing-room is a shady, pleasant, home-like room, and looks more clothed than most, as we have the embellishment of a carpet in the centre, leaving a cool margin of white matting beyond. A row of large doors open on to the deep verandah, which is darkened with green "chicks," or blinds, made of thin strips of reed, so fashioned as to shut out all glare, and yet give admittance to the delicious soft breeze from the gentle south. Our verandahs give a look and feel of expansion to our Indian rooms, and prevent the experience, which otherwise we should have when they are shut up, of being caged. Our verandah is amply supplied with lounging-chairs, and small low tables, and we may be said to dwell in it. As soon as the sun takes himself far enough into shade, the chicks are pulled up, and the breeze allowed to enter at its own sweet will, and we look out to the foliage-skirted garden, or, later, to the starlit dome and glowing Eastern night; while the crickets and grasshoppers make their shrill melody in the grass, and the lovely fire-flies dance and glow among the bushes and trees. One charming kind of decoration we can always count upon for our rooms, and which transforms their bareness into beauty, is the quantity of lovely bouquets which are brought in fresh and fragrant every morning all the year round.

Our nights, now that the hot season has set in, are often, as you may have gathered, a battle with heat and refractory punkah-walas, mosquitoes, and howling jackals. Worst of all, the latter spend their days in sleep, and their nights in unearthly yells, which have more of Pandemonium in the sound than anything else ever heard in the world. You won't wonder, then, that we sometimes get up rather more tired than when we lay down.

However, we repair to our nice little verandah-room, open to the sweet pleasant garden, and have our chota-hazri, or preliminary breakfast, after which our energies begin to revive. We are down generally by six, and redeem a great deal more than time by getting up so early. We see the beautiful unfolding of the morning as it goes on "shining more and more unto the perfect day;" we hear the happy birdies sing their early songs of praise; we have the first freshness of the flowers while they are full of their dewy fragrance; and we have an opportunity of watching many of God's works and ways, which people lose who spend the morning hours in sleep.

"Oh! timely happy, timely wise
Hearts that with rising morn arise!
Eyes that the beam celestial view
Which evermore makes all things new!"

Our morning hours are indeed delicious and most precious. We get through a great deal of real work before the conventionalities of the day begin, and we have to submit to the restraints of a proper toilette. After seven, Dr. M. receives Bengali visitors; and at nine we have prayers and breakfast. When this is over, I do my housekeeping, which consists chiefly in trying to keep the khansāman's daily bazaar accounts within reasonable bounds; and then the world of visitors is let loose. From twelve to two are the hours for ceremonious visiting; and in connection with this we have some of our funny "customs." The durwān is the gatekeeper; and ours, by the way, is quite a character—an up-country man, who speaks beautiful high Hindi, and scorns all Bengalis and their tongue. He has a glittering eye, and a nose like a hawk's beak, and has some very hawk-like propensities. There is a standing feud between him and my durzee, and he takes advantage of his position as custodier of the premises to annoy this man by examining his bundle every evening as he departs from his work, in case it may contain any of the Mem Saheb's cloth! I have constantly to interfere between the belligerents. Well, one of our happy and sensible "customs" is, that when you are busy or engaged this functionary is told to say to all comers, "Darwāzā band hai," or, "The gate is shut;" in which case the carriage deposits its cards, and drives on to another gate. If, however, entrance is permitted, the carriage drives in, and the durwān announces the fact by striking his gong. If the visitor is a gentleman, one stroke is enough; if a lady, she merits two; and if it announces your doctor, then there are three. The next part of the ceremonial is that cards are sent up, because the native servants make wonderful havoc of names; you return your "salām," and the visitor at length walks in. As an illustration of the name difficulty, I may tell you of a friend in Bombay who was a lawyer; and as it is common to indicate a man by his profession, this gentleman was popularly known among the natives as "Liar Larken!"—*liar* being their pronunciation of *lawyer*.

A native visitor never takes his departure of his own accord. Etiquette requires that you dismiss him, which you do in the politest way possible,—not by saying, "Go," but by saying, hospitably, "Pray come again; the sooner we see your face, the pleasanter it will be," or with other speeches, which I hope are always as sincere as polite. I often think how nice it would be if this dismissing rule obtained in all society, especially when idle prosy people inflict their leisure on you.

We have no bells in India; and when we want anything we shout for somebody, and it is a rule that one of the bearers shall always be in attendance. The table-gentry only appear at meal-times.

Before I stop for to-day, I think I must tell you a droll little anecdote our friend Mr. Long told me when dining with us last night. He took Miss Milman to the house of one of his Babu friends lately, to pay a visit in the zenana. She presented one of the ladies with a picture; and the next time Mr. Long went to the house, he found the picture framed and hung up in the Babu's room, with this inscription written below: "Presented by Her Holiness, Miss Milman, the Lord Bishop of Calcutta's sister!" This puts me in mind of a letter Dr. M. once received, which was addressed thus:—"The Right Reverend Dr. Murray Mitchell, Esq., Chief Priest, Bombay"!

I have just been watching an immense adjutant bird, which has paid us a visit, and has been pacing with slow dignity along the top of the garden wall. These birds are most grotesque,—like huge cranes, with tall spindle unfeathered legs, and long neck with *bag* below—the larder of reserve. A wicked little urchin in the village below threw up to it a tiny live kitten, which the horrid creature swallowed at one gulp, and deposited in the bag. These birds and the jackals are the scavengers of Calcutta; and so valuable as such, that a fine of fifty rupees is imposed on any one who kills an adjutant. They love the uppermost perches; and one very favourite resort is the roof of Government House, where they are at most times to be seen, surmounting the highest points. There is one generally perched on the horn of the unicorn in the royal arms, and another on the nose of the lion. They always stand on one leg, and have a very sinister and evil look. Our crows evidently look on this visitor as an intruder, and are making a great noise and fuss, though always keeping at a safe distance from his formidable beak. When one of these creatures flies past, it sounds like a little whirlwind.

Tell dear little R. that we have discovered a jackal, which lives under the steps which lead up from the garden to the verandah-room. The servants wanted to hunt it out, poor little thing, and kill it; but of course Dr. M. would not allow this, and protects it. Its one little voice will not add much to the general howl, when the pack hold their orgies at night over some treasure-trove of carrion.

Tell her, also, that a beautiful kite has made its nest in a little nook on the housetop; which happily we only know of, and we hope nobody else will find it out. There is only one egg,—a very large beautiful one, with a blue tinge; and I watch it every evening, and the mother bird knows us now, and is not much frightened when we look.

Our good old khansāman has a son of his old age, I find,—a Benjamin, the very apple of his eye. One morning, when we went downstairs to breakfast, I spied a wee fellow standing with the servants, grave and dignified, with his arms folded across his breast in imitation of them—a miniature khitmutgar. He was elaborately dressed in a white muslin coat, scarlet satin trousers, and green and yellow skull-cap. I could not forbear a smile at the important little face, with a decided twinkle coming out from the corner of his eye, and a very conscious mouth. "Who are you, my little man?" I asked, giving him a pat on his head. "Yih merā betā hai," answered the khansāman proudly ("He is my son"). "Your grandson," I suggested. The child came up to the old man's knee. But no; he was his own son, and his name was Meetoo. Being thus introduced, Meetoo made a profound salaam down to the ground; and the company having seated themselves, he went round the table doing ditto to each person. A liberal donation of fruit from the table was the occasion of more salaams; and then, on the conclusion of breakfast, he and I had a chat, and I found him a very sagacious and wide-awake young gentleman.

The khansāman had brought his family—consisting of a pleasant-looking, youngish woman, his wife, and this child—to live in the compound; and ever since little Meetoo has been my most devoted squire.

Well, yesterday, again going down to breakfast, Meetoo was standing in the hall in his finery, but this time with a companion. A tiny mite of a girl-child stood beside him, whom, but for the gleam of her lustrous black eyes, you might have taken for a doll. She was arrayed in crimson gauze, with spangles of gold. "Whom have you got here, Meetoo?" I asked in my wonderment. "Yih merī bibī hai" ("This is my wife"), said he, with a profound salaam, and with the air of a knight of renown. "Your wife!" we all exclaimed in a breath; and the servants behind had to retire a little to get their titter out. The youthful pair did not look at all abashed, but the precocious husband ordered his wife to make a salaam, and showed her how. It was exceedingly droll, and looked like playing at marriage. Plenty of fruit, and a rupee in each hand of the small bride, which the tiny fingers could hardly double over, made them depart hand in hand, in great glee. It is very pretty to see them playing together about the doors; and it is very nice having the little creatures about. He patronizes her in the funniest way.

XII.

Female Schools.

IN the time, not so very long ago, when female education in India was a thing unknown, and every effort to introduce it was met with determined opposition, a system of orphanages, or schools for destitute girls, seemed the likeliest way to make a beginning of the work—to get in the thin end of the wedge, so to speak. Foundlings and poor little outcasts were, unhappily, too easy to find. No wonder, in a country where girls were often counted as nothing, and the birth of a female child was considered a curse rather than a blessing; where female infanticide was fearfully prevalent among not a few classes even of high position; and where the parents still dedicate them to temples—"marry them to the idol," as it is called, which means abandoning them to a life of infamy. Where such things existed, it seemed a very plain duty to institute houses of refuge—nurseries for Christ—where these little ones could be gathered in, and lovingly cared for, and trained for usefulness and happiness here and hereafter. Miss Cooke, afterwards Mrs. Wilson, who arrived in Calcutta in 1821, soon established the "Agurparah Refuge;" and she has been followed by many workers in many societies ever since. No schools, I believe, have been more successful and far-reaching in their usefulness and influence than those established by our Scottish Ladies' Society—the Free Church "Society for Promoting Female Education in the East." My heart thrills as I look back on the many happy hours I have spent in them. The very happiest work of my missionary life has been in connection with the training of the highly intelligent and interesting girls gathered together in Bombay and Poona. The Orphanage here is equally important.

Every Sunday that Dr. M. can arrange his work for it, we come round by the Orphanage from church, and he gives the girls a short address, questioning them as he goes on. The sight, as we enter the schoolroom, is very pretty. The whole school is collected together, the little ones seated in the gallery dressed in their Sunday's best. This consists of a simple white frock, and a *chudder*, or veil of white muslin or net, carried over the head; though not arranged to conceal the face, like the chudders of the non-Christian women. The simplicity of this attire, which is a real covering for the person, contrasts favourably with the gay colours and jewels, and often rather scanty clothing, of the ladies we see in the zenanas. The dress of the women is certainly one of the things which should be included in the much talked of "reforms;" and it is cheering to see that, in deference to the opinion of the zenana lady-teachers, a modification as to attire often takes place in the homes in which they teach. The native Christian women of all the missions have adopted a uniform style of dress, which is very much what I have just described as worn in the Orphanage, and is exceedingly pretty and graceful, as well as befitting those whose "adorning" ought to be "the meek and quiet spirit." There are now about sixty girls in the Orphanage, of all sizes and ages; nice pleasing girls, some very intelligent, most of whom have been baptized on their own profession of faith.

This "Orphan Home," as Mr. and Mrs. Fordyce delighted to call it, when it was under their loving care, has done a great and good work in Bengal. It has had many earnest workers connected with it. Several of our missionaries have lived in the upper floor of the house, in order that their wives might devote themselves to the charge of the poor little children in the floor below; and no one who has not tried this work knows what the labour, the anxiety, and wearing sense of responsibility are which it involves. But these ladies have done it bravely, often in sickness and weakness, and amid many family cares, from love to Christ and pity to the orphan children; and their work has not been in vain. The well-educated, well-trained Christian women that these orphans have been transformed into, are now scattered over Northern India, filling most useful spheres in native Christian society, as wives, and mothers, and teachers, and Bible-women, and heads of Christian households.

Of all influences at work in the native community, none tells more powerfully than that which goes forth from these native Christian households. Nothing preaches more eloquently to a young man than the sight of one of these homes, where love and confidence reign, and where the wife takes her own rightful position. I have often noticed the profound impression made by this simple spectacle. A Hindu comes in of an evening to visit a native Christian friend. He is welcomed by his friend's wife, as well as by himself. She presides at her own tea-table, while the children play or sit round; and (if there is no one to tell) the visitor also partakes of the tea. The evening is concluded by the most beautiful and touching of all services, united family worship. "The Book" is brought out: the hymn of praise is sung; the Word is reverently read, generally verse by verse in turn, all round: and prayer is offered to the unseen but present Father of all. I have heard this scene spoken of almost with tears by heathen young men, who, in their hearts, sigh and long that their homes could be the same as these Christian households.

Orphanages and boarding-schools in past years have been of incalculable service in providing wives for the Christian converts. Now, happily, there is another source of supply for this pleasant need—namely, these very Christian families which have sprung up, and to which I have been alluding. What nice girls there are in some of these families!—sweet, modest, pretty creatures, who take one's heart by storm.

One little girl lies in the Orphanage, slowly sinking under consumption. She seems very near her end; but it will be a happy change for her, as she knows and loves her Saviour. She is one of the little castaways I alluded to. Her cruel relatives—perhaps because she was "only a girl"—exposed her in the jungles, where she was discovered by some humane person, who sent her to the Mission. She is very happy. It is quite touching to go in and look at her beaming face, in the midst of all her weakness and pain, and hear her speak of the joy she feels, because "she is so soon going to be with Jesus."

Of all the day schools I have seen, I think Dr. Duff's day school for high caste girls interests me the most. To one who knows anything of the almost insurmountable difficulties which have attended all efforts to educate the women, the very existence of such a school means so much. It is so significant of progress, and of the breaking down of prejudice and opposition.

What you see is simply a group of wee creatures, ranged on

gallery seats, in the prettiest of fancy costumes, the innocent little faces set in surroundings of gauze and tinsel, the large dark dreamy eyes gravely fixed on your face without shyness or fear, but with a look of intense inquiry, almost scrutiny. The quaint little figures so daintily robed and bedizened, and covered with beads, bangles, and anklets, and nose-rings, and such unusual embellishments; and the novel sight altogether is extremely interesting. And yet this is only a small part of the interest, for these are the children of the highest castes, who come out of the secluded homes where the women live their imprisoned lives, which have been so firmly closed against all enlightenment for ages. They come in the morning and return in the evening, carrying back with them the lessons and impressions they have received,—spreading an influence which must be like a fresh breath from heaven in these shut-up homes, and which will work in time its own silent but sure way. At the age of eight or nine these children leave school to be married, or, as we say, betrothed; after which they must not be seen again without the zenana walls. It is very grievous to think that these poor young things are so soon caught in the meshes of relentless fate, which rules everything here, and married when they ought to be in the nursery, thenceforward to be cooped up for life in these cruel zenanas. Hindu etiquette is inexorable on this point; and as yet a girl has never been allowed to remain in school after her betrothal has taken place. Here the system of zenana, or house to house teaching, comes in as the boon it is. The teacher follows these children to their homes; and after they become little "*bows*" (married women), their education, which has had the foundation so happily laid in school, is carried on.

This school was founded by Dr. Duff in 1857, and was an important addition to the orphanages. An intelligent Koolin

Brahman, with wonderful liberality, and from personal kindness to Dr. Duff, granted him the use of two rooms in his own house, in which to make the experiment of a female school for the higher castes, in which the Bible should be taught. He commenced with three pupils. The numbers, however, soon increased under his personal care and supervision; for he paid a daily visit, fostering the little nursling, and watching its growth, which, though slow at first, went on steadily and most encouragingly. Now there are upwards of forty pupils in attendance every day. [Before we left Calcutta in 1873, the numbers had nearly doubled; and the children *paid fees*, which is a significant fact in a school for girls.]

The Bethune Institution, close by, is the same sort of school; but with this great difference, that in ours, as I said, the Scriptures are taught. To give women a wholly secular education is a grand mistake. It is perilous for the men, but far more so for the women. With education and enlightenment would come liberty; but liberty without a controlling and sanctifying influence along with it would be no boon.

I think I shall often find my way to this charming school. It is quite a comedy to watch the grave little consequential faces, as the small creatures get up with stately dignity to point out Edinburgh on the map—the *Ultima Thule* of their imagination, where the great "ma-bap," * Dr. Duff, now lives, who gave them the school. I could not resist giving one bright fair winsome wee thing a surreptitious hug, which would have been highly perilous to its caste, I am afraid, if it had been seen. These children are brought daily to and from school in large, close omnibuses, under the charge of careful servants. To walk even a hundred yards in the open street is a thing inadmissible to a woman of caste.

* Father and mother.

The original teacher was Mrs. Chatterjee, a Bengali Christian lady connected with the Mission. She nobly seconded Dr. Duff in his efforts for this school; and to her chiefly it owes its present prosperity. Associated with her is a dear old pundit, whose love to the children is beautiful to see. He might well be called the "ma-bap," also, for his care of the little ones is quite motherly, not to say fatherly; and the younger pundit, who assists the old man, quite partakes of his spirit, and shows that his mantle is descending upon him.

Let us hope that this "little one will become a thousand, and the small one a strong nation." May the Lord hasten it in its time.

XIII.

Incidents.

CALCUTTA, *April 11.*

TO-DAY the Churruk-pooja, or swinging festival, was celebrated. As we were sitting down to chota-hazri, the māli, or gardener, an old gray-headed man, came to the door, and asked if he might go to the *tamāshā* or show. Presently another came and made the same request, and I wondered if the whole establishment were going to march off—the native servants are such babies. But this made Dr. M. inquire what it was all about; and he found it was the celebration of this great festival, whereupon he and Mr. D. went to see the *tamāshā* too.

This used to be one of the most brutal and brutalizing of all the idolatrous spectacles in India; and it is by no means a far past time when bloody rites marked the observances at this debasing rite. The victims who in former times "had a vow," and "took the hook," were frequently women. The hook was really inserted in the flesh, whereby the person was suspended and whirled round; but it is too horrible to speak of. There are no such practices permitted now in Bengal. The strong arm of British law protects these poor deluded victims from themselves, and their torturers, the Brahman priests.

Dr. M. looked narrowly to see if the orders for the suppression of the bloody part of the ceremonial were attended to; and one is unspeakably thankful to know that nothing of the old loathsome rites was anywhere visible. Even in the matter of sacrificing animals there is a considerable change. He and Mr. D. stood beside the sacrificial post, in the cleft of which the head of the victim is inserted; but, except one poor little kid, they saw no creature put to death. Some few years ago the blood of the poor victims would flow incessantly for hours. There were plenty of simulated appliances—hooks, and rods, and ropes, and all the instruments of torture; but it was a make-believe: even what looked like blood at first were only great patches of red paint! Thanks be to God, the glory of the infamous Kali—that atrocious ten-armed goddess, who wears a necklace of skulls—is waning. There were, of course, great crowds assembled, and a fearful din of horrible music, and plenty of tom-tomming and tom-foolery. Men were dressed like women, and painted like tigers and leopards; there were dancing and singing,—objectionable enough, I am told,—and ridiculous pantomime; but let us be deeply thankful that the dreadful Churruk-pooja, the very saturnalia of Satan, has dwindled into this kind of childish carnival, or stupid, vulgar show.

April 22.

Last night Mr. D. and my husband went to see the public worship of the Adi Brahmo-Samaj; that is, the older section of this body. You must know that the Brahmos, like too many other societies, have split into two sections; which may be designated respectively as conservative and progressive. The latter is led by Babu K. C. Sen; the other chiefly represented by the head of the Tagore family. Both acknowledge the celebrated Rajah Ramohun Roy as their founder. It is nearly forty years ago since this able and earnest man promulgated the doctrine that there is one spiritual God and Father, who should be spiritually worshipped; and both parties of his followers hold this as the principal part of their creed.

Both sections have chiefly drawn the truth which their creed contains from the Holy Scriptures, although I am aware that the conservative Brahmos would stoutly deny this regarding themselves. Unhappily, both cast from them that which gives life to the whole. They acknowledge the one invisible God, but they reject Him who is the "image of the Invisible," "the first-born of every creature," in whom "it pleased the Father that all fulness should dwell."

The worship was conducted in an orderly fashion, but was very cold and formal. The place of meeting was in a private house, as the original body has no "mandir," or church, as yet. The gentlemen were most politely received, and conducted to a long, narrow room, the centre of which was railed off and paved with marble, the top and bottom being occupied by benches for the audience. On a small raised and carpeted dais in this centre place, two officiating Brahmans sat, cross-legged; before each was a low, marble-topped stool, on which lay prayer-books and hymn-books; opposite these was a sort of desk, in which sat the singer; and behind was a harmonium, at which Mr. Dijendernath Tagore presided,—the eldest son of the leader of this branch of the Samaj. The service began with the short recitation of a kind of creed, in which all the congregation joined. Prayers were then read by the officiating Brahmans; a short sermon in Bengali was also read, and extracts from sacred Sanscrit books; while all was intermixed with hymns sung and chanted, accompanied by the harmonium and a tom-tom or drum. This was the whole service, and it lasted nearly two hours. It is thus celebrated every Wednesday evening. The room was pretty well filled, but no woman was present.

April 23.

We had a visit this morning from Mr. D. Tagore, the gentleman who presided at the harmonium during the Samaj service last evening. He is the grandson of that Dwarkanath Tagore, who visited England two or three times a good many years ago, when it was not so common for Hindus to cross "the black water" as it is now. His brother is a member of the Bombay Civil Service, and is now judge at Ahmedabad. I was much taken with our friend to-day; he is exceedingly refined and gentlemanlike. The conversation was deeply interesting. How near the kingdom of heaven some of these earnest, inquiring men seem to be!

Mr. Tagore has asked me to visit his zenana—an invitation of which I shall certainly avail myself. His sister-in-law, from Bombay, of whom Miss Carpenter speaks so much, is paying a visit there at present, and it will be very pleasant to meet her.

April 24.

A nice young man has breakfasted with us, Mr. K. P. G., one of the converts of our Mission. He is a medical student, and I feel quite proud to think that he has distinguished himself more than any student of his year.

Yesterday, the annual distribution of prizes and honours took place at the Medical College, and our missionaries had the great satisfaction of seeing one of the *alumni* of our Institution, and, better still, one of the Christians connected with the Mission, receive some of the highest honours. He has gained two gold medals, and has got a watch and several volumes as prizes, besides two certificates of merit. He and one other student were singled out by the chairman, Sir R. Temple, to receive special congratulations on their success. He is now going to England to compete for an appointment in the Government service, and I hope he will succeed. I also hope that the kind people at home will not spoil him! He is modest as well as intelligent, and has a great deal of determination in his face—a quality perhaps rare in his race.

There are five of his countrymen who now have appointments in the medical service, and of course they can rise as high in its ranks as Englishmen can. Strange to say, they are all converts, and good influential Christian men. Two of them are in Bombay, and three in Bengal.

April 26.

I have been glancing over Miss Carpenter's book, and am so amused to find, in a kind notice of my dear old Poona school, the following remark:—"Some of the jackets worn by the little girls were somewhat after the fashion of Joseph's coat of many colours." Of course they were! In manufacturing them, the children used to joke about their "Joseph coats." The gay morsels of chintz, out of which these little garments are fashioned, were given to us by our kind merchant-friends, who gladly sent us bundles of these "samples" when they had otherwise served their day. Many a useful bundle of this sort I have had; and our good matron, Mrs. Miller, always hailed the arrival of such. They made at once delightful work-material for the little ones, and supplemented the scanty little wardrobes of her children. Miss Carpenter also notices our magnificent tamarind-tree in the Mission compound, beneath which the dear children have their pleasant, shady playground, and where they sit of an evening and work, and sing their pretty hymns. Miss Carpenter says of their singing, what so many others have noticed, that it is "peculiarly sweet and beautiful."

Dr. Duff's girls' school here bids fair to rival the old Poona one in my affections. It is one of my favourite haunts. The children all belong to the higher castes and classes, and some of them are such bonnie wee things. They have sweet little gentle faces, wonderfully fair, with necks and arms and ankles, ears and noses, ornamented with beads and bangles, and jewels of all sorts, according to the poverty or riches of their fathers. Most of them are so small that it seems more natural to take them on my lap and play with them, and fondle them, than to teach them; and they look up in my face with their great lustrous eyes, half frightened, but easily reassured. I long to give them cake and sweet biscuits, which would, of course, break up the school; but we may give them sweetmeats if made in their own way, and by a Brahman confectioner. One English sweetie would break any child's caste for life.

Meetoo is intent on study. I have given him a slate, and he sits under the stairs, inflicting his ardour on me, and shouting his sums at the top of his voice. Kite-making, however, is a rival occupation, and he may soon desist. It is very droll to see the good old father flying the kites with him, and scrambling among the trees to find a missing one, and doing anything the young tyrant may take it into his foolish little head to order him to do.

April 28.

My letters were most unhappily cut short yesterday by a visit from a German lady, who did not comprehend the value of mail-day hours, and stayed half the forenoon. She came in, in spite of the formula "Durwāzā band hai," or, "The gate is shut;" which is our truthful way of saying "Not at home" in this country.

This has been the hottest day, I think, I ever felt, and it is a most trying kind of heat; whatever air there is has a hot electric feel, as if it came from the mouth of a furnace, and yet the sensation is of being in a perpetual steam-bath. The moisture bursts out all over one in innumerable rills, producing a stinging, prickling, irritating sensation, which is not pleasant, to say the least. One's head feels weighted with lead, and life is hardly more than an endurance. My never-failing recipe in weather like this is to have plenty to do, only one's hands don't do anything comfortably any more than one's head; they have a boiled feeling, like a washerwoman's who has been manipulating all day in the tub. Outside there is a white-heat look on everything; the sun has a fiery fierceness in his glare, as if everything he looked upon must be scorched and scathed. Nature is perfectly still, as if awed; the leaves hang limp and parched; the grass crumples up and disappears; the poor birds hide themselves away in any corner where there is a bit of shade; there is not even a fly abroad; all life seems frightened into quiescence, and mankind—at least the native portion—is asleep. I think we are sure to have a storm soon. These storms, called "nor'-westers," are most seasonable and merciful visitants in heat like this. They come very suddenly, and with the most impressive grandeur; thunder and lightning and tempest, "blowing and roaring, and roaring and blowing," like the poet-laureate's "New Year," and then the flood-gates of heaven are opened, and what a blessed cooling descends upon the earth! Everything at once seems to live again.

One of these storms came upon us rather untowardly one

evening. When we don't drive, or take a stroll in "the Secretary's Walk" in the cool of the evening, we sit in the garden, and have tea on the croquet-green. On Tuesdays we are always thus at home, and our friends know it, and come to see us; it is much pleasanter than forenoon visiting, which is one of the stupid things people do here. As soon as the sun dips sufficiently to ensure shade, a number of low, light chairs are carried out, tea is brought to us, and we sit under the darkening sky, while the sweet south breeze, which is always delicious in the hot season, cools down our fevered frames.

Last week we arranged a nice little garden entertainment for our native friends, and invited some people to meet them. The green was set with numbers of small tables, covered with cakes, and tea, and ices, and flowers. Seats of all sorts and bits of carpet were put down everywhere. Some of our friends had come, and our garden-party promised to be both pretty and pleasant, when, lo! Mr. Don said quietly, "Look there!" and truly enough a cloud like a man's hand had risen in the west, and we knew what would follow. Consternation seized us; we all jumped to our feet; each one snatched up something—chair, table, cups, fruit, everything—and rushed pell-mell into the house. Not a moment too soon. The heavens grew black as ink; the birds flew in terror to some cover, filling the air with their screams; the wind swept past with a low portentous sigh; and we had hardly our goods and ourselves under shelter, and the doors and windows secured, when the storm was upon us, and raging in mad tumult without.

The air becomes thick with sand, and lurid like the yellowest of London fogs; the wind rises into fury, and the dust is driven hither and thither as by a whirlwind. The sun seems blotted out, and in the appalling darkness you see the lightning play and dart, and zig-zag from heaven to earth, without one moment's intermission. The thunder comes, not in distinct explosions, and then a pause, but in one continuous roll of terrific reverberating noise, while the rain descends with an *abandon* quite in keeping with the other forces of the storm. It generally comes in horizontal sheets of water, instead of drops, and is driven by the mighty wind as you have seen sea-spray driven from the wave-tops in showers of foam. A storm like this is a magnificent spectacle, and its effects are delicious. In a wonderfully short time the conflict ceases—the thunder rolls away into the distance, the wind is hushed, the sun shines out, and nature, though tearful, looks happy and refreshed. Everything literally rejoices on every side; the air feels cool and light, and for some days there is pleasure in existence.

Our little fête was spoiled; but when the war without ceased, we made up by doing what we could for the pleasure of our guests within, and all is well that ends well.

Dr. M. has been away for some days in the villages with Mr. ——, visiting schools, and preaching to the people, and he has evidently been a prey to more than the heat. He has come back a mass of bites, and half-starved; the creatures feasted on him while he fasted, which was hardly fair. During his absence I paid a most pleasant little visit to the P——s, who have gone to a pretty place over the river for a change. This is near Howrah, which lies opposite Calcutta, on the Hooghly, and is now an important suburb, being the terminus of the East India Railway.

The house my friends have taken is a pretty quaint old habitation, standing in a large green compound, and with a verandah going quite round the house, from which, at different points, you have the most varied and beautiful views of Calcutta, the river, and the shipping. It was cool and delicious, and Mrs. P. is charming, and I enjoyed myself thoroughly. Mr. P. took me there and brought me back in a pretty little green boat, threading our way through the great ships and steamers which lie closely moored in the stream, sometimes six abreast. This beautiful river is very treacherous, however. The currents are so strong, and the channels between the sand-banks so narrow, that accidents are of very frequent occurrence. The other evening two magnificent ships were going out, homeward bound, one to Liverpool, the other to Dundee, with the largest cargo of jute which ever left the Hooghly, when the wind suddenly shifted: a collision occurred; both touched the terrible quicksands, and in almost less time than I take to tell it both had disappeared and were swallowed up, covered over with the shifting sand!

My husband feels the heat grievously. The long drives in the fiery sun to the Institution (where, observe, there are no punkahs), and the intolerable blinding glare, try him terribly. But the college recess is at hand. It is always a puzzle to me why the schools don't meet in the early morning, instead of the hot noontide, as is the sensible custom in other places. Up country all the heavy work is done before the heat of the day comes on. People at home fancy that life in India is a luxurious *dolce far niente* kind of existence. On the contrary, everybody is overworked. This is true of all office-men, merchants, missionaries, and editors; and even the high Government officials, with the Viceroy at their head, are no exception to the rule—all alike have their energies overtasked. I suppose the reason is that a few do here what the many do at home. So it is that people break down, and either have to go home or die. This is, of course, attributed to the climate; but to say that *it* is the cause of so many overworked brains and shattered nervous systems among us is simply a libel.

The work which the missionaries of our Church have to do is an example of the "pluralities" which exist here. They are professors of a college and school with about fourteen hundred on the roll, having to teach several hours of every day; they have a great deal to do with the University and the examinations for degrees; they are expected to be members of the Bible, tract, and other societies; to be ready on every occasion to lecture, and to speak at public meetings; then they have to preach, and, when possible, to itinerate; they have to write for all manner of periodicals, and to watch every utterance of the native press on religious subjects especially, and be ready with an answer; besides home correspondence; they have to search out and deal with inquirers;—and the number of men who call and expect advice and help, or desire friendly conference with the missionary who is kind and sympathetic, is simply endless. Then some think it their duty to study the native languages and literature, without which the native mind cannot, indeed, be thoroughly understood and dealt with; and this brings translation of the Scriptures, composition of tracts, and other work of this sort.

This looks a startling catalogue, but it is not an exhaustive one. Every man who is a real missionary is worked, or works himself rather, up to the last point of endurance.

Dr. Ogilvie dined with us last night, and as we were alone, his natural shyness wore off, and he was very pleasant and entertaining. He related some of his experiences with the lads of his college, which were very droll. A young fellow came to him one day, and asked if he could teach *Russian.*

"Why do you want to learn Russian, my lad?" asked the doctor, opening his eyes very wide.

"O sir, because, you know, the Russians are expected to take this country, and whoever knows their language will get the best appointment!"

Another asked him if he could teach the "sublime sciences." Another expressed a wish to read Homer.

"Yes, my boy; but why do you want to learn Greek?"

"Oh no, sir, not Greek—I want Pope's Homer; can't you teach Pope's Homer?"

The anxiety the poor boys show to "pass" in the University examinations is extraordinary. Their future career depends so much on the place they take at these examinations, and they make the greatest possible sacrifices in order to pay the fees. They also resort to the most ingenious devices to find out the questions they are likely to be asked, and even make minute inquiries as to the habits of mind of the different examiners, that they may guess what sort of questions they are most likely to put. It was found so impossible to prevent these clever Bengalis, who were by no means very scrupulous about the means they used, from discovering and copying the questions, that now examiners have to go in person and give their papers in to the registrar; and it is part of the printed instructions that no copy shall be kept. These papers are then locked into a strong box or safe, and sent to England to be printed! It was so impossible to help bribery and corruption from doing their work, both in the post-office and printing-press, that this extreme caution was found to be necessary; and now Mr. Sutcliffe, the registrar, himself takes the strong box on board the P. and O. steamer, to be shipped for England. Dr. Ogilvie told me of one printer who had taken an impression of some questions off on the inside of his white coat. What clever fellows they are!

A gentleman has just told me that in his office—one of the largest and most important connected with Government—there is a situation now vacant, and that six hundred young men have sent in their names as applicants!

There seem to be very few outlets for the talents and energies of "young Bengal." Situations in Government and mercantile offices, with the professions of law and medicine, especially the former, seem to provide the only openings they care for.

XIV.

Zenana Life.

CALCUTTA, *May 1.*

WHAT a contrast is our first of May to the joyous day you are having at home, so full of brightness and hope, and promise of the coming summer! Our associations with May-day are not of your delicious *caller* air and fresh dew, and the singing of birds, and the fragrant white blossoms of the may-thorn. All we can think of is this sickening heat, with the consequent languor and weariness. But perhaps I am more than ordinarily home-sick to-day, having had some sleepless nights of pain.......

I think I can count on a quiet forenoon in this furnace-heat, and will tell you something of the Hindu homes I have had a peep into lately. I know your sympathies will flow out to the deeply interesting inmates, as my own never fail to do. I have spent several mornings with our own excellent teachers, and also with the ladies of the Normal School, in visiting among their pupils. I will, then, select one morning, and relate to you what I saw; as this will enable you to form a correct idea of what the zenana is, and what zenana work really means. I am sure my kind Bengali friends will not think that I violate either courtesy or confidence if I raise the purdah just a little, and let my friends at home have a glimpse of their sisters in the East, so that they may know them better, and think of them with kindness and sympathy.

I ought first to say that the word "zenana" (*zanān-khānā*) simply means "the house of the women;" or, in other words, the harem of Bengal. As soon as a woman marries, etiquette, or rather hard custom, requires that she must then retire within the zenana, never more to come into the outer world; and you know that her marriage—or betrothal, which here is held as marriage—takes place when she is still quite a child. From the age of eight or nine, then, the women of the higher and middle classes are doomed to a life of seclusion and ignorance, and, as in the case of widows, very often also to degradation and misery. The more enlightened native gentlemen are now anxious to change this state of matters. They are not only willing to let their wives and daughters be educated, but they earnestly desire that they may be trained so as to become intelligent companions for themselves. The younger ladies, too, are eager for knowledge, and wish to be taught to read and work, and employ themselves as we do. They have longings and desires after change, and seem to be seeking for something, they hardly know what. But they cannot come out to schools and colleges to receive the training they wish for. We must carry it to them, and, by the visits of qualified teachers to their secluded homes, give them the blessing of a good Christian education.

Well, now, we shall start on our expedition; and I think, if you will accompany us, you will be interested and pleased. There is no use in beginning our visits earlier than eleven o'clock, as the women are engaged in the earlier part of the day with cooking, eating, and household duties. Our starting-point is the Mission-house, in Cornwallis Square, which is delightfully close to all sorts of mission work. We must drive, of course, as walking under this fierce sun is out of the question. You observe the gharree is a very narrow one, and cool, with cane-bottom seat, and no cushion. As we drive down the narrow lanes—which can hardly, even by courtesy, be called streets—you will perceive the advantage of the small conveyance, as we shall manage to thread our way through the long strings of bullock-carts we are sure to meet *en route*, whose drivers are exasperatingly slow in getting out of the way. Most of the lanes are skirted by those fragrant drains I have spoken of before; but we soon come to a small arched doorway in a high blank wall, and here we stop. The durwān admits us; and we find the unpromising exterior belied by what is within.

We find ourselves in a quadrangular court, paved with marble, open to the sky. Round this the house is built, and balconies and verandahs on all sides and on all the stories face inward, off which the rooms open. On the side opposite, as we enter, you observe that instead of the verandah there is a pillared chamber, with a low flight of handsome steps leading up to it. This is "the god's room," in which worship—"pooja," as it is called—is performed, and where at the different festivals the images are set up and offerings made. During the "Doorga-pooja," for example, it is here that the image of the goddess will be fashioned, and in this court the different ceremonials connected with the worship will take place. Every respectable Hindu dwelling has a family temple such as this. Of course, we shall not enter the room—we shall not be allowed to go nearer to it than the foot of the steps; and even if it were right to look at what we are not meant to see, the "dim religious light" inside would prevent our perceiving anything further than the line of handsome chandeliers which hang from the ceiling. Opposite to the god's house you notice there is a verandah carefully screened off with venetian blinds. This is where the ladies of the family come during the celebration, whence they can see what goes on below without the possibility of their being seen.

We shall now be conducted upstairs and through the house, probably by one of the Babus, who always receive us with great politeness and cordiality. The rooms we pass through on the first floor are very handsome: one, at least, is furnished in European fashion, with mirrors and pictures, and chairs and sofas, set down as thickly as possible; and the next to it in Eastern fashion, where handsome Persian carpets are spread, and large, thick cushions are placed against the wall. Here the Babus will recline and have their chat when their day's work is done. The English apartments, I fancy, are purely for show; but all the rooms containing this comfort and grandeur are sacred to the lords of creation. You would never find a lady of the family in one of them.

Leaving these, then, behind, we go on through some more verandahs, cross one or two courts—where one feels the sun rather uncomfortable, even though you are protected by the novel and rather unbecoming head-gear called a sun-topi—and, finally, we stop at a door in the wall, where the Babu hands us over to a female servant; for this is the boundary which closes in the zenana from the outer world. We ascend a short stair; and lo! we are in "the house of the women." At the top we are met by a gentle, timid-looking, rather pretty, and wonderfully fair young creature, dressed in an airy, wavy costume of purple gauze, spangled over with gold. Her beautiful glossy black hair is plaited into a large knot behind her head, in which pretty silver ornaments dangle. She has a large nose-jewel, with pearls and emeralds, ear-rings and necklaces, bangles, and heavy silver anklets; and round her waist she wears a beautiful zone of massive silver. She receives us rather shyly, but with evident pleasure, and takes hold of your hand to lead you to her room. Doubtless you would expect that this room should resemble somewhat those we have seen in the Babus' quarters. On the contrary, this is bare and comfortless in the extreme. The walls have once been whitewashed, but now are dingy and spotted, and liberally garnished with cobwebs; for it is considered a sin to kill a spider. A tiny window, high up, and grated with iron stanchions, looks on to the tiled roofs of other houses. There is some matting on the floor, and a cot at the upper end covered with a white sheet and some round bolsters; there is also a box of some sort. And this is the furniture of the apartment; there is really nothing else. This, and many other rooms like it, open off a verandah, which looks into a court—or garden, rather, for there are three or four sickly-looking trees—and a well or tank, which seems stagnant, for it is covered over with green slime. This melancholy garden and the tiled house-tops make up the whole view which the poor women who dwell here from year's end to year's end have of the outer world. And this is only a type of other zenanas, where the surroundings are very much the same.

Chairs will be brought for us, as we do not take kindly to the floor; but the lady in the spangled gauze, and her teacher, Miss F., will deposit themselves on the matting. And now the lesson proceeds. Not, however, before an old, hard-looking woman has taken up her position on the door-step, eying us very suspiciously, and keeping jealous watch over every word the lesson contains. This is a very orthodox and most bigoted widowed aunt, whom no courtesy or kindness on our part can tempt quite into the room while we pollute it with our presence. The pupil, however, does not seem to mind her much.

The reading, which is from the Bengali version of the "Peep of Day," proceeds in the most steady manner in spite of the duenna. The young creature asks questions which show much intelligence and deep interest in what she is taught. She is naturally very quiet and shy; but it is pleasing to see how her eagerness for knowledge overcomes the timid shrinking which she showed at first, and which is natural to her.

The scene in the next house we go to is quite a contrast to this. We are received with a storm of delight by six or seven bright young girls, who throng round Miss F. as if they would eat her up, so demonstrative is their joy at seeing their teacher. She chatters Bengali as fast as they do, and makes me envious who can do nothing but smile and shake hands, and reciprocate in expressive pantomime their kind greeting. I avail myself, however, of my companion's Bengali tongue, and have nice little chats with each as she is presented by name. These are the daughters and daughters-in-law of the house. The mother soon makes her appearance,—a pleasant, clever-looking woman, wonderfully young and fresh, but evidently a widow from the plain garments she wears and her shaven head. She has no clothing on the upper part of her person, and is simply enveloped in a coarse white chudder, or sheet, edged with a black border. She wears no ornaments of any sort. This is the "bow-ma," as the head of the house is called; and Miss F. says she is a person of great influence in her family. She has a number of sons, and these young creatures whom we see are their wives, and are called "bows." The eldest son is in England, which is a great concern to the old lady, as she fears he may be too "high" for them, as she expresses it, when he returns, and will not fall in with the old ways. She does not seem to fear his becoming a Christian, and does not mind his losing caste; she only dreads his affections becoming estranged from her and the family.

I had seen his young wife on a former visit, when she touched me much. She then brought her books and her work, and sat down by my side. She displayed a gay cap she was crocheting for her absent lord, and a pair of slippers she had finished. She read a few verses in the Bengali Bible distinctly and well, and seemed to understand the meaning of the passage, which was about the sower sowing seed in the different sorts of soil. She said she feared her heart was one of the stony places; but she *wished* that the return should be "an hundred-fold." Then, as the crowning accomplishment, she brought out a small English primer, in which she spelled out a few words with great pride; and then she looked up in my face, and said so wistfully, "Don't you think he will care for me now?" I felt a tear come to my eye; I hope he will care for her. But she is not pretty. They were betrothed, of course, as mere children, and don't know each other in the least.

You will be quite astonished at the number of women who will pour into the room in this house; they seem countless. One of them told me that she thought there were about fifty females under this roof-tree, including aunts and cousins and all manner of relations. They are indeed a gregarious people, and live together in this patriarchal way,—grandfathers and sons and sons' sons, sometimes to the fourth and fifth generation, all dwelling in the same family house.

Of these women only six are pupils. All the six are married, and some of them have their babies in their arms. They had known of our coming, and are decked in their finest clothes, and glitter with jewels. Their curiosity regarding everything we wear is most amusing. It is the same wherever you go; and I suppose every one who visits among these ladies for the first time finds herself unexpectedly an object of much interest and curiosity. They question me always about my clothes, my "sahib" (husband), my object in coming to India, and especially my children!

Here, as in the former house, Miss F. squats upon the floor, and is soon surrounded by a ring of eager, attentive pupils, each with a small pile of books before her, and a little bundle containing her work. Most of these can read the Bengali Bible. Even the old lady sits down with her spectacles on; and though she cannot quite read herself, she is a most attentive listener when Miss F. reads a parable over and explains its meaning. They are reading steadily in the New Testament, and the beautiful narratives of the Gospels seem to interest and touch them. Their teacher hopes and believes that the truth has come to some of them, "not in word only, but also in power and in the Holy Ghost."

I was exceedingly taken with this interesting family, and they are among my friend's favourite pupils. They seem to be a happy household too,—which every family, I am sorry to say, is not. The secret is that this "bow-ma" is kind and good. If she were the contrary, she could make the lives of the younger women bitter to them.

We shall visit another family equally interesting, who are very poor, but of very high caste. A friend comes in, rich, but of a lower caste, and she bows before the head of the house, a gentle, sweet-looking woman,—making obeisance and touching the high-caste woman's feet with her forehead. This woman was once taken from her home in a sinking condition, as it was thought, to die beside the holy water of the Ganges. Happily, however, she revived, and was rescued before exposure and the holy mud which is put into the mouth and nostrils had done their work.

The position of the young Hindu lady is sometimes hard enough. After marriage, while still quite a child, she must live in a strange house, among strange women, and must not even visit her own mother but by the will of her mother-in-law. She must yield the most unquestioning submission, not only to her husband, but to this mother-in-law, and indeed also to her elder sisters-in-law. If she is a woman of character and some strength of mind, this changes as she grows older, especially if she becomes the mother of sons. But while she is young she must not speak in the presence of the older women unless spoken to; she must not unveil herself; she must not eat with them, nor even sit down unless expressly permitted to do so.

The simple truth is this—the life of millions of women in India is one lasting cruel wrong from their birth to their death. One of their own nation has thus described it: "The daughters of India are unwelcomed at their birth, untaught in childhood, enslaved when married, accursed as widows, and unlamented when they die." I am afraid this is too true a picture. They are the slaves of tyrannical and absurd superstitions, which take away their freedom both of mind and body.

In the outer life of the nation, then, the Hindu lady has no part, no recognized position at all. And what has she to fill her own everyday life? Alas! little indeed. She has no knowledge nor cultivation; she has nothing to do: so the dreary hours are spent in sleeping, or cooking, or making garlands for the gods, or looking at her jewels, or braiding her hair. This is her condition at the best; but if she be a widow, then woe to her! She, may have been betrothed as a mere child to a boy who sickens and dies. Or she may have been married to an old Koolin Brahman with one foot in the grave, who may have fifty wives besides; but he is of the highest priestly caste, and therefore an alliance with him is highly honourable. But he dies. She may not have known him, hardly seen him; nevertheless she is now a widow for life. She is thenceforward held as one forsaken of God and man, and fit only to die. British law has done this for her, that she cannot now be burned on the funeral pile with her husband's dead body; but I am not sure that this is not the more merciful fate—to endure the real rather than the life-long dying. She is stripped of her good clothes and jewels; her hair is cut off; she must sleep, not now in a bed, but on a mat on the floor; she must eat only one meal in the day, and that of the coarsest food, and by herself, not with the family; she must fast often besides; and while the fast continues, she must not drink a drop of water, even though she should be dying. She must do the meanest work of the house, and be the servant and drudge of every one. And worse than this,—henceforth no love nor sympathy can come into her life. No one must say a kind word to her, nor even give her a pitying look; for their superstition tells these women, that if they are kind to the despised widow, they will probably be visited by a like calamity themselves.

Now, what we want to do is to change all this; and by God's blessing on zenana work all this *is* being changed.

One thing which is very pleasing is the manner in which the zenana teacher is received and the position she holds in the families to which she goes. She is invariably welcomed with the most demonstrative joy. Her visits seem to bring life and brightness to these dull homes, and her pupils long for the hour when she is to arrive. When there is sickness or trouble, her sympathy and help are counted on and prized, and she is the adviser in every difficulty. One old widow told her teacher it was "sunshiny" the day she came, and "cloudy" when she was absent.

The older women, if they are not very prejudiced, now look with interest on the studies of the younger ones, though they are sometimes jealous if they occupy themselves much with reading and work. What a blessed change even these little arts bring into the lives of many who are as highly gifted naturally as any of us, and have tastes and capacities which only require cultivation!

The zenana, I ought to have said, is hardly an institution of Hindu origin. The Hindus owe to their Mohammadan invaders this blemish on their social system and family life. In olden times Hindu women were not the victims of superstition they now are, nor hidden away and down-trodden and enslaved. Some of the more intelligent among the men will tell you this, and add with pride that the time was when mothers and sisters had position and freedom, and were reverenced nearly as women are in Christian lands. Indeed, a few of the Bengalis would advocate "female emancipation" in the sense of now opening the cage doors and letting the imprisoned inmates take wing and go free. But this sort of emancipation would be no boon. A preparation is needful before freedom can safely be given. Let us make haste and give the education and Christian training which will bring mental and spiritual emancipation; and then the other will of necessity follow. The more one knows of zenana work, the more important it will appear. The arguments for it are drawn usually from the state of the poor neglected women, and too much cannot be said from this point of view. Their condition is as sad and sorrowful as can possibly be pictured. A Hindu lady once said of the life they lead: "It is like that of a frog in a well: everywhere there is beauty, but we cannot see it; all is hid from us!" There could not be a more apt illustration.

But there is also another side, where the arguments are equally cogent,—namely, the influence on the men which the elevation of the women would exercise. At present they are a hindrance to progress among the men. There is no obstacle the missionary has to dread so much as the influence of mothers over their sons. It is a great mistake to suppose, because the women are shut up within their zenanas, that they have no influence. A wife has not much power with her husband, but a mother has unbounded influence over her son. She says to him: "Take all the geography and history, all the learning the padre can give you; but when he speaks to you on religion, do not believe a word he says." His teacher hopes he has made an impression on the heart of a young man, who has left him seemingly thoughtful and solemn. He goes home; his mother's keen eye detects his state of mind, and she speedily counteracts the whole. It is the older women chiefly who uphold superstition. In many cases where the men of a family, being educated and enlightened, do not care for the observances of their faith, the women do; and all the more that the men are indifferent, thereby grievously offending the deities, as they suppose, they zealously perform all that the Shastras enjoin. Their religion is all they have; and they cling to their superstitions, and their goddesses, and their Brahman priests. They are jealous of innovation, and are the props of orthodoxy and "custom." Indeed, the zenana may be said to be the stronghold of Hinduism. Therefore let us attack the citadel if we would fully vanquish the foe.

Let us teach the women equally with the men. Our great missionary societies equip their colleges, and send forth their missionaries, and set up the most perfect organizations,—but chiefly for the men. Until in *equal measure* the great undertaking is faced of giving Christian education to the women generally, we cannot entertain any reasonable expectation of evangelizing India.

A woman we lately visited has interested me profoundly. She is a sweet, gentle, gracious old lady, with a happy gleam in her face, and is clothed differently from the usages of the zenanas; she wears a jacket with long sleeves, and buttoned to her throat, and has a shawl over her shoulders. I felt she was a Christian when I saw her. Her room, too, is different; it is very neatly furnished, and has a small round table on which lie a well-used Bengali Bible, and one or two simple English books, which she reads with ease. I have had delightful talks with this most interesting woman, and find she is indeed resting on Jesus as her Saviour. At first her husband greatly opposed her reception of the truth; and this was a very sore and bitter grief to her, as she and her husband are much attached to each other. She made this sorrow a matter of constant prayer; and a severe illness so changed him that he opposes no longer, and now they read God's Book together. I am sure she is one of the Lord's precious hidden ones; and I believe there are many such in the homes of Bengal—Christians, though unbaptized.

XV.

Humble Life.

CALCUTTA, *April.*

HERE comes mail-day again. Time seems to be marked by mail-days; and they do chase each other with marvellous rapidity.

What did we do in bygone times, with only a monthly budget from home, sweet home? How did we exist without our weekly feast, can any one tell? And how did those poor people do in more ancient days still, when India was really a land of exile; when poor Henry Martyn made this mournful entry in his journal: "I have written to Lydia, and it will take eighteen months before I can have her answer"? This was to tell him whether she would be his wife or not! We live in happier days now. We can tell almost to an hour when your dear little messengers will come in to brighten us with their words of love and tender greeting.

It is scorching heat, and it gets worse and worse every day. I have already left off, article by article, every scrap of dress which it would be decorous to do without; but it is of no use. Punkahs and all other appliances seem to come short in the one point of making us cool; and we are hoping that one of those beneficent storms may soon come to our relief; the air is so electric that I think it must soon explode.

I wish I could photograph Uncle J. for you—himself and his equipage—as he set off to the Institution just now, leaving many messages of love for you all. For himself, he is attired in a yellow silk coat, cool and thin as gossamer; his nether man is encased in white drill; and on his head he wears a huge sun-topi, which gives him the look of being thatched.

What would certain of his home friends say to such a transformation? His equipage is quite in keeping. It is a "ticca gharree," which means the hackney-coach of Calcutta, and is the most queer little nondescript concern you can picture. It is an oblong box—like that little palki which stood on the side-table at Alness—set on four little wheels, with sliding panels instead of doors, through which you scramble in; there being a kind of well for the feet. This machine is drawn by a pair of wee ponies, only a little bigger than Brownie (our dog), and much of the same colour. The harness and traces are often made of rope, but our "ticca," as it has the honour of carrying such a "burra sahib," has leather traces; though the pole is spliced and bandaged, and all is freely tied up with ropes. Uncle J. is reduced to this sort of locomotive for college-work, as we have not yet fallen in with a horse to suit us. But the spirit the little things have is wonderful to see. They fly off like an arrow from a bow, urged on by their elf-like driver, and go the four or five miles, he hardly drawing rein.

The driver is quite a boy, and sits on a little perch at the top of the gharree. At first he was naked to the waist; but as this was inadmissible, he now comes arrayed in a cotton sheet, which floats behind him in the wind like a flag; and on the top of his tangled locks there sits a white skull-cap shaped like a cocoa-nut. Would you not like to see the turn-out?

My window sometimes makes me idle. I have just been watching the rise and progress of a furious quarrel. The combatants are women; but their tongues are their only weapons. They do not proceed to the extremities our furies do at home in the terrible lanes and alleys of our cities. The only use these poor creatures make of their fists is for gesticulation, which is quite dramatic. But oh, their voices! Nothing on earth is so shrill and incisive as the sound of these women's tongues when they are in a downright fight.

The men are squatting round, having suspended their gossip, and smile complacently at their wives' prowess, but take no part in the quarrel. The children have ceased their noisy play to look on; and even the poor little cow, that has worried me all the morning with its plaintive calls for its calf, which is cruelly tied up within sight, has ceased its lowing, and gazes in wonder with the rest. I am sorry to say these quarrels are of very frequent occurrence, and are all conducted out of doors, like everything else among the lower classes of this strange people.

Last night, as we were leaving the drawing-room, an appalling sound of shrieks and cries rose from the village, and filled the air. "Oh, there is some one dead!" we all exclaimed at once. This was the cry of the women; and anything more mournful I never heard. It pierced my heart, and to sleep was impossible. The chorus of wailing went on all night and this morning till now, when I fancy the body will be borne to the funeral pile. Somebody said it was the cry of the hired mourners, but it sounded too real for that. The low wail constantly broke into a shriek of agony; these poor children of nature have no idea of self-control. There is far more genuine grief among the Hindus than is believed; and then, they sorrow without hope.

Ah, this is the sorrow of sorrows! They have none of the precious healing hope of reunion which the blessed gospel gives. They do not know anything about the golden gates, and the many mansions of the Father's house, nor of Him who went to prepare a place in them for his own.

I was right. That was the voice of a mother weeping for her first-born son. But the family are Mohammadans; and now there is a large group gathered round the door of the hut, waiting to carry the body to the grave; for the Mohammadans bury, they don't burn, their dead, as the Hindus do. These poor people, really poor, and living in this miserable hut, with hardly a thing inside its walls, will have to make a great feast the day after to-morrow,—for this is "the custom,"—and not only feed all their relatives, but many idle fakirs and religious beggars, who call themselves holy, and delude the people. Oh! that He who spoke so tenderly to the widow of Nain would whisper words of healing and comfort to this poor woman, who is lying with her head in the dust, and refuses to be comforted. Oh! to bring the gospel, as Christ did, to the poor; were it to do no more than heal their earthly woes—though there were no hereafter, though there were no undying soul to think of—only these broken hearts to heal!

The feast I told you would take place is now going on. Outside the hut door a mat is spread on the ground, round which the company sit cross-legged. A row of small fireplaces, made with two or three stones put together, gipsy fashion, lie beyond, surmounted by huge pots filled with curry and rice, dāl and ghee. A little further on a man is engaged in baking great piles of very good-looking cakes, like thick *scones*. Before each one of the guests a piece of fresh shiny plantain leaf is placed to answer for a plate, on which are heaped quantities of rice and curry, with little piles of chutney and chillies and other relishes placed round the margin. Everything is put on to the same leaf, and the men of the house serve. Not a woman is to be seen, either among the guests or attendants. This khāna, or dinner, has taken place between eleven and twelve in the forenoon, which is the native dinner-hour. Before a native dines, he always bathes; he never eats with "unwashed hands." Our servants are always absent most of the forenoon bathing, eating, and finally sleeping; and appear again, like giants refreshed, about two or three o'clock. This is the chief meal of the day; they do not eat again until quite late in the evening.

It would be impossible to tell how ignorant the lower people are; and the worst is, that so little seems to be done for them. When you ask any of these poor women the very simplest question about God, or their souls, or sin, or a hereafter, they stare and say, "How should we know? we are *gureeb lok* (poor people); we know nothing;" or, as I have heard them say more than once, "We are only women—how could we know?" as if the simple fact of being a woman was enough to account in this wretched land for any amount of ignorance. What we want is a thoroughly organized woman's work to reach the women of every class. Not only those of the higher classes, who live in the zenanas, but the poor, who have to live in huts and cook and work, and have no one to care for them or teach them anything.

My husband has been speaking and writing much about the education of the masses. Much need there is! With all the boasted education of Bengal, and all the multitude of schools, Government-aided and indigenous, they say that not even one per cent. of the population can either read or write. And if this is the case with the men, what of the women? and there are, in all India, more than a hundred millions of them! The very thought oppresses the heart with a sort of despair. But with God all things are possible.

Saturday.

I have had the most charming little woman spending the forenoon with me; a native Christian lady, Mrs. C., wife of one of our nicest Babus and native professors, and mother of a fine, manly, clever lad in whom I am greatly interested. She looked so neat and dainty in her pretty white veil of spotted net, clasped tight round her sweet face. She talks English perfectly, and very prettily, and is a thorough little gentlewoman. Better than this, she has the happy faculty of letting her light shine, and she exercises considerable influence in our own and other missions. I have frequently been in her house, and it is quite as neat as herself; it presents a striking contrast to the houses of the poor zenana women, which are utterly comfortless. The sight of this dear little woman, and her neatly-furnished, pretty room, always makes me sorrow more over the hosts of the untaught.

Just now a gentleman has said to me,—"Oh! you teach native women *tatting!* I care nothing for this sort of teaching." One glimpse of these joyless, unoccupied lives would make this scornful gentleman believe that it is true philanthropy to teach even tatting.

An old Musulman beggar, with a very venerable beard, and almost blind, sings a bit of the Koran for his breakfast every day in the hamlet below. Leaning on the top of his staff, he chants a monotonous refrain, the same thing over and over, until I am nearly out of my wits. He receives a dole, which is deposited in his beggar's wallet, and on he goes to the next door. The old creature must make a good thing of it, for he seems to receive something from the very poorest; indeed, I often notice how good the poor are to the poor, here as elsewhere; besides, alms-giving is always a holy act here, especially feeding religious beggars. This one is clothed and respectable. The holiest devotees are usually nude, and the most disgusting objects you can conceive. The regular Hindu mendicant is more like a wild animal than a man. He is naked, except for a tiger-skin which hangs down his back from his shoulders, and strings of berries and beads which ornament his neck in rows to his waist. His body is smeared with lines of chalk and red paint and ashes, and his hair and beard are matted into an unsightly, filthy mass. He is, indeed, a horrible object; and these wretched men not only mortify the body, but reduce their minds to vacuity, and call it contemplation of the divine! They cut themselves off from every social tie, live generally in the jungles or in a temple, and set at nought the affections and even the natural instincts which God has given them.

One thing in the "manners and customs" of Calcutta which depresses one much, is the way in which Sunday is kept. It is a Continental, not a Scottish Sabbath. Instead of being the day of rest, it is the day of visiting and tiffin-parties.

Another depressing thing is that so many of the Scotch people forsake their own good old Presbyterian Church; it is more fashionable, I suppose, to go to the English Church. I wonder often what has become of their *esprit de corps*, not to speak of anything higher. I had the audacity to tell a very nice young

Scotchman the other day, that I thought it "snobbish" in him to leave the Church of his fathers for the cathedral, and that I should expect him next to be ashamed of his country. Whoever is ashamed of either has no business to be a Scotchman.

This is a great day commercially among the Bengalis—"New-Year's Day," they call it, or "lucky day."* The box-walas have been doubly importunate: "You buy from me, mem sahib—then all year will be lucky;" "This too much lucky day;" "This day buy, then all the year goodwill;" "To-day sell one price, mem sahib—not cheat;" "Never sell two price to-day;" "All truth to-day;" "Not tell lie, mem sahib, this day!" These were some of the utterances of the men who brought their wares to the door to-day. The financial prosperity of the year seems to depend on this one day's honesty!

Dr. M., accompanied by Mr. P., rode out last evening to visit a famous Hindu saint he had heard of, or I think had seen at some festival. He wanted to speak to this man, and also address the people, who would be sure to gather about to listen to the talk. He was seated on the ground outside the temple at Kali-ghaut, and had no other attire than a coat of white ashes and mud, which smeared him from head to foot; strings of beads and berries hung in rows round his neck and down to his waist; and his uncut hair was matted and full of ashes, and coiled on the top of his head. His only shelter from sun or rain was a small canopy of matting supported by a bamboo post. Here the poor deluded man sits day and night, and never enters a house. He has many disciples, who worship him and

* Lakshmî, the goddess of wealth, is called by the Bengalis *Lakhi*, which is pronounced almost as *lucky*. They play upon the word.—*Edit.*

bring him offerings, and he has the reputation of being learned as well as religious. He is also far-travelled; he has been all over India "seeking rest," but alas! poor man, "finding none."

He was very willing to listen to the Christian padre when he told him where true rest is only to be found,—with Him who has said, "Come unto me, and I will give you rest." But though he said he believed in the Supreme God, and had heard of Jesus Christ, who he thought perhaps might be one of the many incarnations of God, yet he could not allow that "in Him is life," nor that "as the Father hath life in Himself, so hath He given to the Son to have life in Himself."

Many people gathered round as the conversation went on, and Dr. M. spoke until he was hoarse. When he was taking leave the sage thanked him, and begged him to come again; which of course he promised to do. My husband says that something is gained when a kindly relation is established between the Christian missionary and the heathen, even though no conviction is produced at the time. Mr. P. has told me of another devotee, on whose head, like Samson, no razor has ever come. His hair is rolled up into a huge, unsightly, towering mass, which serves as an ample turban. Mr. P. made him unroll the coil, and when it was measured it was found to be seven feet in length! They said this was all the natural growth of his own head. Perhaps so; but these matted locks often owe much to addition from without.

May 18.

I have just been listening to a conversation between the gentlemen and some missionaries who have breakfasted with us, on the subject of the feeling which exists between natives and Europeans, and also between the different castes and classes of the natives themselves. What a problem it seems to be!

I am afraid that there is a great gulf fixed between the European and native communities here; far greater, I think, than exists in Bombay.

We were present at a large dinner-party the other day at the house of the Hon. Mr. P., who, with his wife, takes a great interest in native advancement. Two native gentlemen were among the guests—one a judge of the High Court. I felt quite pleased when our host asked me to sit next to this gentleman at table; he was most pleasant, and conducted himself exactly as any other gentleman would do, though he ate nothing but ices. I was rather surprised then after dinner when one of the ladies observed, with considerable sharpness, "When native gentlemen bring their own wives into society, it will be time enough to invite them to meet European ladies." It is thus partly their own fault that this feeling exists.

If coldness or want of sympathy existed between European Christians and native Christians, it would be doubly deplorable. It is surely our duty to befriend and welcome into our social circles those who have had to forsake father and mother and brother and sister, and in many cases wife and children, for Christ's sake and the gospel's.

But talking of race antagonism, surely caste-antagonism in the same race is infinitely worse; and this is what we have all around us here. Our native friends must take this beam out of their own eye before they complain of the mote in ours. It is vain for them to say, as they often do, that there is caste among Europeans. If there be, it is a totally different thing from caste among Hindus. There is far too little sympathy between the upper and lower classes; the higher castes despise the lower, and oppress them when they can. I am afraid this is true from the Brahman downwards.

The education of the masses seems to obtain little favour or support from the upper strata of Bengal society; though there are some honourable exceptions, and a few men are doing all they can to battle with this unworthy exclusiveness. It is high time that the blessing of education should be extended to all castes and classes alike.

June 4.

We have been a scattered family for the last week or two. The gentlemen were spirited away by Mr. Long to a favourite hill-resort of his, where they took advantage of the recess at the Institution to get some needed rest and fresh air; the latter is an article not to be had in the furnace Calcutta has been of late.

The hill they visited is called Parisnāth (the final letter is not pronounced), and is hardly a day's journey away. It has beautiful woods, and there you entirely escape from the heat of the plains. The visitor, however, has to rough it, for there is hardly a house to speak of—there is only a barrack and a small bungalow. "Man wants but little," however, when there is no lady in the question, and the climate makes up for every deficiency.

Parisnāth is a sacred hill, and belongs to the Jains. This is a sect which may be called an offshoot from the Buddhists, and the chief tenet of their creed is *non-killing;* which means that it is a sin of equal magnitude to kill a man or a beast, or even an insect. There are twenty-four shrines on the long top-ridge, and one considerable temple a little way down the hill. Pilgrims resort here in multitudes every year from great distances to worship. The three gentlemen were much in their element, examining the shrines and talking to the priests, and preaching when they could find audiences. It was hoped some years ago that this hill might prove a sanitarium for soldiers in Lower Bengal; but it is not high enough to rise above the fever-region.

June 15.

We have had repeated and very tempting invitations to go to Simla for the season. There are many Scotch friends there who are anxious to have a church of their own, and others who are neither Scotch nor Presbyterian, who are ready to unite with them in the movement. Among these is Mr. Carey, a grandson of the great missionary, who is already doing all he can to bring this matter to a point.

It would indeed be delightful to visit the friends and see the glorious Himalaya; but duty forbids at present. I wonder if we shall go next year.

We find the house-top a delightfully cool retreat in the evenings, where the sweet south wind seems to come to us fresh and untainted straight from the sea. This breeze blows strong just now, and tempers the heat deliciously. You would be amused to notice on this flat roof of the house a long well-marked pathway reaching from end to end; this is where my husband takes "his constitutional" every morning before sunrise. It is so carefully trodden that it puts one in mind of Wordsworth's "path of perseverance."

XVI.

The Rainy Season.

CALCUTTA, *June 18.*

I WISH you could see how it rains! For eleven whole days it has come down incessantly, and the compound is like a lake. People are beginning to grumble; but I like it: the air is so much fresher and pleasanter, and one feels so much more alive, than in the terrible heat which preceded this down-pour.

Up-country the monsoon has not commenced quite so favourably, and at Mirzapore I see that the Hindus have been propitiating the weather-god after a fashion of their own. The people there, it seems, believe that a great black frog is "clerk of the weather." So the Brahman priests got all the foolish little urchins of the town collected together, and made them leap about in the dust and personate frogs! They rolled about and leaped, and chanted appeals to the deity, the burden of which was "*pāni de, pāni de,*" or, "water give, water give;" while the by-standers threw chatties full of water over them (which, I am sure, the boys enjoyed, whatever other virtue there was in the operation), and soon they became balls of animated mud, and sufficiently like frogs to please the deities.

The Nassick people took another method of obtaining the

coveted blessing. They propitiated their god by carrying him round the town in grand procession, and then gave him a good bath in the sacred river Godaveri. They imagine that this honourable treatment will put him into such good humour that he will command the heavens, and they will give forth abundantly of their watery treasures!

Is it not very sad, dear, that these poor people are still so steeped in superstition? Would it not be a joy to teach them our sweet song, so different from their own?—

> "So Thou the year most liberally
> Dost with Thy goodness crown;
> And all Thy paths abundantly
> On us drop fatness down."

Would indeed that these poor ignorant people knew who it is that blesses them—who makes the outgoings of the morning and evening to rejoice; and also that this beneficent Father is equally willing to open the windows of heaven and pour down a spiritual blessing, until the whole land is filled, and there is not room to receive it.

I think you would enjoy the pleasant, easy hospitalities of Calcutta. Some people dined with us last night in honour of the wedding of one of the pillars of our Church; and all the company were special friends. There is less ceremony here, I think, and fewer conventionalities, than in our own country. We ask our friends without that dreadful extra fuss of preparation which people seem to find needful in entertaining at home, and which is such a trouble to the poor lady of the house. The viands are brought in and handed about by the servants—who are numerous, at any rate, for every guest brings his own khitmutgar (table attendant); one of the features of an Indian feast being the row of swarthy domestics, clothed in spotless white, who stand like so many statues behind their masters' chairs. There is not much time lost, either, in this sociable sort of entertainment.

One thing we rejoice in is the quantity of lovely flowers we may cut, without fear or reserve, the whole year round. The fruit of the country, too, is beautiful—guavas, and plantains, and oranges, and just now plenty of delicious pine-apples, which cost only a few pence each.

But the real *burra khana* (or grand state-dinner) of Calcutta is a very dreary piece of pleasure! You sit at table, tired and hot, often for two or three mortal hours, while the endless dishes go round in weary succession. If the man who sits next you is intelligent, and cares to talk, you are tolerably happy; if not, then, to say the least, it is not lively. Indeed, here, as elsewhere, "life would be very tolerable but for its amusements."

One of our strange "manners and customs" is the way we do our ordinary shopping. We give orders to the durwān to admit a box-wala, or pedlar, who goes about with a grand medley of goods carried in boxes and bundles on the top of some coolies' heads. These gentry pass your gate constantly, shouting, "Mem sahib, want anything to-day?" When you do want anything, and order a box-wala to be admitted, the durwān levies a tax upon him which is called *dustooree.* This is a sort of black-mail, which the man is too wise not to pay, or he would never be suffered to enter the gate again. The bearer also gets dustooree, and the ayah ditto; all which is added on to the cost of the article, and we, helpless miserables, have to pay. This system of dustooree, which is simply bribery and corruption, goes through every sort of transaction among the natives. Your cook, in making your daily purchases in the bazaar, charges a per centage on every article he buys, down to what is only the value of a pice; and this they by no means count as cheating—it is their lawful gain, and we must just submit, and add it on as an item in our everyday expenditure.

I have just had a visit from my peculiar box-wala, who manages to gain admittance, having made it all right with the power at the gate. This is a tall, exceptionally lean Bengali (for most Bengalis are lean), with bent gait, very dark skin, keen eyes, and hands like claws. He comes upstairs with a stealthy, cat-like tread; and being privileged, appears on the landing unannounced. Seeing me, he puts his hands together in a pleading attitude, makes salām, and begins: "What want to-day, mem sahib? I got plenty tings, cheap tings, *wely* putty. New tings, mem sahib; mem sahib, see." All this time he is spreading out his wares at my feet—a most singular medley. I choose what I require, and we haggle over the price. He declares what I offer is not "prime cost," and eventually persecutes me into taking the article at a quarter of the sum he originally asked. Here is a list of some of the contents of his box, which I took down just now to amuse you:—bells, lozenges, handkerchiefs, cigar-case, note-paper and envelopes, pomatum, Shakespeare collars, towels, soap, essence of rose, dog-collars, cosmetics, lace, China fans, hooks and eyes, walking-sticks, tape, cash-box, whips, sugar-plums, sponges, tea-spoons, pipes, tooth-picks, perfumes, braces, sewing-cotton and buttons, tooth-brushes, dresses, thimbles,—and this by no means exhausts the *multum in parvo* which this pedlar's box is.

Are the crows among dear little R.'s favourite pets? They are very impertinent here. I have been missing my pens lately, and wondering why they should so often disappear; and to-day I have discovered the depredators. When I came in a little while ago, I found a splendid black crow perched upon my writing-table, turning over the contents of my pen-tray. "Ah, *you* are the culprit," said I. The creature uttered a caw of triumph, and flew off through the open window, carrying my best quill in his beak—to make a cross-beam, I fancy, in the great black nest which he is constructing up there among the trees.

I must tell you a funny little story about the crows. There was a great caw-cawing overhead a few days ago, and I felt sure there was something important going on in the crow community. I watched, and presently two great fellows were detached from the crowd there was over the compound; they gave a swoop down, and then I saw a poor unhappy-looking wretch, evidently guilty of something, standing on the top of the garden-wall. The two crows each gave him a good peck, which he bore without moving or attempting to get away. Then two more were detached on a like errand. He was not only condemned, I perceived, but the execution was actually proceeding. This I could not stand, so I flew to the rescue; but he was more frightened at my approach and vigorous shouts than at his executioners, and flew away. I only hope he made good his escape. How angry the creatures were! They stormed and screeched in the funniest way, and I hope I really cheated crow-justice for that time.

While on the subject of crows, I must tell you another clever thing I once saw them do in our garden at Poona. Our māli, or gardener, had a standing feud with the crows, who used to build perseveringly in our trees, and were noisy and troublesome. He pulled down their nests without mercy, and otherwise made war upon them; so they determined on retribution. I had given the good old man, who was a great favourite with us, a comfortable red Kilmarnock night-cap to keep his poor bald head warm; and one day, when he and I were busy over the flowers, I heard the most deafening clamour from the crow gentry over our heads. Evidently they were holding a *punchā-yat* (council); and you may imagine our surprise and amazement when one of them, after whirling about in the air, suddenly made a dart downward on the māli's head, picked off his red night-cap, flew off with it in his beak, and deliberately dropped it into the middle of the tank, which lies at one side of the garden!

Another time, in the same garden, one punished Uncle J. with a good slap from his wing on the back of his head, when he had ventured to disturb one of their nests.

June 22.

I was out this morning paying some visits; and the pleasantest was to Mrs. V. of the Church Missionary Society. As I sat with her, a number of native Christian women came dropping in, each one taking a low seat at the upper end of the room. Work-bags were produced, and they quietly set to work: some doing plain sewing, some knitting, and others fancy work. Mrs. V. would presently read to them, and meanwhile they and we had a pleasant talk. The work, when finished, would all be sold; not for the benefit of the workers, but to add to the mission funds. These were not school-girls, but all married women, who, having completed their morning work in their homes close by in the Christian village, now came in to spend an hour or two with the missionary's wife. It was a most pleasant sight.

A melancholy little tragedy occurred lately, which greatly upset us all. I told you we were looking for a horse—a quest which has gone on unsuccessfully for long. At length, however, we congratulated ourselves that we had found just what we wanted. A friend was going home who had a charming bay mare, on which I set my heart. The pretty creature came to us a day or two ago, and we drove it yesterday with a delightful sense of possession. I could not help putting my head out constantly to admire her paces and notice how steadily she went. She neighed prettily when we told her how pleased we were, and patted her, and promised her pieces of bread. Poor thing! we little thought our first drive with her should be our last. While she was being groomed we heard a most unusual commotion in the compound, rushed out, and found the poor horse galloping madly over the garden. At length she stood still, trembled violently—she was in a fit! We sent for a surgeon, got quantities of ice, poured water on her head, and did all we could; but it was of no use. It was terrible. We made a comfortable bed for her where she fell, and tried to tempt her with some fresh green grass; but she only looked up in our faces, as if she would thank us, though she couldn't do more. The servants were all kind and concerned, and helped us to watch and care for her all the night through. She has just died, and I am very thankful her sufferings are over. She died of sun-stroke. I am glad too that we had not had her longer, or we should have been even more sorry to part with her, and see her die.

CALCUTTA, *June 28.*

We have been spending a few days with our friends at Serampore, who kindly asked us to come up and see the *Ruth-pooja*, or car-festival of the great god Juggernath, which is celebrated there just now. Notwithstanding the tremendous heat, we enjoyed the little expedition exceedingly, and had an excellent view of the festival.

We have been accustomed to connect the worship of "the Lord of the World," as the name Juggernath (Jagannāth) signifies, and the drawing of his car, with the annual celebration at Pooree in Orissa, which for ages has had such a terrible renown; and of course Pooree is the great place of pilgrimage to the votaries of Juggernath. But this god has also worshippers, and cars, and temples in Bengal; and the melá, or religious gathering, which is held at Serampore is considered next in importance to that which is held in Orissa, and is certainly very popular with the people of Lower Bengal.

Wonderful stories are told of the origin and deification of Juggernath; but I do not think these would interest you much, nor would you care to hear about the mythology and legendary lore of the Hindus. I will simply tell you something of what we saw at Serampore, and describe the idolatrous observances which *now* are practised among the people around us, and which will show you, alas! that the old idol-worship of India still holds its own.

The festival occurs in June or July, when the moon is in a particular stage, and has two grand ceremonies, eight days apart. On the first day the idol is taken from his temple, enthroned on his car, and dragged by the pilgrims about half a mile to another temple, where he pays a visit of a week to a brother-idol. The last day sees the termination of the saturnalia, when there is the return progress of the god, who is then restored to his usual quarters for another year.

On our arrival at Serampore we found ourselves accompanied by crowds of people bound for the melá, whom we had picked up everywhere by the way. I could not help observing then, as I did more fully afterwards, that great numbers were women —many of them old, forlorn creatures, with a look of unrest on their poor faces which was very sad to see. There was an anxious, wistful expression, as if they were looking for something they could not find, which made one long to lead them to Him who could indeed speak peace, His own peace, to their weary hearts. Most were poor, but some were evidently of the better classes, from the way they shrouded their faces in their long scarf-like garments, clinging to the skirt of some bolder one who was battling her way through the crowd. Women who hardly otherwise are seen without the walls of their zenanas, yet often, instigated by the priests, venture into these pooja gatherings.

After lunch we started for the scene of the festival. We prudently kept to our conveyance, and in no other way could we have penetrated through the vast crowd we found assembled, and which was becoming denser every moment. The gentlemen stood, or scrambled on to the roof of the carriage, while I stood on the box, and there had an excellent view of the strange and impressive spectacle below,—a scene of mingled merriment and superstition, fun and worship, which, once seen, could never be forgotten.

As we passed through the town into the narrow lane beyond, leafy and green from the recent rains, we found a regular fair going on. All along, on both sides of the way, low booths were erected, wherein divers sorts of small wares were temptingly exposed for sale. There were bangles and strings of beads, and brass vessels, and the most primitive of children's toys; but what seemed most to abound were eatables, especially sweetmeats and fruit. I never saw so many pine-apples together before, some of which we bought for a few pice each. A few of the stalls were filled solely with plants and young trees of sorts considered sacred; and quantities of picked flowers, chiefly marigolds and roses, which were eagerly bought to weave into garlands for presentation to the god. But of all the motley collection of goods, nothing was so noticeable as the queer little doll-images of Juggernath, which stood in rows everywhere. These were rudely fashioned in clay, and painted in all the colours of the rainbow—handless, legless stumps, like their prototype, and with his great leering goggle eyes, most hideous to look upon. The gods of Greece and Rome were at least beautiful; but who can tell the grotesque ugliness of this frightful image? There were also quantities of dauby pictures, indecent-looking things, representing the god and his friends, the cars, and also incidents in the lives of the gods, which did not tell much for the purity of their reputation among their worshippers. Further on we find merry-go-rounds in full swing, filled with men, and women too; which I could not but wonder at here, where women are supposed to be exceptionally retired. A great deal goes on at these pilgrimages which is unseemly and indecorous, to say the least. Still the crowd was far more orderly than such a vast assemblage would ever have been at home.

There are two cars at Serampore, which I understand are opposition institutions. The smaller is, in fact, a little bit of dissent on the part of a high Brahmanical family, who were rich enough to set up a rival car on the occasion of some fancied offence. We did not halt long by the smaller one, but proceeded to the centre of attraction, the great original car, where the chief ceremonies were being performed.

All cars are of the same construction—huge, pyramidal, pagoda-like structures, about fifty feet in height. They are of wood, painted fantastically, having a reddish-brown hue, and fashioned in three tiers or galleries, each succeeding one being smaller than the one below, and over-topped by a canopied tower, which is the chamber or shrine of the god. Everybody has seen representations of this ponderous erection, with its terraces and niches, and horrible figures. Above all, its sixteen awful wheels, one glance at which sends a sickening shudder through one, as we remember how, times without number, they have been dyed with the blood of poor deluded human victims.

Just as we got to a good place of observation near the car, the idol was brought from the temple, and the attendant priests proceeded to haul him up to his place; which was done after rather an ignominious fashion, by a thick common rope tied about his neck. As he was landed on to each stage in the ascent, the vast crowd gave a tremendous shout, while garlands and flowers, and other offerings, were thrown into the air, and the Brahmans chanted songs in honour of the god. All those who were engaged in officiating in any way, I observed, had little strips of red cloth tied round their heads as a badge of office. When the god was fairly installed, two companions, a brother and aunt, or sister, perhaps, were in like manner, but with far less ceremony, elevated to places beside him; while attendants stood by waving the tail of the yak or Tartary cow. Next, two absurd wooden horses were attached to the machine; and a no less absurd figure of a modern coachman in livery was placed over them. Then came the uncovering of the god, for hitherto his glories had been veiled in wrappings of red flannel; and again the air was rent with plaudits and shoutings, and cries of "Hari bol! hari bol!" which means, "Cry Hari, cry Hari,"—that being the name of the god.* The Brahmans on the car tried hard to excite the people to enthusiasm; but we thought the crowd was listless.

We were very glad to find several missionaries, both Euro-

* Much the same as *hurrah!—Edit.*

pean and native, engaged in preaching in Bengali, and also distributing tracts and books, which seemed to be eagerly received. Afterwards we noticed several people sitting on the roadside reading these books, who seemed to be greatly pleased to be spoken to regarding their contents. Dr. M. had much talk with some English-speaking young men; especially two or three of our acquaintance from among "young Bengal," whom we were surprised to find taking part in the ceremonies, and wearing the red badge.

"Ah, Babu!" I could not help saying to one of these, "one week you give a lecture on progress and mental improvement, and the next you assist at the dragging of this idol-car."

"What can we do, madam?" he replied, looking rather ashamed of himself; "it is the custom of our fathers."

"Why, then, don't you throw yourself under the wheels? That too was the custom of your fathers."

He laughed at this as a good joke, but would not see its application. One of these young men, we found, was the author of the song or hymn, as they called it, which was then being chanted in the heart of the crowd, and a copy of which he promised to give us. And yet they said, "You surely do not suppose we believe in all this?" No; they knew it was a lie; and yet they could not, or would not, see that they were only the more culpable in thus doing what they could, by their influence and presence, to uphold this degrading and demoralizing festival, which year by year destroys the souls and bodies of their more ignorant fellow-countrymen. They cannot get beyond "the customs of their fathers!" And yet, if our Government would boldly come forward and put down pilgrimages by its own strong hand, the better class of natives would only rejoice, though it might be secretly at first.

But now a shout more deafening than any which had preceded told us that the car was about to move. And, to be sure, amid the beating of drums and clashing of cymbals, and, above all, that appalling roar of the multitude, which seems to be the indispensable accompaniment of this the crowning act of the day, and which is heard more than a mile off, the monstrous machine was slowly drawn from its stance. Hundreds of the now excited pilgrims seized the huge ropes, while others struggled forward, elbowing their way through the throng, striving to have a part in the meritorious work. Others danced and shouted or sang in front of the procession, working themselves into what seemed a very real fever of excitement; while yet others, who followed after, bowed themselves until their foreheads touched the sacred tracks, or prostrated themselves wholly on the rut the wheels had left. It was now easy to conceive how in that moment of supreme and frenzied superstition the poor devotees would hurl themselves beneath the deadly wheels. I held my breath, feeling as if they must do it; and a horror seizes one like nothing ever felt before.

And yet there is far less of enthusiasm than in former years, and none of the wild fanaticism. So everybody assured us, and so it was easy to see. Dr. Smith told me that the crowd is smaller, and the celebration quieter, every succeeding year. There are plenty of police and European constables about. It is whispered that sometimes cases of self-immolation do still occur; which, however, are always attributed to accident.

What I have described is the Juggernath festival at Serampore. But this is nothing to the same festival at Pooree. The numbers without number that were congregated there reminded Dr. Claudius Buchanan of the universal judgment; and I have heard that this year there is no falling off in the numbers.

Two years ago, Government issued a proclamation regarding Pooree. "There is no more room; no more pilgrims must go!" But "too late," said one of the papers. Already cholera and fever had broken out, carrying off their victims by the thousand.

A native gentleman told me, that as the time comes near for going on pilgrimage, respectable natives watch their homes carefully. Designing priests entice away the poor credulous women, who go to Pooree, but who often do not return. This is not alone because of cholera and such diseases; other and worse evils lie in wait for them, and they, poor things, believe that if they die in this holy place, they go straight to heaven and happiness.

A friend of mine told me that one day a servant of the house, a very respectable man, rushed in to her in a state of intense agitation, begging for a few days' leave; his wife had disappeared, and he had reason to suppose she had been induced to join a band of pilgrims bound for the melá at Pooree. He pursued the fugitives, and found he was right. The Brahmans had persuaded her to accompany them without her husband's knowledge, deluding her with the vain hope that by such a meritorious act as going on pilgrimage to Juggernath, she would secure to herself the favour of the god for ever. Poor thing! I dare say she was seeking after peace, and did not know how better to find it than by listening to the deceiver's voice.

And yet people have been writing pathetically on the cruelty it is to interfere with the innocent amusements of the people, grudging them their holiday and their annual melás! No one would think of grudging the people their amusements. What one *would* wish is, that these should be dissociated from idolatry, and with all the horrible past in the worship of such monstrous images as Juggernath, Doorga, and Kali.

Why should not these festivals, which now are such a powerful means of upholding idolatry and prolonging the power and influence of the Brahmans, be superseded by others which are innocent and good? This has been done with most excellent effect by the German missionaries among the Christian Koles of Chota Nagpore. As, for instance, the Kātanī-kā-parab, or feast of the harvest-home. At the conclusion of harvest, the heathen Koles have for ages held one of their most important festivals. It occupies several days and nights, and is characterized by frightful debauchery—eating, drinking, dancing, and every sort of revelry. Instead of quite abolishing this feast among the Koles who have been converted to Christianity, the missionaries have altered its character, and turned it into a beautiful Bible-like celebration, which puts one in mind of "the feast of weeks" in Jewish times. Like the true Israelite of old, the Christian Kole brings part of his increase, and offers it to the Lord: "every man as he is able, according to the blessing of the Lord his God." When the day of this festival comes round, the great body of the Christians meet together. They are then formed into a procession, along with the children of the schools, boys and girls, and headed by the missionaries in gown and bands. Each individual brings something: some have baskets or brass vessels, containing rice and other grain; others bring sheaves or roots; and others bring pice (pence). Thus they march to the church, where they deposit their offerings on the floor opposite the pulpit; and very soon there are good big heaps of both grain and pice. After this there is regular service conducted by the missionaries, when there is a great deal of singing, in which the whole congregation join most heartily; and indeed the music is wonderfully beautiful, these wild people have such sweet and harmonious voices. They seem to make their offerings very gladly, and quite to understand that they are acknowledging the bounty of God, who has crowned the year with His goodness. All the contributions go to the support of catechists and schools, and to the general operations of the mission.

Is not this a happy substitution for the wild orgies and drunken revelry of their old heathen feasts? When will the time come when something of the same sort shall be possible in Bengal, to displace the vile Juggernath and his terrible car!

As we returned from Serampore next day, we found, in the only available carriage there was, two fat natives set cross-legged on the cushions, and, shocking to relate, more than half naked. It was the first time we had seen natives in carriages intended for Europeans, and I confess I felt a strong repugnance to enter: not, however, because they were natives; certainly not; but because of their nearly nude condition. Their loins were girt about with fine soft muslin; but this was all! However, it was not so bad as will seem to you, because the rich brown skin comes in as a very tolerable substitute for clothing. A half-clad native has not nearly such an indecent appearance as a white man in the same condition.

One of these travelling-companions was a huge man, very fat, with coarse features and thick lips; the other was as good-looking as the first was plain, with very handsome refined features, but a bold eye from which one rather recoiled. I am afraid we made some disrespectful remarks, and immediately felt reproached when the big man said, with the utmost courtesy, in beautiful high Hindi, "Pray talk on. We do not understand English; be not disturbed by us." When he spoke his face lighted up, and there was a pleasant expression, with a look of power and self-respect, which made him almost attractive. Dr. M. and he at once became friends. He found that the big man was the great man, and a very great man indeed. The other was his follower. The former was the grand high guru or priest of the Jains; and he and his companion had come all the way from Lucknow to solve some high dispute about the possession of the sacred hill Parisnath, which his sect claims as their own. This was the hill I told you my husband visited in May, on the top of which there are so many Jain temples. It is peculiarly sacred ground to the Jains, because they believe that one of their great saints ascended from its summit to heaven; and indeed it takes its name of Parisnath from this *Teerthunker*, or holy man.

The men were wonderfully communicative; and the guru was greatly delighted when he found that Dr. M. could converse with him in Sanscrit. His own volubility in the sacred tongue was wonderful to hear. Much learned talk followed, and the great Jain doctrine of not-killing was discussed. This sect holds that it is as sinful to kill a fly as it is to kill a man; but they get over the difficulty of the wholesale murder it is to drink a glass of water, very cleverly. The water is boiled before they drink it; and, of course, the servants do the boiling, so that the sin does not lie at the master's door! One practical argument which rather ruffled the big man's equanimity was drawn from the great number of deaths which occur every year in India from tigers. "Which is better, to kill the tigers, or let the tigers kill men?" asked Dr. M.; and I don't think he had been quite able to answer this when we drew into the station at Howrah. He took leave of us quite affectionately, complimenting the "Pundit," as he called his antagonist, and asking for his card, though he was sorry, he explained, that he could not himself call on Dr. M., being much too great a man to call on anybody.

Next day, however, his follower called, bearing the salaams of his chief, and begging for a visit; which, of course, Dr. M. has paid him. Mr. D. accompanied my husband, and they found the guru, now respectably clothed, seated on a sort of throne, and surrounded by an assemblage of his co-religionists in Calcutta, who are generally wealthy bankers, merchants, jewellers, &c. Much conversation followed of a very interesting character, during which Dr. M. set forth the claims of Christianity as simply and clearly as he could. The chief objections which the guru urged against it were that it sanctioned murder and drunkenness: murder, inasmuch as it permits the killing of animals; and drunkenness, because tasting one drop of alcohol is as heinous a crime as drinking to excess.

It is wonderful how many nice young men we meet here whose relations we have known at home. We give them all a general invitation to spend Sunday evening with us after church; to which, I am glad to say, not a few respond. These Sabbath evenings have a breath of dear old Scotland about them; and some of the lads tell me that the tea-table, and the hymns we sing and read, and the family worship at the close, put them in mind of their homes, and waken chords which keep vibrating through the week. It may help them, perhaps,

> "To carry music in their heart,
> Through dusky lane and wrangling mart;
> Plying their daily task with busier feet,
> Because their secret souls a holy strain repeat."

XVII.

The Lanes; the Eclipse.

CALCUTTA, *August 11.*

THIS is a holiday in all the offices, which is not favourable for my letters. Gentlemen improve the leisure forenoon to make calls on their friends, and we have had a busy morning. There were so many people in the room when a shy friend came upstairs, that he lingered on the landing; and when Dr. M. went to bring him in he whispered, "I did not know you had a meeting to-day!"

One of our visitors was the daughter of a venerable missionary at Kishnaghur, Mr. Blumhardt, who with his like-minded wife have been working there for more than thirty years. He is quite the father of the station.

August 12.

The rain is most persevering. It comes down not in ordinary drops, but in sheets of water. The whole place is ankle-deep, and I have just been watching the servants wading through the slush with queer little wooden umbrellas over their heads, bringing in the dishes for breakfast. All Indian kitchens, you know, are at a little distance from the house. Everything is damp, and disagreeable, and mouldy. It is quite an occupation to look after one's books and clothes; and, after all, no care avails to save them. The books would break your heart; their faces, so fresh and fair when we left home, are spotted and spoiled. The very pillows smell as if they had come out of a charnel-house; the gloves you wear to-day are white with mould to-morrow; your boots the same; and your very hair seems mildewed.

Still, no one shall say that Calcutta is a bad place to live in. It is *the* place in India, like London at home. Its climate is greatly maligned (though this may seem inconsistent with what I have said), and it is not unhealthy; the free action of the skin (to put it delicately) seems to do one good, though of course it is not agreeable.

In low bungalows you sometimes meet with little frogs hopping about in the rains; here they generally keep to the garden, which is pleasanter. The flying cockroaches are rife just now; and they have a special love for one's hair, and a liking to nestle in the chignon. Last night, tell little R., we had a grand hunt after three bats, which kept flying through the drawing-room, and trying to slap our faces with their wings. One was at length vanquished, and it measured over a foot from wing to wing. The wings were the finest gossamer, but the head was like a rat's, most hideous to behold.

There are some lovely drives into the country about Calcutta, quite out of the usual *Course*—and very much nicer than the Course: there is so much more to see away from the beaten track; and I think we have rather the knack of finding out new roads and pretty lanes, where nature just now is wildly luxuriant and beautiful,—the effect, of course, of the bountiful monsoon.

The woods are full of rich loveliness; for besides what the trees have of their own, aspiring creepers, and beauteous things which love to cling, wind themselves up the strong stems, fling their tendrils in graceful festoons from bough to bough, and then send forth in wanton profusion, and "fantastically tangled," the most delicate and exquisite flowers. The very ditches are turned into beds of beauty, covered thick with the beautiful caladium leaves, blotched and streaked with crimson, and purple, and brown; the way-sides are carpeted with soft velvety green, or lovely wild flowers, and fringed with beautiful grasses, and ferns, and arum leaves. The lanes are often like long avenues, lined with flowering shrubs and trees, with here and there clumps of the feathery bamboo. This is a most graceful tree, and they grow together in groups, like gigantic bunches of wavy feathers. Then you constantly come on pretty little tanks covered with lotuses and various water lilies; or miniature lakes, which in reality are rice-fields, in which, if you are sharp-sighted enough, you can descry the delicate light tint of the young plant peeping out from the water. The natives are now busy transplanting and bedding it out. I have often come on boys and poor women fishing in the little pools by the wayside, and sometimes getting a good basketful of tiny little fish to make curry of for their evening meal. It is very droll to see them catching their supper out of the slime. The fish are rather like eels, but very good to eat.

I had a gift of a magnificent fish, a day or two ago, from a native gentleman who comes to see us sometimes; he wrote to say that it had been caught in the tank in his garden, though it looks as if it would quite want the ocean to swim in. It was a yard long, and something like a sturgeon.

August 17.

We are in a state of great excitement, looking forward to the wonderful eclipse which is to take place to-morrow. After having rained straight on for a week it cleared a little yesterday, and we were full of hope that the sky would brighten, and we should obtain a good view of the rare phenomenon; but to-day it pours as diligently as ever, and not a morsel of blue sky is to be seen. We have thought ourselves so fortunate to be here, to have a sight of what so many are taking long journeys to observe; and it will indeed be tantalizing if the sun does not show himself.

August 18.

The great eclipse was visible, and we had a pretty good view after all. We had almost given up hope of seeing anything, but the sun struggled manfully out, and while the observation lasted we had some satisfactory glimpses through our stained glasses from the house-top. I was greatly amused to see the servants down on the lawn gazing intently into basins of water, in which, I am afraid, they could see little more than the reflection of murky clouds.

It was not quite total here; about three-fourths of the disk were obscured, and what remained looked like the young crescent moon. There was a deep mysterious twilight look over everything, and it became perceptibly colder; but I did not notice any of those wonderful sights said to accompany an eclipse,—the birds going to roost, and the flowers closing their pretty heads. The sparrows and crows were just as busy and loquacious as ever; and the beautiful hibiscus, which closes its bright petals and goes to sleep every evening, was as wide-awake as if the sun had been in his usual condition.

There has been a holiday over the whole place, and the natives are still in a state of intense excitement. They have a wonderful legend, which accounts satisfactorily for eclipses; and now they are busy performing the religious ceremonies which are enjoined by the Shastras. The legend is this: a demon pursues the sun, in order to devour him, and so plunge the world in darkness. This monster happily has no *body;* only a head which Vishnu once severed from the trunk. So, when he has swallowed his adversary, there being no place below into which to put him, behold the great luminary emerges again triumphant. And then, what a rejoicing there is!

As, when a death occurs, all the members of the family, and all things in the house, become unclean, so when the sun is swallowed up the whole community becomes unclean; there is therefore a general destruction of cooking utensils (which is no great loss, as they are made of a coarse unglazed cheap pottery), and a consequent fast, until the sun, having triumphed and become his glorious self again, a general rush is made to the holy river to bathe and receive purification, and then new pots are procured, and the fast changes into a feast.

The appearance at the river was most extraordinary. Hundreds on hundreds of people were in the water to their waists or necks, muttering prayers, and washing themselves and their clothes, and worshipping. Having done this, they would go home, and make abundant amends for the fast preceding.

The educated natives do not believe all this rubbish about the demon; but they too break their cooking things, and fast and worship notwithstanding.

If the men of this country had only the moral courage to act as they believe, what a different place it would soon become! This stifling of conviction is terribly perilous,—most deadening to conscience.

August 26.

At the close of the prayer-meeting this evening in the Free Church, Dr. M. baptized a Mohammadan woman. She was instructed by Hajji Khan, the Scripture-reader, himself a convert from Mohammadanism, who works exclusively among the followers of the false prophet. No class of the community is so hard to influence as these proud Musulmans; and therefore a trophy won by the power of the gospel from amongst them is a double encouragement. Dr. M. conducted the service partly in English, but chiefly in Hindustani.

We witnessed another baptism a few days ago; that of an intelligent, educated young man, who was brought into contact with the missionaries at the Institution. The service took place in the Bengali Church, and was conducted by Mr. M'Donald.

Thus the Master grants to his servants from time to time some tokens of his presence and blessing in their arduous work; but how hard it seems for these intellectual Hindus and haughty Musulmans to enter into the kingdom of heaven!

September 9.

This afternoon we had the pretty spectacle, in the Mission church, of a native Christian wedding. The bride is one of the Orphanage girls,—a quiet, gentle, good lassie whom we all like, named M. She looked very modest and nice in her simple white muslin dress and spotted net veil, with a marvellous profusion of hair very prettily dressed. Her bridegroom is one of the Bengali Christians connected with the Mission, and is a particularly fine, steady, intelligent young man. The chapel was filled with a large congregation of Christian men and women of our own and other missions, and crowds of natives were grouped about the doors and windows looking on. Mr. Don performed the ceremony, and it was a very pleasant Christian service; at the close we sang the second paraphrase, "O God of Bethel," &c.

When all was over, and we had shaken hands with the young couple, and witnessed the signing in proper form, we all repaired to the native manse, where a little entertainment was provided of fruit and sweets, including a very pretty wedding-cake, which was cut up and distributed among the guests. These were pretty numerous, including the lads from the Mission compound, the girls from the boarding-school, the native Christian couples with their children, several European friends ; and all mingling in happy social intercourse. It was one of the pleasantest gatherings I have seen for a while.

I am going to another marriage to-morrow in connection with Miss Brittain's "Home." A wedding is in itself an interesting sight ; but the union of two Christian people in the midst of a heathen community like this, forming as it does another Christian household, and another centre of Christian influence, is a peculiarly cheering and happy event.

XVIII.

The Doorga-Pooja.

CALCUTTA, *September 28.*

WE present rather an unusual spectacle as a community at present,—a whole city on holiday. Not the native part only. Counting-houses, banks, schools, and offices are all closed; business is at a stand-still, and everybody is "out of town."

The reason is, that we are now in the midst of the "Doorga-pooja," or worship of the goddess Doorga; and from time immemorial this great annual festival of Bengal has been held as a general holiday, by Eastern and Western alike. It is a happy breathing-time for the toil-worn office people who grill and grind at their desks for the rest of the year; but one cannot help wishing that their well-earned holiday had other associations than those connected with this horrid festival in honour of the cruel Doorga. It is a pity, too, that it does not take place at a cooler season, when people could enjoy a trip, and see the country comfortably. September, I think, is our most disagreeable month as to climate; there is both rain and heat. The rain comes down in tremendous pelts; then the strong sun shines out, and the hot steam rises from the earth, producing a langour and oppression which makes one feel very good-for-nothing.

The goddess Doorga is the wife of *Shiva*, and is chiefly famous for having slain a terrible giant who had conquered the gods and subdued several worlds. She is represented with ten hands holding implements of war. She is accompanied by her children and friends, rides on a lion, and has one foot on the neck of her foe, the prostrate giant.

Although mixed up with so much legendary absurdity, and accompanied by a great deal that is exceedingly repulsive in the mode of observance, this festival seems to be one of the least objectionable of Hindu celebrations. At all events, if we could only divest it of its debasing idolatry and sickening exhibitions, there would be much in it both pretty and interesting. It is the special time for family reunion and social gatherings. Other festivals are public; this is more private and domestic, and is celebrated not at the temples, but in private houses—especially those of the rich. In fact, what Christmas is to us, this time of festive rejoicing is to the Bengalis. All the scattered members of a family reunite under the parental roof. Daughters who are married and away return to their homes; the younger members of the family wait on the head of the house and pay him respect; every one is dressed in new clothes; and the servants and dependants receive presents of cloth, shoes, money, and sweetmeats. Nor are the poor forgotten—many who have often been hungry since last "Pooja" fare sumptuously now.

In the houses of all respectable Babus there is a room called "the dwelling of the gods," which opens from the inner court below. Here the construction of the image which Doorga is to inhabit goes on for some time before the festival occurs. It is fashioned in clay and wood, painted gorgeously, and decked in tinsel and finery according to the taste and means of the family.

A grand ceremonial takes place, which is called the "awakening," when the goddess, who is supposed to be asleep, awakes and enters the image. Then follow salutations and well-wishings on every side, much as we wish each other a merry Christmas and a happy New Year. The pooja, or worship, is now considered to have commenced, and it lasts for four days. Food is cooked in large quantities, which is first offered to the idol; and when she is supposed to have eaten her fill, the priests first, and then the family and friends, receive their portion; then the servants, and afterwards the poor: all are fed, none are sent empty away. All day long offerings are being presented at the shrine, of money, rice, fruit, and flowers; the worshippers having first been purified by bathing in the holy water of the Ganges. When the women are making their offerings and performing their worship, purdahs, or curtains, are hung across the entrance to the shrine, to secure their privacy.

On the third day bloody sacrifices are offered, when the most revolting scenes take place. Buffaloes and sheep are sometimes offered, but generally it is a poor little bleating kid which is led into the court for sacrifice. The head is fastened into a groove on the floor, below which stands a vessel to receive the blood, which, with the head, is afterwards presented to the idol. The art is to sever the head at one blow. For once the goddess is merciful! If this is not effected, it is not lucky; the sacrifice is abortive, and the goddess is displeased. The devotees meanwhile shout and sing and dance, and work themselves into a state of frantic excitement; the multitude of spectators catch the infection, and rend the air with acclamations, while the horrid din is swelled by the deafening noise of tom-toms and the shrill notes of screeching wind instruments. The days which witness all this frightful idolatry are fitly followed by nights of revelry and license. Nautches and spectacles are held in the court, which is decorated and brilliantly lighted. The galleries which surround it on every side are filled with spectators; sometimes including, in one or two of the greater houses, European gentlemen, and even ladies. For the ladies of the family, places are reserved behind venetian screens, whence, though not seen, they can see all that goes on below.

The last ceremony of all is when the "dismissal" of the goddess is pronounced by the officiating priests, and she is supposed to depart to the place whence she came. The shrines are now dismantled, amid the sorrowful farewells of the poor women especially, who grieve to part with the goddess, and also with each other; the deserted images are carried forth, and processions are formed to carry them to the river. The scene by the river-banks on this finishing day of the festival is one of the most extraordinary I have ever seen. Tens of thousands of people fill the streets and line the banks, and the throng and crowd of all sorts of vehicles, jammed together in inextricable confusion, is a sight in itself. Then along every road, and down every lane, all advancing to the river, come the processions. First the music—the clash of cymbals and those dreadful tom-toms; then, borne aloft on the shoulders of a dozen men or more, and preceded by others dancing and shouting, and throwing themselves into the most grotesque attitudes, come the huge frameworks bearing the images; in the centre stands the goddess, with her ten hands; and on each side the attendant deities. Next come the priests and devotees; and last of all, the men of the house to which the erection had belonged. Some carry gay umbrellas, while others fan the goddess with punkahs, or wave over her the tail of the yak cow.

All the processions take one direction—to the river—where the images are thrown into the water. I noticed that there was always a scramble among the irreverent crowd for the finery and tinsel. They tore off whatever they could get hold of, and all the river received was a bare unsightly framework of wood.

Thus ends the great festival; though the general holiday does not end now. It goes on for a fortnight; and then the people return, and work proceeds for another year. The Rajah Kali Krishna kindly invited us to witness the tamāsha (or show) in his court, which I believe was exceptionally grand; but of course we declined to be present as guests at idolatrous ceremonies. Dr. M., however, saw in different places the nature of the celebration; and called on the rajah, who was most polite and kind, but apologised for not shaking hands that day, as "he was pure," having bathed for worship. I also was allowed to look into a court where the worship was going on; but no one must approach nearer the goddess than the foot of the steps leading to the shrine.

The thought which came into my mind as we stood at the ghaut last night, watching those multitudes mad on their idols, was this, *By what means* shall these people be taught to worship the true God, and Jesus whom He has sent? How shall these masses be reached? This question has been echoing through my head, and knocking at my heart, ever since. What is to be done?

It is no wonder that these people should be what they are. Having for ages worshipped this wretched Doorga and the cruel Kali, is it any wonder that they should be like them? It is the old principle, "They that make them are like unto them;" how should the worshipper be better than his gods?

But the transformative power is in our hands—to teach them to worship, not these senseless images, but "the image of the invisible God, the man Christ Jesus;" that, *so* worshipping, "they may be changed into the same image, from glory to glory."

Surely, if our ministers and students saw what we saw last evening, and *took in* the reality of all this, they could not stay at home. Why is it that men of every Church seem to prefer the smallest charge at home, with perhaps only a few hundreds to minister to, to coming to India? Here they might preach Christ to thousands, almost to millions, who never heard of Him, nor of the salvation which He wrought for man. I wonder *why* men are so slow to come. What do they fear? or what is the hindrance? Is it climate? Or do they fancy that the work and life are less interesting? Oh, let them come and try! All I can say is, that some who have spent most of a lifetime in missionary work, only wish they were young again, that they might begin anew—though with a double ardour and consecration, and far more of the spirit of the Master when He wept over impenitent Jerusalem.

September 30.

Now that the rains have somewhat abated, the visits of the young Babus become more frequent again. I occasionally read portions of the Bible to some of them; and more attentive listeners could not be. Those who have been educated in Christian schools are familiar with the Scriptures; but some of our visitors who come from the Government College have scarcely heard the Word of God before, and it is deeply interesting to watch the effect on their minds of what is to them so new. When they ask a question, really wishing for information, I answer to the best of my ability; but when they show a cavilling or merely argumentative spirit, I quietly shut the book, and say that controversy is not my object. I tell them plainly, that what I want is to sow the good seed of what I know to be truth in their hearts, hoping and praying that God's Holy Spirit may cause it to take deep root and bring forth fruit; and instantly they become serious and attentive. What seem to interest them most are the beautiful narratives of the Gospels, especially those which illustrate the life of Christ. The beauty and deep meaning of these seem fresher to myself as I simply read them to these young men, who certainly *seem* to receive them as if there were a thirst in their spirits which only these living waters could quench.

I never shall forget the effect on a Musulman lady once, when I told her in rather broken Hindustani the story of Christ raising Lazarus, and of his love to the family at Bethany. The tears rolled down, and she begged for more, more.

We have been very glad to hear, from several intelligent Bengalis, that the pooja celebrations are undoubtedly declining, both in splendour, and the interest they excite. The families who have the image set up are far fewer in number; there is less money spent on the decorations; and the observances which accompany the celebrations are not nearly so barbarous as in former years. Dr. M. asked the young men what they thought was the reason of this decline. "We think there is less money, and we know there is less faith," was the answer. Whether the money is less or not, there seems to be no doubt that the faith in the Shastras is less, and that what is most objectionable in the ritual of Hinduism is steadily passing away.

Not, indeed, that this stupendous system is yet "crumbling to its fall," as some sanguine people would persuade you. Ideas alter faster than institutions; and religion in this land is so interwoven with the family and social life of the people, that change and revolution must be slow. Still, it is indisputable that a great and rising tide of change has set in, which must sooner or later carry all before it. Education, missionary influence, railways, commerce, civilized law and government, and a hundred other things which are of European origin, and which British influence and rule have introduced, must have unbounded power in pulling down old habits and beliefs, deep-rooted though they are.

The grand question for Christian men to solve will be, how to direct and guide all this; and if heathenism is really breaking up, to see that the religion of the Son of God is put in its place. If not, a very real danger will arise, if it has not already risen. There is considerably over a million of the youth of this country now receiving a liberal English education, but an entirely secular one, except in so far as the missionaries can counteract this state of things. All this education, if not intermixed with the leaven of religion, will assuredly work harm; and non-religion, infidelity, and immorality will come in like a flood. Already some of the most respectable and far-seeing of the Hindus are themselves afraid of this; and if things do not mend, the last state of this great country may be worse than the first.

The cure, however, seems plain enough: *all* education should be mingled with moral and religious truth, so that spiritual training may keep pace with intellectual. A good, pure, healthy literature is also much wanted, full of sound principles, and conveying the same moral and religious lessons as the school-books, and at the same time as entertaining and attractive as possible. Above all, we should have an army of evangelists—European they must be at first, I suppose; but as soon as possible let them be drawn from among the people—sons of the soil, who would scatter themselves everywhere, and speak to their countrymen in their own tongues the wonderful works of God. With all this, and God's blessing, a new and blessed era would soon dawn on India.

I may quote here the following striking testimony to missionary education from the organ of the progressive section of the Brahmo-Samaj, the *Indian Mirror*:—

> Though Government is probably as anxious as we are to make native youths truthful, honest, and moral, and though there are not wanting good teachers, head-masters, and Principals capable of exercising healthy influence, yet the inevitable effect of the general system of teaching in Government institutions is unfavourable, and even adverse to morality. If we turn our attention for a moment to missionary institutions, we find there is an altogether different state of things. We regard it as an indisputable fact that there is a higher tone of morality amongst the students of missionary schools than those of Government schools. Why is this? Not surely on account of the peculiar dogmas of Christianity; for, with solitary exceptions, the pupils seem unwilling to accept them. The reason is, there is positive religious teaching with accompanying moral instruction; and then there are superior Christian teachers, whose force of character is sure to be felt. The students constantly hear of God and immortality, listen to prayers, are every now and then reminded of their duties and obligations, and subjected to moral discipline; so that, though they may not accept the doctrines and tenets that are taught, they unconsciously imbibe the high moral influence of Christian education. In stating our convictions on this point freely and impartially, we do not mean to advocate the introduction of the Bible into Government schools; but we believe that without teaching Christian, Hindu, or Mohammadan dogmas the Government can enforce moral discipline.

Nothing seems to be so indicative of the change I spoke of, as the circumstance that the education of the women has taken such a start within the last few years. When I look back to our first years in India, and our experiences in this field, the change looks as if from death to life—the beginning of life, it is true, but yet life. Then, we could hardly induce a few very young girls from among the poorest people to come and learn the alphabet, even when we tried to attract them by giving money and clothes.

How well I remember my first little girls' school in Bombay. We got a room erected close to our house, the walls made of thin planks of wood, and the roof thatched with dried palm-branches—the most primitive of schoolrooms, put up at the cost of a few rupees. Here some dozen poor wee lassies were collected by an equally poor schoolmaster, whose pay depended on the number of pupils he brought. Every child was paid for coming; and she demanded her pice at the end of the week, as if she had been working for her bread. Even with the pice inducement, these children could not be made to come regularly; and every now and then a boy was found occupying the place of a girl, and trying to escape observation by hiding behind a sister. It was a fight, too, to get them to learn anything beyond the alphabet, which they first mastered by shouting it in a sing-song chant in a class, and then were advanced to writing the letters with a little style on a board covered with sand. The multiplication table was learnt in the same manner; and this, with little simple lessons I gave them by word of mouth, as I learned Marathi myself, such as, "Who made you?" and, "Suffer little children to come unto me," was all that could be taught at that time in female day-schools in Bombay.

Yet God graciously blessed such faint and feeble beginnings as these. One of the best and noblest native Christian women we ever had in India, received her first impressions in just such a school as I have described. Among the earliest experiences of my missionary life, and one which has left an indelible impression on my memory, was when this girl, then little more than eleven years of age, first took her stand as a convert to

Christ and his religion. In God's strength she braved a crowd of a hundred men and more, who had gathered in our compound to intimidate her, and withstood at once the entreaties and threats of her relations, and their whole caste, being enabled through grace to hold fast her profession without wavering. She became a thoroughly educated woman; spoke English beautifully, conducted the Free Church boarding-school in Bombay for some time, and was married to our dear friend Mr. Vincente A. Da Cunha, assistant-secretary of the Bible Society. She was one of the best of wives and mothers, as well as a missionary to her people, until it pleased God, when she had hardly passed the noontide of her life, to take her to Himself.

I could not refrain from giving this sweet little reminiscence of the olden time, brought up by the glimpse of the past of our work; for I loved dear M. as a child. At that time female education was an almost impossible task, and, as far as the higher castes and classes were concerned, quite impossible. To get into the houses of the rich was a thing not to be thought of. Even as late as ten years ago, the native gentlemen could not be said to be more than just willing to have their wives and daughters educated. Their opposition had declined; but they were still indifferent, to say the least. And now? What of the wonderful present? There is hardly an educated Babu in Bengal, I fancy, who does not desire education for the female portion of his family. I should even go further, and say that the majority desire it with eagerness, and *will have it.* They want their wives and daughters to be their companions; they want them to be like English women; and they will welcome us even with the Bible in our hands, and give us access to their zenanas, if we also bring general education.

And what of the women themselves? What do they feel on this, to them, vital question? Ah! these poor things have had their eyes opened; they have seen their fetters, they know that they are bound, and they are now crying out in their bondage; and their cry has gone up into the ears of Him who is the helper of the helpless. It would melt a heart of stone to see how they welcome the zenana teacher; how they look for her and wait for her, and come to meet her, and accompany her as far as they dare to the little door, which, as I said, is the boundary dividing them from the great and attractive world without. Her visit brings brightness, because it brings knowledge and occupation; and a fresh breath, which does them good, from that *other*, Christian woman's world, of which they get glimpses through such visits, and which as yet is so different from their own: not to speak of yet another world still, and a better life, which we can help to fit them for, by leading them to the feet of Jesus, and teaching them that He came to seek and save them as much as us. What we want now is, not so much to find pupils, as to find teachers who are willing to go out and instruct those who are waiting to be taught. We want also those who are willing to give money that teachers may be sent. Only women *can* do this work. The time has not come when men, however devoted and successful they may be as missionaries, can go into the zenanas. This will come in time. but it has not come yet. Even medical men cannot go into these secluded homes.* If a physician be summoned to attend the sick-bed of a native lady, he must not see her face. He may look at her tongue, if this can be managed through the veil! And he may feel her pulse, but it must be through the purdah. We must have women to do the work; and *all* the work for the bodies and souls of the women, at least of Bengal. We must have lady teachers; yes, and lady medical missionaries. The

* Except into those of the Parsees in Western India.—*Edit.*

East supplies the strongest plea for the medical studies of ladies. *No* agent can do the work in the zenanas from such a vantage-ground as an educated medical lady missionary. And I say *lady* advisedly. The gentle-born, gentle-mannered, cultivated Christian woman may do a work for our poor sisters in the heathen world which an angel might covet. Joyfully, we must believe, would the angels accept the commission to go and teach these helpless women; to tell them that there is hope and life and deliverance through the Crucified for them. How their bright wings would speed on such a message of love! But it is given only to us to tell it. O precious task! If we would only accept it, and take it up, and *do it.* "Here am I; *send me.*" When shall this be the language of Britain's favoured daughters? For it is to Britain's daughters peculiarly that this work of raising India's daughters *is* given. America's daughters are nobly aiding in the work. And those who cannot go should help with their prayers and means to send others. If every woman in Scotland gave something, even as the Lord blessed her, what a revolution we might effect! We might occupy not only the zenanas of the high-caste and rich, but we might go into every village and hamlet, and carry the gospel to the whole of India. Women are now doing much at home; their energy achieves great results in every department of Christian effort. Let us put forth the same power for India, and "the acceptable year of the Lord" will then have come.

October 23.

Dr. M. had a great discussion with a very learned Brahman last night. This man had requested an interview, and as his object did not seem to be mere controversy, my husband was glad to go and have a conversation with him. There were other Brahmans present, and about forty or fifty of an audience. The conversation was carried on in Hindi, and partly Sanscrit. The men were polite and quiet, and seemed really anxious to have their questions on religious topics answered, and various difficulties solved. The Brahman who had solicited the interview was chief spokesman, and was more skilled in his own sacred books than any one Dr. M. has yet met in Calcutta. When pressed with the difficulty as to how the different systems which are comprehended under the name of Hinduism were to be reconciled, he candidly said he would like some time to think over the question. The great systems of philosophy, he thought, were good for such learned men as himself, while image-worship was suited for the common people; but he begged for time to think about it, and also to consider what he had now heard from the Christian Shastres. So they are to meet again. The conference lasted from five till eight. A solicited and friendly discussion like this is very cheering to a missionary.

We have had a most interesting visit from two German gentlemen,—Dr. Hardeland, director of the Leipzig Mission; and Mr. Meyer, one of the missionaries. This mission works much among the Shānārs of the south, who are demon-worshippers. The progress of the gospel among this people has been wonderful. Since the first commencement of missions in the south, some hundred and sixty years ago, more than a hundred thousand of these Shānārs have been converted to Christianity; and now the number of baptisms averages about five hundred a year.

It is very delightful, too, that Dr. H. bears the most emphatic testimony to the Christian character of these converts. They have churches and schools, and Christian villages, and native pastors, and are quite an organized Christian community. The work also among the aboriginal races is everywhere becoming daily more interesting and hopeful; * and we are full of expectation about our own mission to the Santals. A very interesting man—Mr. Boerresen, a Dane—has been with us, who, having some little means of his own, has come out with his wife to live the rest of their days, and work, among the Santals. What an example is this! Would that it became infectious. This Dane has got a Norwegian, Mr. Skrefsrud, for his colleague, and they are breaking ground among this interesting people. They belong properly to no European society. They live in the jungles, and inhabit a hut of leaves, while they are building their house.

Indeed, the work among the wilder races is much more hopeful than any other. God seems to be blessing it more. Strange if these outcasts should yet outstrip the wise, philosophical, high-caste Hindu, and the proud, fanatical Mohammadan! Such things have often been. It is God's way to choose "the weak things of the world to confound the things that are mighty." "It is written, I will destroy the wisdom of the wise, and bring to nothing the understanding of the prudent." Who knows, then, but that God may "choose" the poor foolish Santals, and Koles, and Shānārs, and the rest! They have no *system* of religion; all is a vague dread of demons, which soon gives way before a calm, clear declaration of the power and love of the great Father in heaven. They are unfettered by caste, and have no sacred books. If they adopt the religion and civilization of the West, they may at no distant day become a great power in India. They will be important politically, helpful to our nation and Government; but, above all, helpful to the spread of the gospel, and the winning of all India for Christ.

* The Shānārs are not properly aborigines; they are of the same Dravidian stock as the ordinary Hindus of Southern India.—*Edit.*

XIX.

Inner Hindu Life.

CALCUTTA, *October 29.*

MY feelings were sorely tried by a little child-wife in a zenana to which we went to-day. It was Miss H.'s regular day for visiting in this family, and I accompanied her, but was not expected. The lady of the house herself met us just within the door which leads to the apartments of the women, as if she had been waiting and watching for her teacher, and gave us a most joyous greeting. This lady is singularly sweet-looking, and is gentle and very fair. She has a pensive expression in her face when it is in repose, and a sort of wistful look, as if appealing to one's sympathy. She conducted us to her own room, a narrow strip of a place, but not so bare as some of the rooms I have been in. It had some matting on the floor; there was a small round table, and a cot set across at the upper end covered with a bright quilt. There was a single chair, which, with one accord, was assigned to me as the guest. Leaning on the cot, there was an exceedingly pretty, bright child of eight or nine, who looked shyly and smilingly at Miss H., whom she had not seen since her marriage; for this poor child, who ought to have been playing with her dolls in the nursery, was a married lady. The red mark, which is made with powder, above the forehead, and the slender circlet of steel round her waist, showed that her betrothal had taken place. I spoke to the bonnie little thing, and would have taken her on my lap; but she slipped away, and sat down beside a woman who had just come in, circling her arms round her, and putting her head lovingly on her breast. No wonder! This was the child's mother. The chief "bow" explained that she was only on a visit to them, though this was her father's house; that she had only come for "the pooja"—this being a time for the members of a family to reunite—but that very soon she must return to the house of her husband's family, to be under the control of her mother-in-law. When the poor child heard this, she burst into a bitter cry, and sobbed as if her heart would break; the tears streamed down her face, while she clung to her mother, and would not be comforted. I could hardly keep from crying along with her. If I had known Bengali, I should have broken out into a vehement protest against the cruelty of sending a poor little child away from her own mother and her own home; but, of course, it would have done no good, as they would simply have said, "It is our custom; what can we do?"

This is no exceptional case; the same tale could be told of every Hindu girl from the age of seven or eight, though, of course, some are happier with their new relations than others. From the day a girl is married, she belongs far more to her mother-in-law than to her own mother.

Another thing which roused my indignation to-day, and awoke my heartfelt pity for the women of this land, was hearing of a beautiful young girl of twelve, whose home is in one of the zenanas we know, having been married to a wretched old Koolin Brahman, who has already, nobody knows how many wives.

The Koolin, you know, is the very highest division of the Brahmanical caste; and a rich Bengali, for the honour of the alliance, will often give his daughter in marriage to one of these men, although he may be old and poor, and perhaps already have fifty wives; for a Koolin Brahman may marry as many women as he pleases.

Think of the condition of the girl who is thus given away! She may see this husband of hers, or she may not; better for her, perhaps, if she does not. But when he dies, then she is a widow for life; and, God help her!—you know what this means.

I think I have already described the condition of the Hindu widow, and I need not go over it now. The sadness and misery which thenceforward overshadow her life are terrible to contemplate. I know a woman in Calcutta, who is intelligent and educated. She lived a happy, rational life. Her husband, who was a singularly enlightened man, loved her, made her his companion, gave her every indulgence, and had her carefully taught. But he died. Her superstitious relatives at once reduced her to the ordinary condition of a widow. Her clothes and jewels were taken, her hair was cut, and so on. Worst of all, she was deprived of her beloved books, her needle-work, and all her pleasant occupations. *Now she is mad;* and who can wonder!

Who can tell the amount of hidden wrong, of evils which no one can possibly know, which exist in these jail-like places? What may not be done under the name of "custom"? We know little of the secret life of the zenana; we know only what they choose to tell us. What law or public opinion can reach these recesses?

Once, when we were travelling up-country, I saw a tall fierce Mohammadan, with a face as black as a thunder-cloud, pulling along a young-looking veiled woman by the wrist, which he did with exceeding roughness, while she filled the air with her shrieks. We stopped, and eagerly asked one of the men accompanying them what was the matter, for there was quite a mob of people. He laughed in an almost devilish kind of way, which made me feel furious, and said, "She is his wife!" as if this were sufficient to account for any sort of treatment he might choose to mete out to her. "But what has she done?"—"Oh, she tried to run away to her mother."

This sight haunted my memory for weeks. "Tried to run away!" What woe must have entered into this shut-up, veiled woman's life, that she would ever conceive anything so desperate as to run away—a step so contrary to all the habits and ideas of Eastern life! And who could follow her, now that she was re-captured, and know what would befall her, especially if her husband was the villain he looked?

These high, blank, dismal zenana walls hide many possibilities in the lives of the inmates which one shrinks from even contemplating. This woman may have done something very wrong; probably she had; but, speaking generally, there is hardly room for anything to occur which would excite the jealousy of a husband. At all events, morality is not left to choice or principle; it is compelled, an affair of bolts and bars. I could plead for ever for these poor Indian women, if I only could make Christian women really take in and take up their cause!

[I have just noticed the following in the *Indian Mirror* of October 17, 1875, and may quote it to show what is now occurring in India:—

A very affecting case of suicide by a young Hindu widow occurred on last Monday. The girl was only eighteen, and had become a widow at fourteen. She could read and write well. The letter in her own handwriting, found under her pillow, contains among others the following passages:—

"Where my mind is, there I am going. What is the use of my living? It is not my intention to go astray. The Hindu religion is very bad in giving early marriage.—She here pathetically bids farewell to her mother.—Mother, I leave thee in sorrow! Forgive all my misgivings. I am going long before my time. I could not ask forgiveness in words, and therefore do so in writing. I was destined to die in this manner. Let no one grieve for me. I am fated thus to die. It is no one's fault. Mother, on account of me, no one liked you, but now every one will worship you. My aunt, who took care of me, is worth her weight in gold. Take care of her. I am sorry I cannot take leave of her as I ought. Such has been my fate."—Here she earnestly prays to God to forgive her sins and save her soul from going to hell.]

Dr. M. preached for the Wesleyans to-day, this being the anniversary of the opening of their chapel. It is an exceedingly pretty building, and was very well filled. This body has a flourishing mission in Calcutta, and many of the church-members are good and useful men, who seem to assist the missionaries in many ways.

From this service we went round to the Orphanage, where we always have such pleasant little meetings that we do not like to miss one. The children enjoy them too, and are quite disappointed if anything prevents our going. During the week they write short exercises embodying the lesson of the previous Sunday. These are often exceedingly well done, and show, not only that the girls thoroughly understand what they are taught, but that their natural intelligence is of a decidedly high order. They are both quick and thoughtful, and their minds are cultivated a good deal more than those of young women in the same position at home. Their answers to difficult questions often surprise us. I wish that the kind friends at home, who are so interested in their welfare and progress, could see them.

Another little Sunday service we have, is one at four o'clock in the hall, for the servants and people about, when a Scripture-reader comes to read and explain in Bengali; of which, as yet, Dr. M. has not got thorough mastery. None of the people object to attend, except the durwān, who is a very strict Musulman, and holds the Scripture-reader in great contempt. Most come, I fancy, because it is the Saheb's wish; but all are tolerably attentive and quiet, except one irrepressible khitmutghar, who cannot be subdued into humility. He can read a little, on which he greatly prides himself; and so he often tries to enter the arena with the Scripture-reader, determined on controversy, until the Saheb appears and awes him into silence.

The servants' service was shortened somewhat to-day, as we had another "church in the house" for the baptism of the child of one of the native Christians. This is Babu J. Banerjee, who has come from a distant station, where he occupies an important position under Government. There is no Christian minister in the place, so he has had to come to Calcutta on purpose to have his child baptized, who is a fine bright little fellow of three. He has brought his family with him, and his wife is an uncommonly sweet, gentle-looking person. Two or three gharrees full of people arrived, including the whole family of B., and some of our native Christian friends; and we had a most interesting service in the dining-room, which my husband conducted in English. This man made his Christian profession, along with some other converts, the day on which the lamented John M'Donald died; being baptized, I think, by Dr. Duff. Surely it is a touching coincidence, when the disciple enters the Church militant as the teacher is passing through the pearly gates into the Church triumphant.

During the last three days there has been another festival—the famous, or infamous, "Kali pooja." But I am sick of poojas; and I really cannot describe this one, especially as it is peculiarly disgusting. Hecatombs of poor little kids and buffaloes were sacrificed last night at the shrine of the bloodthirsty goddess Kali; who, you know, is represented with a necklace of skulls.

This evening I had a company of five pleasant young Babus sitting with me in the garden, waiting until Dr. M. should have leisure to talk to them. I was expressing great horror at the needless slaughter of so many kids and buffaloes, when one of them said very courteously,—

"Madam, may I be permitted to say something?"

"Certainly, Babu; pray say anything you wish."

He continued: "We, madam, sacrifice for the worship of our goddess; and with much mercy, for the victim is killed with one stroke. You Christians sacrifice, with much torture, for the worship of your belly."

What could I say? Fortunately he did not remember pigeon-shooting—as I did—nor the boasted "bag" of our sportsmen, nor vivisection, or he might have hit us harder still.

This is the festival at which the general illumination of shops and houses takes place, which is exceedingly pretty; but the rockets and crackers which are let off, and resound through the air the whole night through, accompanied by the hideous din of tom-toms and fifes, are really a very hard trial to anybody who has nerves. The idea is, that this is the season especially when ghosts and demons are abroad, and that the lights will at once propitiate and frighten them.

A few days ago a gentlemanlike young man, a member of the Tagore family, called to ask me to pay the ladies of his house a visit. He brought me a photograph, too, of the well-known reformer, Dwarkanath Tagore, who so often visited England.

Yesterday evening I made out this visit, accompanied by Mrs. R. The house is large and very handsome; and in it, in true patriarchal and Hindu fashion, the descendants of the Tagores reside to the third and fourth generations. We were most kindly received at the door by the Babu who had called—Mr. J. N. G., the husband of one of the daughters. He conducted us to the ladies' apartments, which are on the third and top story of the house; and I do not know how many courts, verandahs, and terraces we crossed. At length he took us into a little boudoir, furnished somewhat in English style, with a couch, table, and chairs; and at one end there was a bookcase containing books both in English and Bengali. This is the first time I have seen books in an apartment of the zenana—except, indeed, the lesson-books. There were also some little bits of work about, and other signs of cultivation and womanly employment, which are not as yet very common in a Hindu home.

The ladies soon came in, and welcomed us with stately courtesy. They were very kind, but less demonstrative than most of the women I have visited. Our friend, Mr. D. Tagore, and his family, were absent at their country-house; so, to my regret, we did not see his wife, as we had hoped. Mrs. T., whom we did see, is the wife of an assistant-judge in Western India. She spoke to us in excellent English; indeed, she is quite an educated and cultivated woman, and receives her visitors, and sits at the head of her own table, just as any Englishwoman would do. It seemed hard to believe that she was not a Christian. Her sisters-in-law whom we saw are amongst the most refined native women I have met—very fair, with delicately-cut features. All the ladies were dressed alike; and being in mourning for their distinguished relative, the Babu P. Koomar Tagore, they wore simple white chudders, edged with a border of black. They had also a bodice close to the throat, and with long sleeves—a garment rarely found among Bengali ladies as yet. The only ornaments apparent were thick gold bangles on their wrists. A very pretty, modest young creature proved to be the wife of our friend who had brought us in. It is altogether contrary to Hindu etiquette for a wife to sit unveiled before her husband in the presence of others; indeed, she ought to vanish as soon as he appears. But this lady sat still and talked in the presence of her lord and master, as if she had been an Englishwoman—an impropriety which would have shocked an orthodox Hindu. But the Tagores, happily, have long since left orthodoxy in this sense far behind. They are enlightened and advanced beyond most of their compatriots; though, I am afraid, they are far from the reception of Christianity. How different their conversation was from that of the ordinary uninstructed zenana lady! who invariably inquires how many children you have, and asks the use of the various articles in your attire. These ladies were most intelligent, and we had some very pleasant talk.

They seemed pleased to find that I had known their grandfather, Dwarkanath Tagore—he being a fellow-passenger to Bombay on my first voyage to India. He was the first Hindu I had ever seen; and I shall never forget his gleaming, coal-black, eagle eye, nor my astonishment at his sitting down at table on board, and eating beef just like the rest of us.

We drove out last afternoon to Cossipore, to spend the evening with Mr. and Mrs. W. D., and to greet our friend Mr. J. and his sweet young wife, who have just returned from their wedding trip, and are to live at Cossipore. What a number of delightful friendships one forms in India!

It was a glorious moonlight night. We first strolled about

through a wide avenue of beautiful trees; and then through the sweet, quiet garden, which is a charming mixture of flower-pots, terrace-walks, shrubbery, tangled rose-beds, and pretty green lawn, where the weird shadows from the trees were beginning slowly to lengthen. The company then gathered on a small stone terrace, close to the river-bank, where we enjoyed the delicious cool breeze from the water, and watched the numberless boats glide swiftly past with the current, and the moonbeams play and sparkle, and shed a soft silver light over everything. It was delightful; and it seemed quite Goth-like to go in and dine—which, however, we did finally.

Mr. D. showed me a spot high up in the garden where a wreck had lain. During the cyclone of 1864, the great storm-wave which marched up the river—sixty feet high, I think—parting ships from their moorings, and spreading wreck and disaster on every side, had carried one of the biggest ships in the river, and deposited it like a plaything among the rose-beds in Cossipore garden.

November 3.

Last evening we had our usual prayer-meeting. The Rev. Mr. Hughes, of the Welsh Presbyterian Mission to the Khassia Hills, who was with us, gave us a most interesting account of his work. The Khassias are a simple, aboriginal people, somewhat like the Santals and Koles. They worship demons. They are not a very religious people. They have few ceremonies, and engage in acts of worship only when in any trouble, or driven to such by fear. They are terribly afraid of witchcraft; and they are very intemperate, like the other wild races.

The gospel is making considerable way among them. There are already eight hundred Christians and fifty schools connected with the Welsh Mission.

XX.

Calcutta Sights.

November 4.

THE work in the Mission College is specially hard just now, as the young men are busy preparing for the University examinations.

A question always asked by the University is, "What religion do you profess?" One would not think there could be much variety in the answer among 1200 Bengalis; and yet my husband says it is marvellous how much diversity there is. Most of the lads, of course, write that they are "Hindus;" others write "Theists," others "Deists;" a good many subscribe themselves "Bramhists," and a few "Christians." One young man came to him in great perplexity as to what he should call himself. "I believe that Christianity is true," said he; "but, you know, I am not a baptized Christian." His conscience was relieved by the suggestion that he might just simply state the truth; so he wrote, "A believer in Christianity."

A great many of our intelligent lads would have to subscribe themselves as this young man did, if they told the full truth. Many are "almost," though not yet altogether Christians; and many would be altogether so, but for their mothers. One day a boy, who is very bright and hopeful, and a great favourite of ours, came to school looking so wretched and ill, and so different in the class from his usual self, that Dr. M. asked him what was the matter. "Are you ill, my boy, or is anything wrong?" The poor fellow burst into tears, and said his mother was angry with him, and had given him no breakfast, because he *would* come to the padre's school. "She is afraid," said he, "that I am going to be a Christian."

November 6.

A few evenings ago we had quite a festive gathering—a sort of "at home," to receive our Bengali friends, and especially Bengali Christians. A good many Europeans came to meet them, and seemed to enjoy the little entertainment very much. The drawing-room and wide verandah looked very pretty, decorated with evergreens and well lighted up. We have some fine lads connected with this and other missions, who are as gentleman-like and conduct themselves as well as college lads do whom you meet at home. We had some good music, which was a great attraction; but what all seemed to enjoy most were Scotch songs, and hymns; and in the latter all joined while Mrs. M'Donald played. We finished off with Keble's beautiful hymn, "Sun of my soul, thou Saviour dear;" and as they took leave on the landing, the guests made polite little speeches as to the pleasure they had enjoyed.

I must here observe—and I do so with great joy—that among the Christians connected with the various Protestant missions there is a large amount of brotherly feeling; in fact, one may say there is no sectarian feeling at all. I am afraid we cannot say so much for European Christians. Let me add, that the native Christians look forward to the time when they will all be enrolled into one Indian Church. A blessed consummation it will be.

Next evening we had the Sunday-school teachers and other friends; and then I felt a rest would be agreeable. But it is such a pleasure to see people enjoy themselves.

The temperature is perfectly delicious now. The mornings and evenings are almost cold, and the days balmy and sweet. It is something like an Egyptian winter, or an Italian early summer.

November 9.

Our friends from Serampore, big and little, have come in for a few days, and Mrs. S. and I are very busy. Indeed, I shall have to put a great deal into little time now, for our days in this pleasant abode are numbered. It is now only seven A.M., and I have written fourteen notes already. Notes, or "chits," as they are called, fly about like shuttlecocks, and consume too much of one's day; but they are necessary evils, because the messengers make the most amusing havoc of verbal messages.

Mrs S. and I have just returned from one of the most singular scenes I have ever witnessed—namely, an opium sale. A strange place for ladies to go to, I dare say you will think; but my friend and I are equal to a good deal together, and we were properly escorted by Mr. M., who is the Government inspector of opium, and obliged to be present at the sales. Besides this, we kept strictly "behind the purdah;" a screen having been placed on purpose for us, and so well placed, that, though entirely unseen, we saw and heard perfectly. The sale takes place once a month. It is a sort of auction, when the chests are put up in lots, and disposed of to the highest bidder. Government, as you know, has a monopoly of the opium trade, making as much gain as possible on the deadly export as it passes from its own hands into those of the dealers; who bid for it, and buy it, and send it on to do its work on unhappy China. The purchase, of course, is a pure speculation, depending for the return on the state of the market when the consignment reaches China; and hence the extraordinary nature of the scene we witnessed. The huge hall was one sea of faces. Men were congregated there from every part of the country—Hindus, Musulmans, Jews, Parsees, Europeans, and Indo-Europeans. A good many were up-country men, as one could tell from their different dialect, and their peculiar head-gear. But, whatever the nationality, every face wore the same look of intense eagerness, which it awed one to see. The keen restless eyes were all turned on the seller, who stood in a thing like a school-desk, or small pulpit, with a little hammer in his hand. There was a subdued buzz in the room, as of many eager hushed voices, while the street below was a perfect Babel of deafening tongues. A great crowd of the same sort of men as those in the hall, had assembled below the windows. These were not buyers; their object was to bet on the results of every purchase; and in this they showed the same terrible eagerness as the actual buyers did within. As each lot was knocked down, and the little hammer had given its tap, tap, some one rushed out to make known the result to the crowd below. This was done by marking the number of the chest and the price on a white slate, which was held up at a certain window, and exposed to the anxious gaze of the upturned faces, whereupon the betting proceeded, with frightful din and indescribable excitement.

After watching the scene within for a while, especially the strange and varying expressions on the countenances of the bidders, as the keen competition went on, we went to a little balcony overhanging the street to survey the crowd of gamblers without; and I think the spectacle was even more curious than the one we had left. The men were a rather lower-looking set; certainly the most disreputable company of natives I have seen.

They were a strange medley of races, complexions, and costumes. The Babu element was small. There were some shabby Jews, low Parsees, wily Marwarrees, overgrown Banyans, and, lowest-looking of all, some loafer-like Europeans. A tall Mohammadan, evidently from the North-West, stood about the middle of the throng, with a small red turban set jauntily on one side of his head, and an unpleasant eye. This man caught sight of us, so we thought it better to bring our investigations to a close, and immediately took our departure.

I must say I came off with a blush of shame on my cheek. This sale is conducted by our Christian Government! A most important item in its revenue is drawn from this vile opium trade, so ruinous both to the bodies and souls of the poor Chinese. Nay, we forced the use of it upon them at the bayonet's point. The system of collecting the revenue is different in Bombay and Bengal. In Bombay the drug is simply taxed, which is surely far better than what is done in Bengal, for here it is grown and sold by Government itself. They say that China will not be able to compete with India in the production of opium. The juice of the poppy has not the same flavour, when grown anywhere else than in Malwa and Bengal. The educated taste of the real opium-eater won't put up with the inferior article his own country can produce! There is therefore little hope that China will be left to carry on her own ruin. And the trade seems increasing by reason of the fatal facilities for export. There is now the railway, instead of the old slow bullock-cart; and magnificent steamers, instead of the old sailing-ships. I am afraid, then, it will be less and less easy for Government to listen to the voice of duty in this matter. Yet Britain once did a magnanimous thing when she struck the fetters off the slave; and how proud we are at this day that "slaves cannot breathe in England!" Why cannot we do something as morally great in connection with the opium traffic?

On Saturday Mrs. S. and I spent the forenoon in visiting some Jewish families. I have long wished to know something of this portion of the community, who are so interesting everywhere; and Miss T. kindly introduced us. You know that she had charge of dear Mrs. Ewart's Jewish school for some years, which she conducted admirably, and this connection has given her a large acquaintance among the parents of her pupils.

The Jews in Calcutta are as rich as they proverbially are elsewhere, and they appear to occupy rather an influential position, chiefly as merchants, though none seem to have risen so high as the distinguished Sassoon family in Bombay. I saw a good many Jewish countenances, overtopped by the red fez and long blue tassel, among the keen competitors at the opium sale yesterday. These men were certainly doing their own share of the business.

One of the streets we drove to is called Ezra Street: here we made several visits. The houses are large and handsome, but the surroundings and entrances, and also the fittings in the interiors, are sometimes unpretending and mean enough, considering the indications of wealth which are otherwise apparent. An Eastern house has seldom much in it suggestive of comfort and convenience; and these—with the mistresses clad in satin and diamonds—were often untidy, comfortless, and even dirty. The Jewish ladies we saw are more or less educated, and some know a little English. One of them, Mrs. G., is a most intelligent woman, and speaks English perfectly. I have seen her once or twice at Government House, quite an honoured visitor. I never saw anything like the jewels they wear; they are magnificent. Each Jewess had on a fortune in diamonds and emeralds. Some of the ladies are very handsome, with beautiful eyes, delicately tinted with black—which has a very pretty effect—and lovely soft olive complexions. They are much less shy in manner than the Bengali ladies, and talk freely and brightly. Altogether, their lives seem to be more natural and joyous; and, but for their Eastern garb, they would look more like Europeans of the soft South, than born Orientals. Their dress is handsome, made of the richest materials and most brilliant colours; but the form is not graceful, particularly in the bust arrangements.

Mrs G. has asked both Mrs. S. and myself to the marriage of her sister a fortnight hence; and I shall be glad of the opportunity to see a Jewish wedding. We saw Mrs. G.'s young daughter-in-law, who has just been married to a handsome young man, who came in and talked to us, dressed like an Englishman. She is a beautiful girl, with a lovely little head, prettily poised on her arching neck, and wonderfully fair. Her throat was clasped round by a diamond necklace of immense value, and it seemed odd to see them wear such jewels as everyday attire. These people seem all of the straitest sect of their religion. Christianity has not, as far as I can learn, got the least entrance among them. When the men care for religion at all, they are decided Jews, attending the synagogue, and observing their Sabbaths and new moons and appointed feasts; but indifferentism appears to prevail in a greater measure among them than among the Hindus. Certainly there is less of religious inquiry. The men are much more like modern Greeks than ancient Hebrews.

One of the unique sights of Calcutta is the China Bazaar, which I never visited till yesterday. I am indebted to the stimulating effect of Mrs. S.'s visit for a good deal; her bright energy is infectious. We got up some wants in the shopping way; made ourselves look as ragamuffin as possible, in our shabbiest clothes; got into a ticca gharree, and set out. Had we gone respectably attired, and in our own conveyance, we should have had to pay the penalty of respectability in "burra saheb's" prices. There are always two prices in India—one for the rich, and the other for the poor; and the unerring way in which the natives gauge the relative incomes of those who employ them, is wonderful and most diverting.

We drove into the heart of the native town, and got into a street so narrow that the gharrees had to go single file, and in order to turn had to go to the top of the road. The houses are exceedingly poor and mean-looking; there is no pavement; the streets are dirty; the shops are low and shabby, and looked eminently uninviting. This is the China Bazaar; and here, in the midst of dilapidation, and the most unlikely surroundings, what represents an untold amount of wealth is gathered together and hidden away. In these unpromising dens you can purchase almost anything, "from a needle to an anchor." The most exquisite shawls manufactured in the looms of Cashmere; rich elaborate brocades in silver and gold; wondrous inventions of Chinese ingenuity; lovely articles in porcelain, ivory, and sandal-wood; goodly specimens of Japanese art; curiosities and *bric-à-brac* of every description; beautiful jewellery of immense value; not to speak of the products and manufactures of European countries, which you find here, from Manchester cotton and Paris bonnets, to tapes and buttons and macassar-oil. The moment our gharree appeared we were surrounded, mobbed, taken possession of, by scores of vulture-like Bengalis—the "touters" of the shops—each one determined on making us his own individual prey. We had got out of the gharree, but I precipitately fled back to it, and took refuge from the irrepressible throng. They then poked their goods into the gharree, until there was a promiscuous pile at my feet, which I pretended to appropriate. The din was dreadful, each one shouting at the top of his voice, "Mem sahib, come my shop," "My shop, good shop," "I got cheap ting," "I got pretty ting," and so on. At length we descried a Babu quieter than the others, and less eager; we beckoned to him, and finding his shop was near, we made a dart into it, and, to our surprise, the crowd instantly became orderly, and quietly dispersed. They accepted the situation; their brother Babu had gained the day; their turn would come next. We found ourselves in a narrow strip of a room, lighted only from the door, which was really a passage between two high walls of piled-up goods. Each side was filled from floor to ceiling with bales of yellow and white calicoes, fine broadcloths, gay chintz, gossamer French muslins, and all sorts of stuffs. On a small carpet in the middle of the floor sat the merchant cross-legged, and beside him a venerable man with close-cropped gray head, sharp face, spectacles on nose, and pen behind his ear; this was the cash and book-keeper, who had the emblems of his calling before him in a cash-box and ledger. One end of the shop was filled with commonplace boxes of flowers and millinery; but above, up a rickety old stair, was the most interesting and delightful old-curiosity shop you can imagine, thick with dust, and garnished with cobwebs, and full of the most tempting things, gathered from all corners of the Eastern world. Here I could have stayed for days; and the attendant Babu was very good-natured, letting us examine everything to our heart's content, without a pretence of offering to buy. You folks at home labour under the hallucination that

Indian things are bought for nothing—a very great mistake. Out of old hingeless black boxes came magnificent rings and other jewels; and from the back of a dingy, dusty shelf came rolls of finely-wrought kincob, pieces of soft shiny white silk, and piles of Delhi, Cashmere, and Rampore shawls, and other beautiful things too numerous to name. There was some lovely old china, which the man said belonged to an obsolete art.

We confined our investigations to this and one other shop, and came home as the sun went down, more tired than tongue could tell.

December 5.

I have not had such a heartache for a long time as this evening, when I returned from the river, leaving Mrs. T., who has been staying with us, alone on board the steamer bound for Singapore. Five short months ago she was a happy bride; now she is a forlorn widow. Such, too often, is life in India.

Poor thing! she seemed so desolate, as she stood on the deck in her deep mourning, waving her hand to me, and gazing after the little boat which paddled back to the landing, taking me to my happy home; and she, young creature, going out into the world alone, leaving her husband dead behind! I could only lift a silent prayer to Him who is the widow's God (and is most truly hers), to be a very present help to her in her sore need.

I promised to give you her touching little story; and it is this. About eight or ten weeks ago a pretty, graceful ship came up the river, called the *Pehlwan*, commanded by Captain T., a remarkably fine young man of twenty-six, who had his newly-married wife on board, it being her first voyage. They had been round to Bombay, and brought letters of introduction to us, —surely a striking providence, as matters turned out, for they knew no one in Calcutta. The first time I saw Mrs. T. was one day she called, bringing notes from Colonel Annesley and dear Mr. Bowen, when she told me that her husband was ill in the hospital, and that they had been obliged to let their beautiful ship sail without them.

My husband went to the sick man at once. There was not much seriously the matter, the doctor hoped; and so we got them comfortable lodgings, a kind and skilful medical man to attend him, and we saw them nearly every day. To our joy, we found they were both earnest Christians, with whom it was a delightful privilege to hold intercourse. He suffered much; but his patience was beautiful, and also his perfect trust as to the issue; whatever way God ordered it, it would be "well." He was touchingly careful to spare his wife, who watched him day and night. The kind doctor did all that man could do; but after six weeks' hoping and fearing, early one morning we were hurriedly summoned, and on going in we found the poor wife prostrate over the dead body of her husband.

We brought her away with us to our home; and the same evening he was laid to rest in a quiet corner of our pretty Scotch burying-ground;—how distressingly soon does burial always follow death in India!

It must have been a sore trial of faith for this dying man to leave his poor young wife and coming babe, friendless and penniless, in a land of utter strangers. But he knew in whom he believed, and his faith did not fail; nor did hers. She has never murmured, though she seems broken-hearted.

She has gone to some friends in Singapore to stay until her baby comes, and then she will engage in mission work, for which she has received a training in an excellent school—that of Mrs. Pennefather's Missionary Home. I miss her very much; and could hardly have let her go, but that we leave this ourselves so soon.

December 6.

Dr. M. preached the annual sermon in the Union Chapel this forenoon for the London Missionary Society. This is one of the best attended churches in Calcutta; and there is so much that is interesting connected with its past history, that one cannot enter it without having one's heart stirred. Many names, distinguished in the history of Bengal Missions, have been connected with "Union Chapel." Among those who have recently been connected with the London Missionary Society in Calcutta are the venerable Lacroix, his daughter, Mrs. Mullens,—who will long be remembered, especially in connection with the Zenana Mission,—Mr. Storrow, Dr. Mullens, and others I need not wait to name.

The natives feel the cold very much; they go about like spectres through the foggy air of these wonderfully cold mornings, wrapped from head to foot in sheets of yellow cotton, and have the aspect of people in a snow-storm at home. Our servants sit in groups outside in the day, sunning themselves, and yet shiver in their thin cotton garments. I have had to open a dispensary for flannels and woollen things; and now there are fewer coughs. The poor māli who is ill, is lying on one of the garden-walks. I asked him why he had come out, fearing it was zeal for his work; but he said he was so cold in his hut, he had come to the "dhoop" (or sunshine) to get warm. I suggested his lying on the grass, instead of among the stones. To us the temperature now is simply delicious; the air in the day is like balm, and the mornings and evenings are bracing, and really cold. For the next three months we shall have a perfect climate. I now wear a good stuff dress; and nothing cooler than silk is pleasant at any time of the day.

Did you remember that yesterday was St. Andrew's day? I am afraid you are very degenerate Scots. Calcutta remembered it after a very jubilant fashion; for the great annual dinner in the Town Hall was eaten by all true sons of Caledonia, and these are not few in this great commercial capital of the East.

This St. Andrew's dinner has become quite an institution here, and a very pleasant bit of nationality it is; though the stolid English may be disposed to ask whether the canny Scots have not for the nonce gone mad. It gives an opportunity of commemorating everything Scottish—which is well in a foreign land, I dare say; and floods of patriotic eloquence are poured forth on such subjects as our heroic King Robert the Bruce, William Wallace, Robert Burns, Sir Walter Scott, and the rest; and all this with an enthusiasm, and also jocularity, which would have astonished Sydney Smith. The battle-cry yesterday was certainly that of the Scots Greys at Waterloo—"Scotland for ever!" Three stalwart Highlanders, in "the garb of old Gaul," marched round the tables during dinner, with skirling bagpipes; which would be charming on their native heath, with a deep glen between, but are rather noisy in a room. Somebody with a splendid voice sang "The Land o' the Leal," the most sweet and plaintive of Scottish songs; but it is hardly safe to stir up memories of the "home-countrie." The *heimweh* sometimes is oppressive enough; for, as Heber asks,—

"For who in Indian bower hath stood,
Nor thought of England's good greenwood,
And breathed a sigh—how oft in vain!—
To gaze upon her oaks again?"

Or, as my dear friend, Mrs. Harriet Miller Davidson,* sings,—

"Oh for a breath o' the moorlands,
A whiff o' the caller air!
For the smell o' the flowerin' heather
My very heart is sair.

"Oh for the sound o' the burnies
That wimple to the sea—
For the sight o' the browning bracken
On the hillside waving free!

"Oh for the blue lochs cradled
In the arms o' mountains gray,
That smile as they shadow the drifting clouds
A' the bonnie simmer day!

"I am sick o' the blazing sunshine
That burns through the weary hours,
O' gaudy birds singing never a sang,
O' beautiful scentless flowers.

"Auld Scotland may be rugged,
Her mountains stern and bare;
But, oh for a breath o' her moorlands,
And a whiff o' her caller air!"

Or yet, rather let me say with a much-esteemed German missionary in Western India—if I may borrow my husband's version of his lines,—

"Know'st thou the land, 'mid zones of dazzling light,
Where gleams with pearl and gold the city bright,
Where a new song they pour in triumph high,
And every tear is wiped from every eye?
Thy Fatherland! Away, away;
Short is thy pilgrim-course, yet brooketh not delay."

* Daughter of the lamented Hugh Miller.

XXI.

Cold Weather Life.

BALLYGUNGE, *January.*

DECEMBER has been much too busy a month for letter or journal writing; every day and every hour were crowded with engagements. I do not mean the gaieties in which Calcutta indulges pretty freely at this season, but public engagements, such as school-examinations, lectures, meetings, anniversary sermons, and such like. All this sort of thing has to be crowded into the cool months in India—which, alas! are few and short-lived. The whole circle of schools and colleges have their exhibitions and prize-givings just before Christmas; and we have often attended two, and even three of these, in a day. Our own little exhibition at the Orphanage was very pretty. Mr. Monteath presided; and Mrs. Monteath gave away the prizes, with a few kind and encouraging words to each pupil. The children looked very nice, ranged on the gallery seats, dressed simply in their fresh white; while tables covered with the beautiful prizes sent from Edinburgh by Mrs. Cleghorn, and other tables covered with the children's needlework, made a very pretty and gay foreground. The whole room was decorated by the children with flowers and evergreens, and well filled with spectators.

You should have seen how the dear little things hugged their prizes! I wish the kind friends who select and send out such prizes could see the joyous delight on the little dark faces. One very wee child kissed her dolly rapturously; and the big ones, though less demonstrative, were quite as happy. In none of the schools have I seen nicer prizes given. The girls' work was beautiful. They do this fancy work in their leisure hours, and it forms a little source of revenue to them. It is sold, and the money they thus obtain enables them to contribute to the Bengali Church Sustentation fund, and subscribe to various charities. They are fond of giving gifts to each other, also, and this pocket-money enables them to afford themselves some little extra pleasures.

One of the prettiest sights I have seen in Calcutta was a meeting of the "Sunday School Union" in the Town Hall the other evening. All the Sunday schools belonging to the different congregations (with one or two exceptions) were collected together, and filled the great hall to overflowing. There were more than a thousand children present, besides teachers and parents and visitors. A few ladies were admitted to the platform, whence we had an admirable view of the interesting spectacle below, which Dr. M. rightly compared to a brilliant parterre in a flower-garden. It was, indeed, a striking and variegated picture. Just in front sat a row of Miss T.'s friends among the young Jewesses, arrayed in the brightest colours, and glittering with gold and jewels; immediately behind them, in pleasing contrast, sat our Orphanage girls, clad in simple white; and then backward, row after row, the seats were filled with English and East Indian children, decked in all the colours of the rainbow—their happy faces shining up at us, full of eager expectation. Dr. M. presided, and gave an address, well garnished with stories. Then followed some hymns and pieces of music, very beautifully sung. Then there were other addresses and more singing. The music was the chief attraction; all the pieces were sacred, and the vast assembly joined in singing them. The whole was conducted most admirably by our friend Mr. Stewart, who must have worked hard at the various practisings to bring so many young voices into such beautiful harmony.

The Sunday scholars look forward to this treat the whole year, and their kind teachers take a wonderful amount of trouble in organizing it for them. This was followed by a trip in a special railway-train, and a fête at Barrackpore, where they were allowed to have unlimited fun in the park, by the kind permission of the Governor-General, who, with his usual kindness of heart, himself honoured the gathering with a visit. Some of our orphan children were allowed to join the expedition; and the little forlorn creatures who were left behind were made happy by a huge basket of plantains, oranges, nuts, and cakes, which we carried to them. We gave them some swings, played a few games, heard them sing their hymns; and I am not sure that they did not think they had, after all, had the best of it.

Ballygunge is one of our prettiest suburbs. It boasts of a maidān, or esplanade, all its own, stretching down to country roads, fringed with beautiful trees, which show through the leafage some handsome houses standing in grounds prettily laid out in gardens and shrubbery.

We are the guests of Mr. and Mrs. Craik, who, like the kind friends they are, insisted on our *flitting* bag and baggage to their bright and pleasant abode, when we had to bid adieu to our own.

January 10.

We have had a new and rather uncomfortable experience to-day—namely, the shock of an earthquake. We were sitting in the drawing-room in the afternoon, quietly chatting, when there was a heave, and a rock, and a low rumbling sound, as of very distant thunder. We all started to our feet, and one of the gentlemen exclaimed, "An earthquake!" The punkahs began to swing, the chandelier-drops rang against each other, doors flew open, the pictures started from the walls, and for ten minutes nothing seemed steady again. It was very odd to see the punkahs swinging of their own accord. They say we shall probably hear sad news of this convulsion from different parts of the country.

My husband preached the annual missionary sermon in the Free Church yesterday; and there was a collection of 1500 rupees (£150). The Free Church congregation is not large, but it has always been noted for its liberality. Besides liberally supporting its minister, it largely contributes to the maintenance of the Mission Schools.

Calcutta is unusually gay and stirring at present. Numbers of high natives have crowded into the city from all parts of India to bid farewell to the retiring "Lord Sahib," and assist at the reception of the new (Lord Mayo). All is loyalty and enthusiasm. The whole place has blossomed into scarlet and gold, and the fantastic tag-rag and bobtail which constitute the following of these petty sovereigns and chiefs. Durbars are being held, and all manner of state ceremonies are going on. One of the parting fêtes which we witnessed was exceedingly pretty,—an evening entertainment at Government House, where we had an opportunity of seeing these grand native princes and their picturesque retinues. Every second man seemed to be a maharajah. Government House itself was a beautiful sight. The handsome staircases and entrance-halls were laid with red cloth, and lined with the troops of the Viceroy's body-guard. Scarlet-robed domestics, whose dusky countenances were becomingly overtopped by the broad, spotless white turban, stood everywhere around. The magnificent reception-rooms were brilliantly lighted and decorated, and filled with a dazzling throng. Ladies, shining in all the hues of the rainbow; officers in their bright uniforms; everybody in full dress; some with the decorations of the Order of the Star of India on their breast; and, above all, the crowd of distinguished natives, each one more gorgeously attired than another, and sparkling all over with countless gems. One rajah had a black velvet coat embroidered with gold and studded with diamonds; another had a coat of cloth of gold, and a crown of gold and jewels; another very insignificant man, with a bad face, had a splendid Cashmere shawl, and his jewelled turban was fringed with diamonds—very valuable, no doubt, but what an uncomfortable weight to carry on one's head! Some of the men were handsome and quite statuesque; but most were small-made, and slight, though their flowing robes gave them presence, and a semblance of height.

By far the most novel and striking in the picturesque crowd were the Nepaulese ambassadors and their suite. There were about twenty of them, the chief being a brother of Jung Bahādur. They wore red coats, a costume half-English, and therefore not pretty; but the head-dress quite made up in fanciful effect. Each man wore a beautiful bird-of-paradise plume, stuck straight up in his helmet in front, drooping over the back. These plumes were perfectly lovely, and some of the ladies made rather covetous remarks. The ambassador-in-chief, in addition to his plume, was decorated with a row of priceless emerald drops, which fringed his forehead, and had a diamond star above. "There are three lacs on that man's head," the Viceroy quietly remarked; and somebody else said the finest emerald in the world was upon his person somewhere.

Amid these bedizened and strange-visaged men, what a contrast the grave apostle of the Samaj presented, in his simple long black coat, reaching to his heels, his bare head and spectacles, and his thoughtful, serene face! We talked much with him, and with my friend Mr. Tagore, and his nice young brother-in-law. In no other place than India, I suppose, could you have witnessed a scene of this description—so full of striking effect and varied interest.

XXII.

Chota-Nagpore.

HAZARIBAG, *January 20.*

WE are having our first experience of Mofussil life in this charming station; and its leisurely, regular, unconventional ways have a great fascination, and are a delightful change from the pressure of the last busy year in Calcutta. We are the guests of the kindest and most hospitable of Irish people, Dr. and Mrs. Coates, whom we had never seen before we arrived at their house, and yet they received us with the heartiness of old friends, and at once made us feel perfectly at home.

We are now in Chota-Nagpore, the district in which the gospel has made such wonderful progress among the Koles,* one of the aboriginal tribes of South Bengal; our chief object in coming here being to see this work, and make acquaintance with the people and their missionaries.

There are millions of aborigines as yet scarcely affected by Hinduism, who are scattered throughout different parts of India. Long ago these tribes were driven from the fair country which was their own by the conquering Hindus, until

* Under this name are generally comprehended the Mundas (who are closely allied to the Santals) and the Oraons. The races are distinct, though very friendly to each other, and with their villages intermingled.—*Edit.*

they had to take refuge in the wilder regions, and often amidst hills and thick inaccessible jungles. They worship bhoots, or *bongas* (bad spirits or demons), who are often supposed to live in trees; consequently each village has its sacred grove where their sacrificial rites are performed. All the wilder races are dreadfully afraid of demons; and a belief in witchcraft is also universal. They have some vague notion of the Supreme* —as a great Being who is good and beneficent: and because he is so there is no need of worshipping him much; he will do them no harm; but the fiends are always on the watch to do them hurt, and therefore it is needful to propitiate them. Many of the tribes also worship the ghosts of their ancestors. They are a simple, trustful, and generally a truth-speaking people; but until late years no one has cared for them, nobody thought of doing anything for their elevation. While the Societies and Churches of Great Britain, America, and Germany awoke to their duty to India, as far as the Hindus proper and Musulmans were concerned, the wild tribes — at least eight millions of the population, hidden away in their fastnesses— were despised or forgotten. The Santal insurrection, which occurred before the Mutiny, emphatically called the attention of Government, as well as that of Christian philanthropists, to the existence of the Santal tribe; but before this the mission of the excellent Pastor Gossner, of Berlin, had been sent out, and had begun missionary work among the Koles of Chota-Nagpore.

The first band of Gossner's missionaries arrived in 1845, and commenced their operations with a few orphan children who had been picked up in the jungles, and sent to them by some humane magistrate. For some years the work of these men

* Generally called by the Mundas and Santals, *Singbonga*, the sun-spirit. —*Edit.*

was one of faith, not of sight; they made no impression whatever on the people; their words seemed as idle tales. They had to struggle, too, with privation and poverty; and they began to question whether their Master would not have them try another field. However, though they did not know it, the night was over, and the morning was at hand. One day four heathen Koles came to the mission-house, making the same request which the Greeks of old had made to Philip: "We would see Jesus." They had heard of Jesus, they said, and now they wanted to see Him. The missionaries invited them to remain to the evening prayer-meeting; which they agreed to do, evidently expecting that their request would be complied with. When the meeting was over, and they had not seen Him, they were very angry, and went off, accusing the missionaries of having deceived them. A week after, however, the same men came back, reiterating their request, saying they could not rest until they had seen Jesus. The poor missionary was in despair; but he took them into a private room, shut the door, and fell on his knees, asking God aloud to open the eyes of those men, that they might indeed see Him who is "the light of the world," and that, following Him, they might "not walk in darkness, but have the light of life." This time they went away more quietly, and considerably impressed by the sight of the missionary praying to the unseen God. They returned again, and again, and received instruction; and the happy result was, that they did come to see Jesus, and know Him, and follow Him, and became the first fruits of this first mission to the Koles. Now, less than twenty-five years after, the converts from among these people number about thirty thousand. Well may we say, "What hath God wrought!"

There is only a small branch of the mission at Hazāribāg—the headquarters are at Ranchi, about fifty miles away; but what we have seen here is profoundly interesting. There are two missionaries, with their wives; but Mr. Batsch being absent, we have only seen Mr. and Mrs. Pohlenz. The mission-station is about two miles from this, and is called Singhāni; a quiet, sweet, rural spot. We spent part of our first Sunday there, attending the forenoon service at the mission-chapel; and it was one of the most interesting days of my life. When we entered the chapel, I was struck with astonishment; here was gathered the largest native Christian congregation I had ever seen, composed evidently of poor simple people, but quiet and reverential, with their Bibles and hymn-books before them, the men seated on one side and the women on the other. It is an exceedingly pretty church; the pews ranged on each side of the centre passage, with the pulpit at one end, and a small organ, surrounded by the choir, all standing in readiness to begin the service, at the other. One of the most surprising things was the beauty of the music. A nice, bright-looking native girl played with a wonderful softness of touch, and a large choir of young men, with the school-girls, conducted the singing; but the whole congregation joined in heartily.

The service began with a beautiful hymn in Hindi; all stood up, and voices softer and sweeter than any I had before heard among the natives of this part of India swelled out into grave, sweet melody, perfectly harmonious and deeply reverential, as if the music was really made in their hearts. I shall never forget that hymn! The grandest music which peals through

"Long-drawn aisle and fretted vault"

never stirred the heart more than did that "cheerful, tender strain" sung by these poor simple people, gathered thus into

Christ's temple from the lowest heathenism. I felt as if the angels must have hushed their songs to hear.

Wonderful power of the glorious gospel of the blessed God! The essence of a hundred sermons seemed concentrated in the sight of that congregation of transformed men and women. They were manifestly uneducated, unsophisticated people; their features showed they belonged to the wilder races; they were clad in the simplest cotton garments, though spotlessly clean and neat; but here they were, intelligently, and with their whole hearts, engaging in the worship of the one living and true God. These and thousands more like them had been redeemed from barbarism, and from the debasing worship of evil spirits. They had begun to live a new life; a good hope for this world and the next shone on their countenances: and all this had manifestly little to do with the teaching and wisdom of this world; it was simply the power of the truth, the reception of that gospel which has told of "peace on earth and good will to men." These things which have been hid from the wise and prudent among the intellectual Bengalis and proud Musulmans, for whom missions have done so much, have been revealed by the Spirit of God to these poor people. They have accepted the truth with simple faith; as new-born babes they have received the pure milk of the word, and they grow thereby. It seemed the fulfilment of many longings and hopes, and the answer to many prayers, to join in this real missionary worship.

The service was altogether very interesting and impressive. During the sermon the preacher occasionally put questions, as if to keep up the attention of the audience, and was readily answered by the men. The women did not speak; but many turned up the texts and passages referred to, as if well acquainted with their Bibles. The whole congregation, however, men and women, stood up and joined in repeating the Lord's Prayer and Creed. At the close all bowed their heads in silent prayer, and then left the church in the most orderly manner, with more reverence of demeanour than I have seen sometimes in the congregations of our own favoured land. The whole people then gathered outside to bid us welcome; and not content with making salaam, they shook hands with us all round, and repeated their beautiful Christian salutation to each of us: "*Yasu sahāy*," or "Jesus be thy help." Does it not remind you of Boaz going forth among his reapers?—"And he said unto the reapers, The Lord be with you. And they answered him, The Lord bless thee."

We have seen as much as possible of these people since, in their everyday life and work. We have also seen the schools for both boys and girls, who look just as bright and intelligent as the children in our city schools. We paid an interesting visit to a Christian village near a tea-garden where the converts are employed, which belongs to our friend Mr. W. Mackinnon; and we were greatly gratified by the emphatic testimony borne by the intelligent and kind-hearted manager, Mr. Liepert, to the improvement in the lives and characters of his Christian workers. They never get drunk! This is sure proof of the wonderful change which Christianity has made in these people; for drunkenness is the grand and characteristic vice of most aboriginal tribes, not at all excepting the Koles. Along with their love of drink goes their love of dancing, which is one of the chief features of their feasts in honour of the bhoots.

My husband's trip to Ranchi has been intensely interesting. He was the guest of Colonel Dalton, the Commissioner, who knows more about the wild tribes of North India than, probably, any other living man, and who is both exceedingly wise and kind in his treatment of them. On one Sunday Dr. M. saw ninety individuals at once receive the solemn rite of baptism; and on the following, sixty fathers and mothers, with their whole families, in the same solemn way were admitted to the Church. He was never so moved in his life as by this most beautiful and touching spectacle. It took the whole time of the service to administer the ordinance, which was varied with much most beautiful music. While making their profession of faith, among the other questions put to the converts were these, "Do you renounce witchcraft? Do you renounce drinking? Do you renounce dancing?" The ordinance was administered to each individual separately, the formula used being: "I baptize thee into the death of the Lord Jesus Christ, in the name of the Father, and of the Son, and of the Holy Ghost." And there was a threefold affusion of water, one at each name of the blessed Trinity. When all had received the rite, and the service was about to close, one of the missionaries lifted his hands over the new converts and blessed them, as Aaron did Israel of old:—"The Lord bless thee and keep thee; the Lord make his face shine upon thee, and be gracious unto thee; the Lord lift up his countenance upon thee, and give thee peace."

It was indeed most beautiful, and carries one back to pentecostal days. Every one seems to expect that the whole Kole tribe will soon come over to Christianity. The heathen Koles are much impressed with the fact that the demons do not punish the Christians with the loss of their worldly goods, and the death of their children and cattle. They see, too, that they are delivered from the fear of the demons, and also that they are better men and women, and evidently much happier, than they were.

XXIII.

Berhampore—Rampore Bauleah.

February.

A GOOD many years ago, a fine old soldier of the proud race of Rajputs came to Calcutta, bringing his two sons with him; for he desired to obtain for them an English education. He heard of Dr. Duff's school, then beginning to be famous, and placed the lads in it. The elder of these is now the Rev. Behari Lal Singh, of Rampore Bauleah.

Under the teaching of the missionaries both brothers soon became convinced of the truth of Christianity, though at first, as Behari expresses it, "they *believed* everything, but *felt* nothing;" subsequently, however, through the Spirit's power, the feeling was added in the case of both. The younger was baptized first, at Benares; and Behari soon followed his example in making a public profession of his faith. He had got a good Government appointment under Sir Donald M'Leod, who took a great interest in the youth, and, by his instructions and the example of his own pure and noble life, did much to water the good seed of the Word which had been sown in his heart while studying in the Christian school. His convictions deepened. He returned to Calcutta, renewed his intercourse with the missionaries; and, finally, Dr. Duff had the joy of baptizing him. Behari was not the man to do things by halves. He gave up the Government service, and his good appointment under his much revered master and friend, Sir Donald—who, however, has been his friend ever since—relinquished his fair prospects and his salary, and thenceforward devoted himself, heart and soul, and for life, to the Lord's work among his countrymen.

Afterwards the old soldier—the father of the now Christian lads—also believed, and was baptized, and, like them, became a good soldier of Jesus Christ.

Behari is now the superintendent and head of the Rajshay Mission in connection with the Presbyterian Church in England. Rampore Bauleah is its headquarters; and hither have we come, at once to visit our old friend Mr. M'Leod, and to see Behari, his family, and his work.

We started from Serampore on the 23rd, at seven in the morning. It was a burning hot, dusty day, and having had fever for some days previously, I found it no easy journey. We arrived at Nulhattee station at 4 P.M., when we transferred ourselves and effects to a branch railway, grandly so called; being a tramway running alongside the public road, so that from the carriage we could fraternize with the good little bullocks which trudged patiently along tinkling their pretty bells, and dragging their queer little laden carts through the heavy dust. Our "first-class carriage" was an old luggage-van, seated with a few basket-chairs, set down among the boxes and parcels and mail-bags. Our speed was hardly more than six miles an hour, so it was dark when we got to the terminus at Azimgunge, on the banks of the Bhagaritty. This stream flows out of the Ganges; it receives another tributary called the Jellinghee, and thus forms our noble Hooghly further down.

Our first halt was to be at Berhampore, to visit our friends, the Lal Behari Days; and they most kindly sent people and a conveyance to meet us. We crossed the river in a huge clumsy ferry-boat, wherein beasts, boxes, and bales were stowed away in one grand jumble. On the further bank we found a comfortable carriage with good horses and lamps lit, which was kindly lent for us from the stables of His Highness the Nawāb Nāzim of Moorshedabad. It was now a brilliant moonlight night; the air was soft and cool and sweet, and as we reclined in the delightful carriage, and sped along at a good round pace, it seemed a delicious, refreshing rest, rather than a continuation of the journey. The heat, and glare, and dust, and fatigue of the horrid day were all past and forgotten. We saw the beautiful country, rich with crops, and noble trees, and green park-like reaches, almost as well as if it had been day, and far more pleasantly. The full, round moon danced out and in merrily among the boughs, and shed down brilliant streams of silver light on the green openings; while deep, mysterious bits of shadow darkened away toward the jungles, and where the majestic trees stood thickest. It was all very weird-like and picturesque, and had a beauty which the full glare of day would certainly have destroyed. We passed through two or three large old native cities, with narrow, unpaved streets—swarming with wild dogs, which howled dismally at us as we passed—high mud walls, flat roofs, and here and there a dome or slender minaret going up to the moon. As we passed through Moorshedabad, our coachman pointed out the Nawāb's palace with great pride, and the beautiful Imambarra, or great Mohammadan mosque.

This city, which afterwards, in common daylight, looked dusty, dirty, and utterly disenchanted, was now glorified by the beauteous magic moonlight, until it seemed something unreal, or as if we had been conveyed into fairyland.

It was about ten o'clock when we got to Berhampore, and found our old friend B. with her husband and three dear little children standing on the steps of their bungalow waiting to receive us. I had only seen B. once since she had left our house in Bombay many years before; and now, instead of the little Parsee girl, here was a wife and mother. You can imagine the pleasure and thankfulness this meeting gave us all.

We remained the guests of Mr. and Mrs. Day for two or three days, and their hospitality knew no bounds. It was as if they could not make enough of us; and by some magic process Mr. Day seemed to lay everybody and everything under contribution for our entertainment. There were horses and carriages at our disposal all hours of the day, and invitations of all sorts—far more than we had time to avail ourselves of. Mr. Ram Das Sen, a rich young Zemindar of the neighbourhood, most kindly sent his comfortable barouche and beautiful grays every evening to take us wherever we liked to go; and, besides this, paid us some pleasant visits. He came in after breakfast the first day, dressed in a green velvet coat bordered with gold, and a little cap of gold embroidery set jauntily on one side of his head. We found him a very intelligent, well-educated, modest man. He brought Dr. M. a presentation copy of a little book of Bengali poems he had written; telling him that years ago he had read his "Letters to Indian Youth" with great care, and ever since had wished to know the author. Dr. M. had much interesting conversation with this young Zemindar, and found him to be a very good Sanskrit scholar. Like most educated Bengalis, he had lost all belief in his own system, while he lacked the courage, if he had the desire, to profess what he seemed to believe to be the true faith.

This part of the country, as you know, is full of stirring memories. One goes back at once to Clive and Plassey; to the struggles of the early European settlers, and the first days of the East India Company. We drove by the field of Plassey; but it has now little to interest save its traditions. Even the mango-tope under the shadow of which Clive considered the question whether he should fight or not, has disappeared, having been swept away by the river. A solitary tree remains, and a low heap of bricks, to show where some of those who fell at Plassey were buried. The Ganges has much to answer for; its encroachments are becoming more serious year by year.

We also visited Cossimbazaar, a most interesting old place, where once stood the largest of the old "factories," and Government House, where Warren Hastings lived. Now there is nothing to be seen but two graveyards, one English and one Dutch, with some moss-grown, weather-beaten, discoloured old monuments which it moved one strangely to see. Those of the Dutch are in better preservation than the English, being large, and very strongly built; they are quaint old monuments, bearing names and dates which are still quite legible.

In the English graveyard, the first wife of Warren Hastings is buried; his daughter also lies here; and Sir Cecil Beadon did his country the good service to order their tombs to be repaired. This pathetic little "God's acre," where so many of our country men and women lie, touched me much. The lonely spot of forlorn graves, so far from the sleeping dust of beloved kindred, surrounded by ruin, filled with sad memories, telling of broken hopes, and perhaps lost opportunities—it was indeed a picture fitted to fix itself on the heart, and teach it many things.

Every trace of the factory is swept away—everything is gone but the precious dust which sleeps below. But though the brave hearts are silent that struggled and trafficked here, their work lives; for they fulfilled the inscrutable purpose of Him who meant to give this great country to Britain—not to enrich her with India's silver and gold, but that Britain should enrich India with the blessings of enlightenment and just government, and the still higher blessing of true religion. The graveyard at Berhampore is also full of old tombs, and among them is that of "little Henry," of whom Mrs. Sherwood wrote so sweetly.

In our drive we passed a high whitewashed wall which surrounds an extensive native palace. Here lives Her Highness* the Maharanee of Cossimbazaar, an enlightened and most charitable lady. She is descended from the Brahman who saved the life of Warren Hastings at the risk of his own, and hid him in his inner room when hard pressed by his pursuers.

One day we visited Moorshedabad, the Nawab's carriage having again most kindly been sent for us. On the way we saw one of the guns which were used at Plassey against us. It is daubed over with red paint, and the Hindus worship it. The palace is a very handsome modern building, and being modern, it is not very much worth a visit. It somewhat resembles Government House in Calcutta; and the centre hall, which is paved with marble mosaic, is a magnificent room. There is the usual quantity of French and English furniture, with glass and gilding and gay colouring, which the rich natives crowd into their rooms, as if profusion and elegance were synonymous. There is a unique little sofa I admired very much, thoroughly un-English; the framework is in exquisitely carved ivory, like

* This benevolent Ranee sent me a yearly subscription after our visit, through my friend Mrs. Day, for our Orphanage in Calcutta.

delicate lace-work, with two little gems of footstools to match. Our dear friend General Colin Mackenzie was at one time Resident at the Court of the Nawab Nazim; and his and Mrs. Mackenzie's portraits, in oil, decorate the walls. On our homeward drive we paid a visit to the Diwān, or Prime Minister of the Nawab, who enjoys the title of "Rajah Prosunno Narayan Deb Bahādur"—a thoughtful man, with most pleasing manners, and a good truthful face. He received the title Bahādur for services to the British Government, I think, during the Mutiny. He has a beautiful house, in a most beautiful situation, looking on to the river. He spoke with a sort of rapturous devotion of the Mackenzies; as indeed their friends are apt to do.

There is some interesting missionary work going on in Berhampore in connection with the London Missionary Society, which the resident missionary, Mr. Bradbury, kindly showed us. Dr. M. also visited the Government College, where our friend, Mr. Day, is a professor. Altogether, we made good use of our time. On the last evening we dined with the kind old chaplain; and when bed-time arrived, we said good-night and adieu to our dear friends, and retired to our palkis.

We were now to cross the country to Rajshay; and there being but indifferent roads, or no roads at all, there was but one mode of transit possible to us—by palanquin or palki, as these little nondescript machines are usually called. As most people know now, this conveyance is an oblong box with sliding panel-doors, through which you scramble in somehow, and lie down at full length, with mattress, pillows, and quilts *ad libitum.* I do not at all dislike this primitive mode of travel; it is certainly slow, but a leisurely mode of progression suits a country so abounding in objects of new and strange interest as this one does. You cannot go a yard without coming on something you want to look at and examine; and it is well for you that the bearers are the patient obliging creatures they usually are, or they would demur to the encroachments you make so unceremoniously on their time. Fortunately, time is not of so much value in this leisurely land as it is in our own fast country.

I particularly enjoy coming on a hamlet or village, where native life is to be seen in aspects often differing much from city life, and, I must say, is far more picturesque and attractive. Then, apart from man, there are wonders at every step; nature is so wildly exuberant as well as beautiful in Bengal, where rivers abound. Here you have everything, from the magnificent giants of the forest, and the lovely blossoms of shrubs and countless creepers and trailing plants, down to the lowliest moss, or grass, or delicate wild flower. Then, again, animal life is perfectly surprising in its endless variety. Suddenly a wild gazelle will dart across your path, or a herd of deer career away into the distance; a whole regiment of monkeys will grin down defiantly at you as you pass through some clump of trees. You pick a piece of moss, and you find the whole alive with ants; you trace them, and you discover a huge colony, and if you only have time to wait and watch, you will see that they are indeed a busy and a wise little people. A crowd of bees which hang in huge black masses from some overhanging rock will perhaps dispute your passage, and make you fly before the fierceness of their attack; not to speak of the whole tribe of snakes and adders, which will steal away from your path if they can. Once a beautiful leopard started from the jungle and bounded *down* the hill, fortunately, from the slope on which we were standing. Another time a cheetah, also on a hill-top, darted through our verandah in search of our dog, we thought, though the dear little thing was safe by my chair. And on one memorable occasion we came on a real tiger, walking placidly on the road along which we were travelling, at night, near Khandāla. Our poor horses were terribly frightened, and trembled and sweated with fear; but the royal beast must have had his supper, for he strode leisurely on, swinging his tail, turned off, and disappeared into the jungle. I thought at first he was a bullock, as I looked out in the moonlight; and we did not know there was anything so formidable as a tiger near us, until the syces cried out to the Saheb in their terror. The loss of life from the prevalence of wild animals—tigers and snakes especially—is something appalling all over the country.

But I have wandered far from our start at Berhampore.

Our palki-bearers came "with their loins girt, their shoes on their feet, and their staff in their hands," rightly equipped for their pilgrimage. Our cavalcade looked rather an imposing one. There are twelve men to each palki, though only four carry at once, and change very often. There is a mussalchi, or torch-bearer, and a couple of banghy-coolies, the men who carry the goods and chattels, which are slung on a stout bamboo across their shoulders. The mussalchi has the emblem of his calling in readiness—namely, a long pole with a bunch of rags tied on one end, well soaked in oil. When lighted, this makes a beautiful torch, which he feeds from time to time from a vessel of oil which he carries. He takes "oil in his vessel with his lamp."

It is surprising how much these slight-built, small men accomplish. Our twelve bearers carried us and our well-laden palkis the thirty miles or so we had to go, at a stretch, and did not look hard pressed either. We always reward our men with the present of a sheep or kid at the end, that they may eat well after their labour. They march at the pace of about four miles an hour.

Our kind friend Mrs. Day took care that our palkis should be well provided; and a most comprehensive receptacle this palki is. Over the feet a broad shelf is fitted, and over that a good strong net is stretched; and these are filled with a collection of articles more heterogeneous by far than that which Pope has celebrated,—

"Puffs, powders, patches, Bibles, billets-doux;"

our dressing-bags, books, slippers, some biscuits and sandwiches, a bottle of cold tea (nothing is so refreshing on a journey), a couple of tumblers, writing-books, towels and soap, some fruit,—everything which our kind friends thought we could by any possibility need, was all stowed away somewhere.

If we had wished to sleep it would not have been easy of accomplishment, from the monotonous *croon*, or chant, which the bearers kept up the whole night. Without this accompaniment I do not think they could march. But I do not advise you to sleep if once in a way you have the opportunity of contemplating throughout the solemn grandeur of an Eastern night—far more impressive, I think, than what you see by day. An awe creeps over the spirit as you lie and listen to the strange sounds, and yet stranger silences; or you take your fill of gazing into the vast dome of shining glories over your head, and "consider" the heavens, the work of God's fingers, "the moon and the stars, which He has ordained." The night wind comes to you, sweet and cool, bringing *wafts* of pleasant odours, which the thick, low jungle-plants breathe out, as they are refreshed by the falling dew. Old memories awake, and you feel that the heavens and the earth are one grand temple to Him "whose name is excellent in all the earth," and whose glory is "set above the heavens." Then the beauteous dawn slowly unfolds itself. The birds carol out their joyous song, and you watch on until the glorious sun himself comes forth, "rejoicing as a strong man to run a race," and lo! all nature has awaked, and—

> "Like a garment, wears
> The beauty of the morning."

By the time it was quite day we had arrived at the river-brink, where our friend Mr. M'Leod had sent his boat to meet us. But the coolies who carried our baggage were nowhere to be seen. Probably you would have thought they had run off. Oh, no! We quietly settled ourselves by the road-side, sent some men in search, and before the sun had become unpleasantly strong they appeared; everything perfectly right—not an article missing. One poor fellow had carried Dr. M.'s portmanteau on his head; a good load to walk with the livelong night. He had sat down to rest—for which I quite excuse him—missed us, and lost his way, and was quite as happy as we, when he was looked for, and found. It is wonderful how perfectly trustworthy these men are. We have travelled over India in every sort of way, and (I gratefully record it) we have never, I think, had anything stolen from our baggage.

A most reviving sight greeted us on reaching the boat. A tiny table was spread in the neat little cabin, which was cool and shady. On the fresh table-cloth were new-laid eggs, tea, toast, and fruit. Did anything ever taste half so good? The never-failing, delicious plantain of this country puts me in mind of what good old Izaak Walton says of the strawberry—"Doubtless God could have made a better berry; but I am not aware that he has done so yet." I am not aware that any better or more useful fruit has been made for India than the good, safe, delicate little plantain.

A good wash, a little rest, and we glided along the sea-like river—the real, great Ganges itself—crossed to the further side, where the white bungalows of Rampore-Bauleah gleamed out from beautiful green trees; and before noon we had landed on the heavy sands below the "Burra Kotee"—that is, the "great house" of the station. This is the residence of our friend Mr. M'Leod.

We have had the most delightful and stirring time at the "Burra Kotee." It is a large, roomy, thoroughly Indian house; which means, that it is the right sort for an Indian residence. The lofty, spacious rooms enter on other rooms; and these on wide terraces or verandahs, shaded pleasantly with dark green blinds, seated with plenty of lounging-chairs, and spread with mats. We have the whole of one end of the house to ourselves, and have more rooms than we know how to inhabit. This is upstairs; the lower part is left to servants, and is used also as go-downs —which is our Anglo-Indian way of expressing store-rooms.

Our kind host entertains us with an hospitality at once Indian and Highland; and more could not be said. His house is eminently the centre of hospitality, not only for the station, but for the whole country round. Our tiffins and dinners are always enlivened by the addition of new-comers, who stray in—unexpectedly, I was going to say; but stragglers seem always to be expected. Gentlemen drop in from the town; or perhaps from a distant factory or plantation, having ridden in some twenty to forty miles; or they have dropped down the river in their luxurious boats.

This is true "mofussil," or out-station life, which is the most social, friendly thing you can imagine. It has its drawbacks, of course. Everybody knows too much, and talks too much perhaps, of everybody else. Your affairs are public property, and your possessions too. A new book, or a new pattern, when some lucky individual receives "a box from England," becomes a common good; which seems to me, however, to be the pleasantest part of a new possession. The charity which "thinketh no evil" unfortunately does not always abound; and to "cover a multitude of sins" is not the natural bent of the human heart. Still, even where there *is* ill-nature, it vanishes before sorrow or trouble. Though you should be the most unpopular person in the community, if you get sick or sorry the whole station will turn out to nurse you, or sympathize with you, or help you in every way possible. The kind-heartedness of Indian people to each other has not been exaggerated. There is a great fascination, too, in the free, unconventional ways which put people on such an easy footing in their neighbour's house.

You must not believe all you hear of the frivolity of Indian society. Some people, doubtless, do take refuge from *ennui* and trouble in so-called pleasure; but, as a rule, life in this country is very chequered, and often full of trouble. There are few homes over which there does not hang some cloud. One thing we all have to bear is, separation from home and beloved friends; and how many there are who have to bear the worse separation from wife or husband, and dear little children! There is often a sweet, pale, pinched little face, giving warning of coming sorrow in one shape or other; or the thought, perhaps, of a quiet little grave somewhere!

You must just bear with me in this little digression, into which I have slid somehow, while I stand up for my countrywomen in India. It has often filled me with indignation to hear how they are talked of. Here life is more open, more patent, than at home; and therefore, of course, you can pick out faithless wives, and careless mothers, and fast girls. But such are not the favourites in society, either among men or women;

and from my own experience I venture to affirm that such are the exception, not the rule. Domestic happiness is often greater in India than elsewhere. Husbands and wives are thrown so much on each other for sympathy, and indeed for society, that they generally become all in all to each other.

I wish I could tell you even a little part of what I have seen among those so-called lackadaisical or frivolous wives and mothers. Sorrow often so meekly borne; the suddenly-ordered journey, and entire break-up of the home, so promptly and energetically carried out, when sudden sickness in one of its many forms seizes, perhaps, the babe of the house; the brave cheerfulness with which the many disappointments are met; or the constant changes, and the weary marchings and wanderings; the patient watching and waiting by the sick-bed: and all in the midst of the languor and prostration which the climate produces. But this is a process by which all that is good and noble in character is refined, like gold that is seven times purified; and what has often been remarked results—namely, that religion here is warmer, more fearless, and more pronounced, both in men and women, than at home. Perhaps the light seems to burn more brightly, too, because of the surrounding darkness.

Our host is the head and representative of the largest indigo business in Lower Bengal. The estate is of great extent, and there are both indigo and silk factories connected with it. Unfortunately this is not the season for seeing the indigo plant, and the operation of making the dye; but Mr. Abbot, one of the managers, has explained the process to me.

Everybody has heard of the great indigo difficulty, and the grievances of the ryot or cultivator. During the tremendous excitement which the controversy occasioned some years ago, the sensational drama was published, called the *Nil Durpun*, or "Indigo Mirror," which I already mentioned. This seemed rather a covert satire on the whole Anglo-Indian community, though its object was ostensibly to show up the misdeeds of the planters, and obtain redress for the ryots. Any way, it is said to have fanned the flame of discontent. Mr. M'Leod tells me that the state of things on this estate was terrible. He and his assistants had to go about with loaded revolvers; their own people, who had gained everything they possessed in their service, were ready to cut their throats if they found the opportunity. They bound themselves by solemn oath not only to do no work connected with the indigo, but to allow nothing of any sort to be sold to their masters; so that for months the latter could get no food but what their own yards produced. No one in the bazaar would sell them even an egg or milk. Many planters were ruined at this terrible time; and no doubt Messrs. Watson and Co. would have been ruined too, had they been less rich and less powerful. Now, happily, this state of things has entirely changed. A reaction has taken place; and the relation between planter and ryot is as friendly as before.

After an early cup of tea this morning, the air feeling delightfully fresh and pure, I went to see the start for a grand shikār or hunt. It was quite an exciting scene. A number of elephants, surmounted by howdahs of varying construction and grandeur, stood waiting; the good patient creatures seeming proudly conscious of all that was to depend on their steadiness and sagacity. There were a good many horses led by syces, and a crowd of natives to act as beaters. One huge elephant, with a primitive howdah made of common wood, the size of a good big spring-cart, was told off to carry the khitmutgars and provisions; and a plentiful supply there seemed to be, judging from the numerous hampers and baskets which were being stowed away in the depths of the capacious howdah. A number of gentlemen were to go from the "Burra Kotee," and they came forth to mount in the most picturesque disguises; the crowning part, literally and metaphorically, being the huge sun-topi, with flaps of quilted white calico all round their heads, which gave them the look of being under tent-walls. They will need it all to stand the sun, which will soon be fierce enough to penetrate anything.

Mr. M'Leod has driven us about a great deal. I have seen prettier stations perhaps than Rampore-Bauleah, but every place is pretty which stretches along this wonderful river—where the grass is green and the trees resplendent with rich foliage, and often with bright blossoms. But the river is making the most daring encroachments, and threatens to swallow up the whole place.

We see a great deal of our dear brother Behari and his work, and are with him and his family part of every day, which makes the chief interest of our visit. We like Behari exceedingly; he is quaint and original, intensely devoted, self-denying almost to asceticism, and is altogether a remarkable man. It is delightful to see the thorough respect in which he is held by the entire community, European and native alike. His wife is a very clever woman, well educated, and speaks English remarkably well; yet she has the good sense to adhere to her own customs, and lives after the fashion of her people. Their daughter seems to have inherited a good deal of her father's character, and promises much for future usefulness; and there are two nice little boys.

The mission is in most vigorous operation. It comprehends all the usual branches of mission work: schools for males and females, an orphanage, regular services on Sundays and week-days in the vernacular, an organization of catechists, and teachers, and colporteurs; and a great deal of thorough evangelistic work, such as preaching in the bazaars, itinerating in the villages, and attending festivals, where there is opportunity of preaching the gospel to thousands of men, and also women. Besides all this, Behari may be said to be the minister of the whole station. There is no resident chaplain; and but for the services of this excellent missionary, the Christian community would be destitute of the ordinances of religion, except that a chaplain from a distant station pays them an occasional visit. There is a nice little church, with a manse close by; and the English services conducted by Behari are very well attended, and much appreciated by the residents, who are all most friendly, from the Commissioner and his agreeable wife downwards. The services which have been held by my husband during our visit have been much prized, people riding in twenty and thirty miles to attend them; which shows how welcome the stated ministrations of a pastor, who could give his whole time to our countrymen, would be to the whole community. The ladies of the station gave a delightful feast one day to the little orphans, which seemed to throw some life and brightness into them, poor things. This was at the close of a very successful examination of all the schools, at which Dr. M. presided; and, finally, in the evening the ladies held a small bazaar, to dispose of a box of fancy-work which had been sent out for the benefit of the mission, by a lady who had formerly lived in Rampore-Bauleah, and had taken deep interest in Behari's work.

A second missionary is urgently wanted here to assist Behari. I would plead that a medical missionary should be added; his services would be an immense boon to the whole place.

On the River.

Our charming visit has come to a close. Most regretfully we bade adieu this morning to the "Burra Kotee," and our kind friends and our most genial host. He came down to the water-edge, and saw us embark in his own gem of a boat, which is to bear us down on the bosom of the majestic Ganges to Kooshtea, where we shall join the railway for Calcutta.

It is indeed "an abridgment of all that is pleasant" in river-craft. This is the daintiest little cabin you can conceive, with green painted window-blinds, a sofa, and a wee table with a cloth and writing materials, and another at which we dine. Inside, there is a tiny bedroom, and a bed draped with mosquito-net—a most welcome refuge from the hordes of these bloodthirsty enemies which infest the river-bank, and buzz in at the open windows as soon as it gets dusk. A small recess at the cabin door is a butler's pantry amply stocked; and an opposite recess is filled with soda water, and bitter beer, and heaps of Crosse and Blackwell's tins. Mr. M'Leod's servants are evidently practised hands at provisioning. But our kitchen is most wonderful of all. It is a hole of about two feet square in the centre of the boat, entered by a trap door, in which there is a little mud "kitchen-range;" and out of this, by some magic process which only native cooks understand, come delicate stewed chickens and most excellent curries. We have a tiny hen-coop, in which are some half-dozen of the feathered race, with whom I should certainly make acquaintance, if I could ignore the fact that they must, sooner or later, fill our larder.

We spent last night on shore at Surdah with Mr. and Mrs. Gordon. We had left them at the "Burra Kotee," but they rode down the thirty miles or so to their own home, and were on the river-bank to receive us when our boat arrived in the afternoon. This is a most beautiful place, more like a baronial English residence than a dwelling in the sunburnt plains of India. You see what looks like a magnificent park stretching away to the river, with clumps of noble trees; and nearer the house a lovely flower-garden, with gay beds of roses and verbenas and other sweet home plants, besides all the show and splendour of Indian flowering shrubs. Some gorgeous peacocks strut about, and pretty gray guinea-fowl fill the air with a merry chorus. A wide verandah surrounds the house, which is a pretty bungalow, with lofty ceilings and marble floors, and a look of pleasant life about it. The easy chairs and low tables in shady corners; the books, and work, and profusion of delicious flowers everywhere, do not give the idea of lonely life; and yet the nearest neighbour is full twenty miles away!

Planters must often feel very solitary, poor fellows! but here there is a lady in the question, and the dull bungalow of the jungles is at once transformed into brightness and *home*. The worst of these isolated dwellings is, that the inmates have not ordinary religious privileges. Chaplains can hardly ever visit them. It is very sad, indeed, to think how many of our countrymen are scattered all over India, without any means of grace whatever. A gentleman told me that one day was so like another in their lives, that he only knew it was Sunday by the non-appearance of his wife's durzie, or tailor.

Mr. Gordon showed us all over his silk factory, where we saw the whole process, from the worm on the mulberry-leaf and the cocoon picked out of the boiling water, which detaches the substance, down to the tying up into hanks of the beautiful soft yellow silk.

It is an endless amusement to me to watch our boatmen, and all the novel scenes of river-life. Our manjee, or captain, is a magnificent Musulman, tall and dignified, and with a beard to his waist. He is the very soul of civility. He has a crew of nine men under him. They eat twice in the day—at eleven in the forenoon, and again when we "lie-to" for the night. They draw the boat to the bank in a shady nook, and having dropped the anchor if it is night, or fastened the craft to a bamboo stuck in the mud if it is day, they proceed to the important operation of cooking. The process is carried on, on shore, and their appliances are most simple. The fireplace is a small portable oven, made of clay, well smeared with mud, in the side of which there is a hole to secure the fire burning. In this a few dry sticks soon blaze up; and at night these little camp-fires, with the dark figures seated round, make a pretty, cheery picture. On the top of the blaze a chatti, or pot, is placed. Some of these vessels are open, some close, but all with turned-over mouths, and made of coarse, cheap, red pottery.

And now the pot is lifted off, and contains a savoury boiling mess of curry, made either of vegetable or fish, which is eaten with a coarse kind of rice. Fish seems to be the favourite food. Our men bring their boat up by a fleet of fishing-boats, and for two or three pice purchase what makes an excellent supper for all the men. One of the number seems to be told off as commissariat officer, who buys the fish, cleans and cuts it up, and puts it into another chatti, to await the general cooking. We have one Hindu in the boat, the others being Musulmans; and he must, of course, cook and eat apart. He sets up an erection of matting between him and his brother oarsmen, lest their shadow falling on his food should pollute it, and so destroy his caste. And what excellent appetites they have! A huge pot has just been emptied of a pinkish-coloured mass of rice on to eight brass platters, twice as large as our dinner plates, which are not only filled but heaped. The poor fellows have toiled at the oar since three in the morning, so they are to be excused if they are hungry. The man who is deputed cook helps the others by diving to the elbow in rice and curry alike! But they do not eat with unwashen hands. Before the ceremony begins, they wash their hands, and feet, and teeth; repeating the process directly the meal is over. The utensils, also, are carefully cleaned; the brass platters being scoured in the mud, and made as bright as burnished gold. The little round drinking-cups are also polished. This done, and the ablutions performed, we are ready to start again.

During the day there is too much glare on the water to let us enjoy the river-view; but in the evening we sit on the roof, and the scene, in the soft light of the setting sun, is lovely. There is not very much of the shore to be seen,—only high mud-banks and a few of the taller trees near the margin; but the broad queenly river flowing ever on, with its calm majestic current, is a sight in itself. Now it looks like a great sea; then it sweeps into a pretty bay, fringed with green low jungle; then it bends to a new channel, stretching away to other districts of country; then, again, the channel narrows, and you find yourself close to what proves to be a "chur," or island of sand, which looks like a bit of sea-shore. These islands are being constantly shifted, and new ones deposited, according to the erratic course and changing mood of Mother Ganges. The landed property on the banks must be constantly changing hands; though, I believe, Government claims for itself any new land formed by the change of current. I have not heard that compensation is made to the unfortunate losers by this unceremonious visitation of the capricious stream.

It is very entertaining to notice the variety in boats, from the pretty painted one like our own, and the handsome budgerow now and then, down to the endless variety of native craft, the generic name of which seems to be "kishtee." The river used to be the highway from Calcutta to the regions beyond, and budgerows were common; now the railways have made these comfortable conveyances nearly as much things of the past as the "Honourable Company" itself. Boats used for merchandize are huge, grotesque-looking things, very strong, the sides walled with bamboo, and thatched from stern to bow. Inside they must be delightfully cool. The fishing-boats are very picturesque. They are long canoes; and two and two are generally tacked together at the long-pointed stem, until they have the appearance of a bridge of boats set right across the stream. We have come on several fish-markets on the banks. The villagers come in great numbers, with covered baskets slung on bamboo poles, and make their purchases, accompanied by an immense deal of gesticulation.

The navigation of this river is a difficult operation. The wind is dead ahead, and when we venture close in-shore, that we may be towed along by ropes, as being the most expeditious mode of progression, we stick fast in the mud. Or, if in their untiring zeal the men row us along, we hear and feel a bump, and lo! we are on a sand-bank. Then follow frantic efforts with long poles to push us off, when the tantalizing wind blows us into the mud again; and so, after hours of tremendous pushing and pulling, we look back at the objects on the banks, and find we have not made half a mile! Dr. M. occupies himself by going on shore, to talk to the people and preach, or help to pull the boat along by a rope attached to the mast-head.

The fitful wind and restless changing clouds we have had all day, gathered toward evening into a magnificent storm. The sunset had a fierce glare about it, and the clouds were broken into rifts, with fitful gleams of lurid yellow light which looked most portentous. A few dull leaden clouds gradually grew dark and heavy, and spread over the sky in inky folds. There was an ominous stillness in the air for a while, as if Nature held her breath in awe-struck expectation. We made our boat fast by the bank, and not a moment too soon. There was a growl, a low muttering, and the hurricane was upon us in all its fury. You cannot imagine how grand these sudden tempests are. The black heavens are riven asunder for a moment, and a dart of arrow-like light leaps out, followed by a terrific thunder-clap; and then the lightning goes on zig-zagging from heaven to earth without a moment's intermission, and the thunder and fierce wind vie with each other in deafening clamour. One is always glad when the rain comes down in good earnest; and to-night it was like a water-spout. But how miserable it made the boat! and the poor men looked dripping and frightened.

The natives are not much impressed by the grand in Nature. Dr. M. pointed out a glorious sunset, wishing either to test their appreciation of the beautiful, or perhaps seeking for sympathy. "Lal hai, sahib," said one—"It is red, sir!"

> "A primrose by a river's brim
> A yellow primrose was to him,
> And it was nothing more."

How sweet and fresh the air feels now! The black river looks quieter, and the stars are twinkling out timidly one by one, and the wind sighs softly, as if ashamed of its frenzy. What a sweet cool sleep we shall have, in sympathy with spent

Nature—only that the frogs have thoroughly awaked, and keep up a tremendous chorus all round us.

We have had a repetition this morning of last night's storm, but in a modified way, and not nearly so impressive. We are passing whole fleets of huge rough country boats moored to the banks, the mariners being afraid to proceed while the spirit of the storm still walks abroad.

One of the sights of the river is a bathing-ghaut. Near every village there seems to be one of these bathing-places, like steps of stairs, which are generally erected by some rich Hindu, who takes this easy way to secure to himself merit, and the favour of the goddess Gunga. Numbers of naked people stand in the water, wash themselves and their garments, and then stand with clasped hands, and bent heads, and mutter prayers to the sacred stream. How one longs to tell them of the river of the water of life, and that precious blood which can really wash away their sins!

Those delightful storms have changed everything. The wind is favourable again; we hope to get to Kooshtea at four o'clock, and to sleep in Calcutta.

XXIV.

Benares.

BENARES, *March 17.*

HERE we are in Kashi, the holy city of the Hindus, the heart of their system, the headquarters of Indian idolatry.

A week of unparalleled bustle has just passed over us, in arranging and packing, and, worst of all, in saying many regretful good-byes. It looks a sort of nightmare in the retrospect, and I would rather not recall it, but that it is so pleasant to tell of the wonderful amount of kindness which our friends have delighted to lavish upon us.

Mr. Duff drove us to the ghaut; and he, Mr. Don, Mr. Sutherland, and several other friends, crossed with us to Howrah, and saw us start. Mr. D., chief of the railway system in these parts, himself came and chose our carriage; and through his kindness, and the potent influence of his name, we had the undisputed possession of a saloon compartment the whole way from Calcutta hither. This was very luxurious. We had each a good, long, comfortable sofa, on which we soon stretched our weary persons, put our pillows under our heads, and were soon fast asleep, as we whirled away in the dark to unknown regions. It is not wonderful, then, that, notwithstanding heat and whirlwinds of dust, we made a most agreeable journey.

Indian railway travelling, indeed, is made as comfortable as possible; the climate and its requirements enter into the calculations of the considerate superintendents, and the worn frames also of too many who are obliged to travel. The carriages are arranged for sleeping, and are not broken up into sittings, as yours are at home. They are well ventilated, have double roofs, venetian windows, and projecting shades. They have sometimes even little verandahs and platforms outside, where one can sit in an evening and enjoy the breeze, which the rapid motion makes doubly strong and refreshing. There is also a miniature bath arrangement—water being introduced into a tiny dressing-room off each carriage; so that every sort of comfort is considered; and if the dust is very bad, which it undoubtedly is, you can at least wash it off as often as you please. The pleasantest time by far to travel is in the monsoon, though people hardly believe this. The country then is covered with a garment of loveliness; it is cool; there is less glare, and there is *no dust.*

We arrived the night before last; and now we are seated in a shady, pleasant room, the guests of Mr. and Mrs. Hutton, of the London Missionary Society, who have received us with the utmost kindness, and are doing all they can to make our visit profitable as well as agreeable. We regret very much to find that our esteemed and accomplished friend Mr. Sherring is absent.

Yesterday was spent in rest, and in making acquaintance with the missionaries of the different societies who work here; and then this morning we began our sight-seeing in earnest. We had dressed, breakfasted, and started before gun-fire (five o'clock), that we might have the benefit of all the cool hours there are in the day just now, in making an exploration of this extraordinary city.

As we got into the gharree, the sweet gray dawn was beginning to tinge softly the eastern horizon, and the air felt delightfully cool and invigorating. We picked up Miss M. and the Rev. Mr. Blake, and proceeded first to the Monkey Temple. This is a very curious but rather revolting place, from the colonies of monkeys, of every size and age, which inhabit it. These creatures are considered sacred; but this temple is not dedicated to "Hanumān," the monkey-god; it is a shrine in honour of the goddess Doorga or Kali. Monkeys scrambled over every wall and filled every tree; and it was very droll to watch the grotesque creatures swing themselves down to the court, as the worshippers continually threw them offerings in the shape of handfuls of rice or fruit. They seemed quite to understand they were privileged, and walked impudently about among the people, adroitly managing to escape up the fretted pillars if they seemed in any danger from the throng. A boy to whom we had given a few pence, shouted to them, threw some handfuls of rice on to the pavement, and instantly hosts gathered from all parts of the building, and with their funny little paws picked up every grain.

Next we visited the well-known Golden Temple, dedicated to the god *Shiva*, under the name of Bisheshur (properly Vishweshwar, or Lord of the universe). The temple itself, with its gilded—hardly *golden*—dome, is not at all large or imposing; and it is a good deal hidden by other buildings, which prevent your seeing it until you are close to the gate. The court, and holy well, and other surroundings, are what really interest. The court was literally thronged with worshippers, and a continuous stream of men and women kept pouring in at the gates. They deposited their offerings, made a profound obeisance before the shrine, and went out again.

The scene outside was very curious. The narrow street was lined with Brahman vendors of flowers, grain, fruit, and every article used as offerings. The flowers were strung into wreaths like children's daisy-chains, and were chiefly composed of strong-smelling white flowers, which scented the whole air. The court was filled with a most strange and motley crowd of pilgrims, among whom were many women, Brahmans, beggars, and devotees. Some of the latter were disgusting objects,—nearly nude, smeared over with ashes and paint marks, and ornamented with sacred berries and beads. A fine, dignified old Brahman, with a beautiful mild expression of face, and fair as a European, came in by the gate where we were standing, carrying a very pretty casket of shining brass. This was divided into tiny compartments, containing rice, powder, and other mysterious articles of worship, including holy water from the Ganges. Another little pot contained the unguents, with which to make the mystic marks on his forehead, arms, and breast, after he had performed his pooja, and made his ablutions. He accosted us with a very polite salaam, and willingly held up his casket that we might examine its contents. He then threw some grains of rice into the holy well, put some more before the idol, hung garlands over it, and finally sprinkled the Ganges-water about, muttering prayers all the time, and prostrating himself, touching the ground with his forehead. He seemed very willing to show us everything; but when we began to talk to him of another religion, and the one Name under heaven given among men whereby we must be saved, his face assumed the smile of polite indifference which is so hopeless; he made his salaam, and walked away.

In and about this single temple there are over a hundred images; and in Benares there are a thousand temples, each one of which has many images, and abounds in sights and scenes of depressing idolatry. Some of them it was, of course, impossible for us to look at; for instance, when a poor little kid was sacrificed, and its blood offered to the idol. Connected with these temples there are nearly five thousand priests, besides colonies of devotees and religious beggars of all sorts. The inhabitants number somewhere about two hundred thousand, besides the concourse of pilgrims who flock to the holy city from all India; and how many missionaries of the cross are there of all societies to meet this overwhelming idolatry? Alas! only eight!

The streets are as curious as the temples. They are comically narrow, paved with stone, and wonderfully clean. The houses are massively built of solid stone from the quarries of Chunar, in the neighbourhood, and are very lofty. I was amused to see small inhabited huts, built on the flat roofs, or on terraces attached to some of the houses. We meant to have made our expedition on an elephant, but I doubt whether the great creature could have squeezed himself through some of the streets we penetrated. Hardly a sunbeam can reach the sombre depths of some of these passages, which must be cool at all seasons; but I am afraid very little fresh air can reach them either.

Benares sweetmeats are considered good, so we halted before a small recess in the wall, grandly called a shop, where a man was sitting squat on a raised little platform. Before him a pan of simmering sugar was set on a tiny stove; and out of this, with a single implement, he was busy concocting the most delicious little confections, like ratafia biscuits, which lay on sheets of white paper, stiffening in the air. We purchased a great leaf-ful for a few pice. In a similar shop a jeweller sat cross-legged on a Persian rug, and, seemingly with no implement but a small file and a pot of glowing charcoal, was fashioning the most lovely silver filagree vase, washed over with gold. The delicate beauty of the workmanship was wonderful, and the designs also beautiful, especially sundry long-necked rose-water bottles, which were very tempting; however, the man soon tired of our investigations when he found we had not come to buy. The famous brocade, or kincob, of Benares, is worthy of its reputation. It is a cloth of gold, exceedingly handsome; and the gorgeous material, with the place where it is manufactured, is quite worth a visit.

But the sight of sights is what we kept for the last—namely, the view from the river. And I must say here, that we could not have seen Benares under better auspices. Both Mr. Hutton and Mr. Blake were delightful cicerones, full of information in everything connected with the holy city, and most obliging in imparting it. We got into a boat, and slowly rowed along the entire river-front of the city; and nothing could equal this scene in singular and striking effect. It is absolutely unique. The city rises from the brink of the glorious river, which makes the grand foreground of the picture, and presents a succession of the most remarkable and varied buildings you can conceive, in every manner and style of architecture. Great men and holy men from every part of India—Hindus possessing the needful, either in money or credit—have built for themselves and families some grand memorial on the brink of this holy stream; and each one according to his own taste, or means, or times. You can imagine, then, the quaint and yet beautiful effect of this mass of nondescript building. The colouring too, gleaming in the bright morning sunlight, added greatly to the marvel of the scene. Now there is a little pinnacled temple, or a slender, graceful, gold-tipped minaret; then a massive dome; then the pointed, turreted, ornamented top of a Jain temple, with, perhaps, a hundred steps of steep masonry descending to the water-edge; next a pillared ghaut, or landing-place, with steps fantastically arranged for descent in any direction; then other ghauts, with porticoes, and courts, and roofed terraces; then more temples with gilded spires; and bathing-ghauts, with steps into the water, of beautifully hewn stone, and solid buttresses. From one ghaut or more, smoke constantly ascends; this is where the burning of the dead goes on in continual succession. Beyond and behind all this are some magnificent houses and palaces, built by princes and kings, who, if they cannot worship beside this river in their own proper persons, and bathe in its holy waters, can yet do so by proxy; they can pay Brahmans and devotees to pray for them; and they can have these mansions to prove that some day they mean to pay holy Kashi a visit. The King of Nepaul, the Rajah of Nagpore, the Gaekwar of Baroda, and other rajahs and grandees far too numerous to name, have built palaces and memorials here. These houses have almost always a temple attached to them, where hordes of greedy Brahmans live, keen-witted and designing, who delude the simple people who flock to this place, believing that their sins will be washed away by a visit to one of these bathing-ghauts; and that if they die in Benares their souls will go straight to heaven.

The wickedness and immorality of this place, as well as its idolatry, are truly appalling. But who can wonder? The Brahmans preach that a dip in the holy Ganges cleanses all sin away.

We have had much pleasant intercourse with the missionaries both of the Church and London Societies, and have seen a great deal of their work. We spent a most interesting morning with the venerable Mr. Leupoldt and his excellent wife, who have laboured here for a great many years. Mr. Smith, a "true yoke-fellow" of Mr. Leupoldt, whom we had also hoped to meet, was absent. They showed us their delightful schools, which are in a great measure industrial. The lace worked by some of Mrs. L.'s pupils is very beautiful, and brings in a considerable revenue to the mission. It is most cheering to hear from the missionaries that they have been greatly encouraged of late by the way in which their bazaar-preaching is listened to.

XXV.

Allahabad—Cawnpore—Agra.

AGRA, *March*.

BEHOLD us advanced another step—or rather two or three steps—on our up-country progress. I find I cannot attempt to give you minute descriptions of anything, our time is so occupied with travelling, sight-seeing, and meeting friends; and when we grow tired—which soon happens—it seems needful to seize any little leisure for rest, rather than for our pens. I must go back, however, and give you a short *resumé* of our proceedings.

We left that magic Benares on Friday, feeling that now we had really reached the *penetralia* of the Hindu world. Our next halt was at Allahabad, where we spent three delightful days with our kind friends the Lieutenant-Governor and Lady Muir, who had most kindly invited us to visit them. I do not need to tell you, that besides being a very distinguished public servant, Sir William is a great Arabic and Persian scholar. He and Lady Muir take the deepest interest in all connected with the highest good of India. We arrived at night, and found we had a charming little encampment all to ourselves. One huge tent with gay cotton walls was our bed-room, another a sitting-room, a third a dressing-room, and a small one for our servants. In this kindly country there need be no limit to hospitality. If your house is full, you can get up bed-rooms *ad libitum* in canvas; and at Government House in Allahabad there was quite a street of tents for the accommodation of the numerous guests......

We had a drive one evening to see the junction of the Ganges and Jumna, near which there is a magnificent railway bridge. This junction of the rivers is one of the most sacred places in India, and "melās," or religious fairs, are held here at different times of the year. At the railway-station the other day we saw strings of pilgrims setting out to and from this spot; some carrying little banners tied to long bamboos, and others having pots filled with the holy water, which they would carry with them to their homes, however great the distance might be. There were some timid-looking, shrinking women among the company. This brought to my remembrance a widow I saw lately in Calcutta, who had her beautiful long hair, still uncut, hanging loose over her shoulders. She apologized for the possession, and explained that it was being reserved to be cut off at this sacred place, as an offering to the goddess, when she could afford to make the pilgrimage. Poor thing! I hope before that day comes, she will have learned "the more excellent way" from the lady who is now teaching her.

At every place we go to, we make a point of seeing all the missionaries and their work, and at Allahabad we were very greatly interested. The excellent American missionaries there have a deeply interesting mission in full organization. A native clergyman of the Church Missionary Society, the Rev. David Mohun, with whom we had a long talk, has a congregation of more than four hundred native Christians, who support him entirely, and otherwise give largely of their means for the Lord's work.

I am deaf, dumb, and blind with a cold. And no wonder; the alternations of climate would try the strongest. For some days we had scorching heat; not the stewing or boiling of Bengal, but a sort of roasting-alive process. Suddenly, the night we were to leave Allahabad, a low boom was heard, and one of those merciful storms burst upon us with the usual wild fury. The whole encampment was flooded; and hailstones nearly as big as hen's eggs were falling thick, when we were obliged to start for the railway-station. I should like much to know how many degrees the thermometer fell during that half-hour: it became bitterly cold, and we shivered all night in the miserable train.

At six next morning we got to that most melancholy place, Cawnpore. Mr. W. Dickson – son of our friend, Mr. Dickson of the Bank of Bengal, and himself a banker—met us at the station, and drove us to his pretty bungalow. After such a night, how delicious seem the quiet and the rest, and how one does appreciate the good bath, and breakfast, and fresh toilette!

By the afternoon, when it got cool, we were quite able to go out to see the place, so full of thrilling, painful interest. In the long drive from the station it had looked so like every other place, it was difficult to realize that it could have been the scene of the fearful tragedy which makes it for ever memorable. My thoughts all day were of our poor, dear cousin......How well I remember his description of Wheeler's encampment!

Well, we saw it all, and it is most beautiful and touching. The horror melts away in a sort of tearful, tender mournfulness, as if you stood by the grave of some one peculiarly dear. When you get within the beautiful grounds which surround the Memorial Well, your voice is instinctively hushed, and you go softly.

I observed that the gentlemen put their horses to a walking pace, as if following a funeral.

A green sloped mound covers the well, which is surmounted by the monument—one of the loveliest creations I ever looked on. There is a beautiful screen, elaborately carved in white marble, which completely encircles the mound; and within this there is a pedestal, also delicately wrought, on which stands the exquisite statue by Marochetti. This is an angel of peace, in pure white marble. She stands in sweet, sad calm; the head slightly bent and a palm branch in her hand—emblematic at once of suffering and triumph. It is the expression of the whole figure which is so beautiful. There is no shadow of dread; only a mingling of ineffable sadness with peace and hope,—like a martyr who in death has realized the fulness of victory, and also as if she breathed the prayer, "Lord, lay not this sin to their charge!" Over the door, which opens inward from the marble screen, the text is inscribed: "These are they which came out of great tribulation;" and inside, on the pedestal, there is an inscription which tells the story of the massacre, with the date, "the 16th day of July 1857." I cannot dwell upon that fearful story; nor is it needful, for what heart is not still full of the sad remembrance?

The grounds about the monument are beautifully laid out in gardens and shrubbery, with broad walks, and some fine palms and other trees, and always kept in perfect order. Water has been artificially introduced in abundant supply; so that at all seasons the grass is green and the flowers are blooming and fragrant. The whole presents a scene of the most peaceful loveliness,—leading one's thoughts rather to the green pastures and still waters of the heavenly land, than to the remembrance of the woes and terrors of earth. No natives are allowed to enter the sacred precincts. The place is shown by an old soldier and his wife—who well remembers all the sad events.

We lingered here long, and then visited the site of the beleaguered camp, whence General Wheeler and his little company were tempted forth by the Nana's treachery. This, too, is turned into beds of roses and other sweet flowers, which are carefully cultivated by the soldiers. The Memorial Church is a large and handsome building, which has been opened for regular English service.

March 25.

I am so impressed with the Taj-Mahal—the wonder of Agra—the wonder of the world—that I do not think I can speak about anything else here until I have told you of it.

We could not sleep until we had seen it; so after we had settled ourselves in this primitive but clean little hotel, we got into a ticca gharree, and gave the order, "To the Taj."

For once our expectations came immensely short of the reality, for no imagination could possibly picture what the Taj is like. I do not know how to tell you of its grace and purity. I did not discover these all at once; every new gaze seems to reveal some fresh beauty. As you read a poem over and over, and each time discover a new and deeper meaning, or a new and subtler music in the words, so, in regard to this poem in stone, you find you never can exhaust the wonders of its loveliness. Somebody, I think, *has* called it a "poem in stone;" at all events, anybody might have so called this marvellous creation. It affects one's heart strangely, and you feel as you do when gazing at a noble picture, or listening to the solemn strains of church music.

Everybody has read descriptions of it; besides, my pen could not presume to picture or interpret it. You know that it is a monument built by the Emperor Shah Jehan to his wife. What you see is a fairy octagonal erection in purest white marble, with a glorious dome of perfect symmetry, and four highly-arched doorways, round each of which passages from the Koran are beautifully inlaid in black marble. It is filled with screens, and panels, and ornaments, exquisitely carved, like the most delicate open lace-work, and curiously and elaborately inlaid with precious stones in every sort of fantastic design. Beneath the central dome lie the beautiful mausoleums of the Begum and her husband, also most delicately carved, and inlaid and studded with gems of great beauty and value.

This beautiful monument stands on a quadrangular elevation, reached by noble flights of marble steps, and is surrounded by a mosaic pavement, with a graceful little column or minaret at each of the four corners, all in purest white marble.

What fills you with astonishment is, that with such wonderful minuteness of detail in the workmanship there should be such perfect harmony and unity in effect. Whose was the conception? and how did the architect find artists in sufficient sympathy with himself to carry out his marvellous design?

Greek architecture has been called "the music of the eye;" I am sure this striking image may well be applied to the Taj.

There is a magnificent entrance-gate, built in red sandstone, opening into grounds and gardens which completely surround it; these are very pretty and quaint, with beautiful flowering shrubs, and terraces, and figures, and fountains. A marble paved pathway, skirted by tiny marble water-courses, and lined with tall dark cypresses, which greatly heighten the effect, lead up to the Taj, which you see gleaming in its whiteness at the end of the lovely vista.

I must not forget to say that we had a last look last night in brilliant moonlight. The moon rose late, but we waited, and sat gazing our fill; and it looked more fairy-like than ever.

March 26.

We spent hours in the Fort this morning, exploring its endless wonders in halls and chambers, mosques, colonnades, and stately portals.

The Royal Palace is within the Fort, with all the apartments of the zenana, which are unsurpassed in beauty and Oriental luxury. These cool marble rooms and shady corridors; delicious baths fed from rippling cascades; gardens, and balconies, and terraces, and sparkling fountains, might well make a palace for fairy queens to dwell in, if this were all. But there are certain mysterious chambers and cells down far below this upper paradise, which are very suggestive of dark and nameless deeds; and if their walls could speak, I am afraid their tale would be of fearful cruelty and wrong. However, I did not visit these subterranean horrors, as some of our party did; and I would rather speak of all the beauty in the upper air, which I confess fairly bewildered me with its variety and endless charm. It looked as if it must be the scene of "The Arabian Nights."

There is the lovely Diwān-i-Khās, or the hall where kings and emperors held their durbars. The Diwān-i-Am (epithets are useless, everything is exquisite), or Court of Justice, where the sovereign himself gave audience to his people. There is the Shish-Mahāl, a unique little chamber, completely lined with tiny looking-glasses, of which there are thousands, surrounded by lovely bits of coloured ornament. The effect of these little mirrors when the room was lighted up, must have been magical. Connected with this apartment is one of those marble baths I spoke of, fed from an ever-playing fountain.

Then you must picture these palaces with alabaster walls; floors of elaborate mosaic, in strange devices; decorations in gilding, and beautiful arabesques; white marble lattices, and screens carved like the delicate open lace-work we saw at the Taj; and ceilings supported by graceful little columns; while everywhere there is that lovely inlaid work in lapis-lazuli, bloodstone, cornelian, agate, and turquoise, forming wreaths of flowers in curious patterns, like Florentine mosaic.

From a very handsome circular apartment, with the sweetest little projecting balcony, we had a lovely prospect without. Numberless ruins are scattered about, gleaming through beautiful trees. Here and there you see a handsome tomb or tripledomed mosque, and other fine buildings: and this, with the wide expanse of country, the River Jumna winding over it, and the city close beneath, made one of the most striking pictures we have seen.

We also visited the Arsenal, and the famous Somnath Gates, which are very curious, the panels being of deeply-carved sandal-wood, and of great antiquity. They were carried off by the great Mohammadan conqueror Mahmud of Ghazni, from the temple of Somnath in Kattywar, and brought back from Ghazni by Lord Ellenborough, who intended to restore them to Somnath, and so avenge the ancient wrongs of Hinduism! Surely a wildly fantastic dream, which public indignation—or ridicule, rather—soon dispelled.

But the chief beauty, the "pearl" of the whole, is certainly the Pearl Mosque, or Motee-Musjid, as it is called, which is most worthy of its name. I am not sure that I do not admire it as much as the Taj. It has a more lofty and ideal beauty, I think, and is more impressive from its perfect simplicity; it is so grand and so pure. One could fancy that the designer's object must have been to embody the idea of purity and reverence in worship. I wonder if he was a Mohammadan, or a Christian! But if the latter, probably he would have introduced some of those ornaments and fripperies which mar so many of the churches of Europe. One great excellence in Mohammadan places of worship is certainly their perfect simplicity, and the entire absence of both pictures and images.

The mosque occupies one side of a square court, which is paved with marble, and divided into compartments by lines of colour; each compartment being intended for one worshipper to kneel on. The building is open to the court, and is surmounted by three exquisite domes. The musjid, the court, and a beautiful colonnade which surrounds it, are all of the whitest marble, and have none of the colouring or of the inlaid stone-work which is so profusely introduced in all the other buildings. At the two ends of the aisles in the mosque there are screens, most exquisitely carved, behind which the ladies of the royal zenana could sit, and see and hear, without being seen.

How impressive the silence which now reigns everywhere! The glory and greatness of the emperors and their courts which filled these halls and palaces, where are they now? Baber, Akbar, Shahjehan, and Aurungzebe, and the rest, with all their intrigues and tyrannies, and the domestic loves and hates, and the jealousies of the thousand queens,—all are gone, and one can only rejoice; and yet there is an oppression and a sadness one cannot shake off, in the midst of the deserted beauty and the strange deep silence, as of the grave.

March 27.

We dined last night with Mr. and Mrs. Vines of the Church Missionary Society, who have been very kind. Mr. Gregson, a Baptist missionary, has also been exceedingly good, taking us about everywhere, and kindly guiding us to all we ought to see, as well as showing us his own mission work. We have just returned from a charming visit to Secundra, where we wished chiefly to see the industrial schools of the Church Missionary Society, and also the magnificent tomb of Akbar the Great. This last is a vast quadrangular pile in four stories or tiers, with terraces round each landing, and pretty minarets at each corner of each terrace. The building itself, and its four massive entrance-gates, which are grand erections in themselves, are built of dark-red sandstone; but when you get to the top story of the tomb, you find a little area of white marble, surrounded by a lovely arcade and wall, covered with fine open carved work, on which reposes the sarcophagus, also in pure marble, and elaborately carved. It is only a fac-simile, however, of the real tomb; for the great emperor lies in a vault beneath the building, and the whole place is full of the tombs of his family.

From this we went to the Mission-house, and breakfasted with Mr. and Mrs. Deiblé, the missionaries now in charge of the Orphanage. The great famine of 1861 filled this and similar institutions with numbers of starving children, and these rescued orphans are now being trained into respectable members of society. There are over four hundred here now. The boys are taught trades, which will enable them afterwards to make their own way in the world. The industrial department occupies the numberless corridors in the tomb of Begum Miriam, Akbar's Christian wife. The interior, where the sarcophagus lies, is walled off and left to its appropriate silence. Extensive premises have been sensibly rescued from the ruins of old Mohammadan state, and utilized for a printing-press and other operations of the mission. I was specially interested in the Christian village. I went into nearly every house, and all were clean and tidy, simply and neatly furnished. The mistresses of these nice little homes were all brought up in the Female Orphanage, and now are married to catechists and artisans. Zenana work has made a decided and successful beginning in Agra, as indeed it has in most of the cities both in the North-West and Punjab.

UMBALLA, *March 28.*

We left Agra at midnight, and soon reached Toondla Junction. But here we had a great scramble for a carriage,—the train being filled with people bound for the grand Durbar at Umballa, which was to witness the meeting between the Viceroy of India and the Affghan Ameer Shere Ali.

We were searching for seats, when two gallant young men—moved by compassion, I suppose, by my woe-begone face—shook off their slumbers, and turned out, themselves and their effects, into a compartment where other men were sleeping, giving us sole possession of their own. My gratitude is strong as I write. I only wish I knew where to find them, that I might make them my salaam.

But our adventures were by no means at an end. We puffed into Ghaziabad, where this particular line ends and that for the Punjab commences, just in time to see the train which was to carry us on to our destination disappear in the distance. It seemed to add insult to injury, thus showing itself so near, and yet, alas! virtually so far.

There was nothing for it but patience. We had eight weary hours to wait until the next train should start, and there was nothing to do, nothing to see; but you will say, I am sure, there was something to learn! My husband wrote letters, but I was too stupid and tired even to scribble in my journal. Besides, the ladies' room was a scene of the most dire confusion,—a perfect chaos of bundles and boxes and ayahs, and poor little tired, screaming children, whose equally tired mothers were trying to get a little rest on the benches round the room. Whole offices, with their following, seemed *en route* for Simla. I am sorry for the victims of this exodus, if this is what they have annually to undergo.

But everything somehow comes to an end, and so did that weary day at that hot, dusty, noisy station. We arrived at Umballa as the day dawned which was to witness the grand sight,—Britain and Affghanistan shaking hands in friendly union and mutual concord.

But I hope it may never be my fortune again to travel when the great ones of the earth are abroad. We were all tumbled out of our carriages, bag and baggage, on to the platform; and as the "special train" was imminent, conveying the Viceroy and Lady Mayo, the Lieutenant-governors, the Commander-in-chief, and many of the great officers of Government, we had to decamp as speedily as possible. We were quite as anxious to go as the officials to get rid of us; but we had our boxes to think of as well as ourselves, and not a cooly must venture within, on pain of the police. A porter was not to be had, nor a ticca gharree, and the waiting-rooms were all "reserved," in decorated grandeur, for the representatives of royalty. I felt for the poor owners of the monster bundles, and helped to carry sundry children to a safe distance without.

"Indeed, madam," said a lofty official, "these portmanteaus *must* be taken away." "I wish nothing more," said I; "but I cannot lift them!" (My husband had gone to look for help in some shape.) We poor women stood shivering over our possessions, for it was bitterly cold. At length we abandoned ours to their fate, trusting to the instinct of our clever khansāman, and walked away. We fared, however, no worse than others who arrived by that train. We left the platform with Sir Henry Durand, who, strange to say, was in a like predicament with ourselves. I ought to add that in process—rather a long process—of time our wonderful major-domo turned up with the boxes all right, and in time for us to array ourselves in suitable apparel for the Durbar.

The kindly welcome from our friends, Mr. and Mrs. H., the hot cup of tea which soon was ready, the charming room so daintily arranged, the refreshing bath, the long sweet sleep after the two nights' travel and all the weary waiting,—shall I ever forget it all?—also the delicious sense of rest, and the hearty kindness of our hospitable entertainers.

The Durbar was a scene of the most brilliant gaiety imaginable. I am so glad I have seen it; but I will not take time to describe it, as "our own correspondents," who muster in force, will do this for you far better than I could hope to do.

Lord Mayo looked more kingly than ever, when he moved to the edge of the dais and received the Affghan chief, who came simply clothed in a dark cloth coat, his keen, coal-black eye gleaming from beneath his high sheepskin cap. His bonnie little son, who is to be the heir, superseding an older brother, made up for his father's simplicity of attire, and glittered all over with beautiful gems. It was altogether the most striking spectacle, in its splendid and picturesque Orientalism, that I have yet seen. It was particularly amusing when the trays of magnificent presents in endless succession were brought in, and especially interesting when the Viceroy presented the little heir with a gold watch, and hung the massive chain with his own hands round the boy's neck.

Umballa is quite a sight in itself. The whole wide plain

over which the station is scattered, and which is intersected with wide roads fringed with beautiful trees—which do look a little dusty from the march of the elephants, artillery, and troops,—appears one great camp. The Governor-General's encampment alone has five hundred and forty tents. Then there are those of the Commander-in-chief, the Governors of the Punjab and North-West, not to speak of endless regiments of cavalry, artillery, and infantry, besides all the native grandees, who have gathered in large numbers from every quarter. Every other man seems a rajah, each with a gorgeous retinue. Some of the native soldiery are exceedingly handsome, fine men, especially the sowārs, or horsemen, in their uniforms of scarlet and gold. Elephants in their gay trappings are at least as common as horses. I went on one of these grand creatures two or three times to see the sights; the most striking by far being a grand review, when all the troops were out. I felt myself a Ranee at least, as we sat in dignity on the back of our elephant, resplendent with gilt howdah, and saddle-cloth of scarlet velvet embroidered with gold.

The whole place, in short, is a scene of the most striking Orientalism, which one could hardly have the chance of seeing more than once in one's life. Every hotel is crammed, every house is full, and every compound has two or three tents pitched in it to supplement the sleeping accommodation; the whole Indian world has flocked hither. We dined at Sir Donald M'Leod's last night with a very large party. There was a huge reception-tent, and one as large for dining in; the two being connected by a wide passage between two red calico walls, and laid with red cloth.

We have had the very great pleasure of meeting the venerable

Dr. Morrison, the senior American missionary here. It was he who originally proposed having the first week in the year for united prayer; what has now happily become almost a world-wide Christian institution. We attended his Sabbath services, one of which was conducted in Hindi. The little chapel was pretty well filled with an intelligent native audience; and we hope yet to see a good deal more of the mission and the missionaries.

XXVI.

Delhi.

DELHI, *April 2.*

AT last in Delhi! I have so long looked forward to setting foot in this far-famed capital of the Great Moguls, that I can hardly quite believe we are here. There is no city, I think—certainly none in India—which appeals so much to one's imagination as this, both from its ancient historical greatness, and also from the thrilling events in its later history, which have so connected it with British power in the East; for who can forget that it was before Delhi, in the memorable siege of the Mutiny time, that, by God's good hand upon us, the fate of our Indian Empire was decided?

We are the guests of our kind and delightful friends the Commissioner and Mrs. M'Neill, who have received us in the heartiest way, and made us at home in their beautiful house, Ludlow Castle. One realizes a little of the romance of Delhi in the house, which is an old palace restored, and has some lovely carving and colouring about its walls and decorations. Colonel M'Neill has himself shown us over it. He seems to me the beau-ideal both of an English gentleman and an Indian officer.* He is the son of the well-known and much-honoured Dr. Hugh M'Neill.

* This admirable man was soon after cut off, in the vigour of his days and the height of his usefulness.

April 3.

We are busy exploring the wonders of this wonderful city. The sights which have impressed me most, I think, are the glorious tower, of which all the world has heard, the Kootub Minār; and next, the magnificent prospect there is from its top. Indeed, perhaps this view is more striking than even the beautiful tower itself. The vast plain which surrounds Delhi, ancient and modern, with the River Jumna winding over it, lies before you; and as far in every direction as the eye can reach, the whole wide area is thickly studded with the grandest ruins. There are handsome palaces, now deserted and silent and crumbling to decay; tombs as massive and magnificent as the palaces, where "the kings of the nations lie in glory, each one in his own house;" endless mosques, with their triple domes; pillars of stone, and curious graceful lāts (or pillars) of iron; old broken forts, which tell touching stories of occupation, and defeat, and conquest; colonnades and cloisters and courts and arches; musjids, with graceful minarets; Hindu temples and remains of very ancient date—before the Mohammadan conquerors had thought of invading the land; and massive old Pathan buildings. Then the ruins of the ancient city and fortifications of Toghlukabad lie a little way off, besides old Delhi, which has been built and re-built many times over, and the handsome buildings and massive wall of the city of the present. It is truly a magnificent panorama.

Of the Kootub one can only say, it is the grandest tower in the world. It is about two hundred and forty feet in height, and at the base is one hundred and fifty feet in circumference. It is built of beautiful red sandstone, is circular in construction, narrowing as it ascends, and is curiously fluted the whole extent to the top. It is in five elevations or stories; and the landing of each story is surrounded by a gallery full of the most exquisite carving, and ornamented by Arabic inscriptions in relief. This matchless shaft stands in the midst of ruins, but is itself in perfect preservation. The beautiful cupola which originally surmounted it now lies at its base; but I think they said it had been taken down for safety.

The Kootub is eleven miles from Delhi; and though it is the wonder of the place, and what you come to see, yet there are many of its surroundings most curious and beautiful, and well worth a visit. The place is exceedingly pretty naturally, and full of leafy loveliness. Fine old neem-trees abound, graceful acacias, with tangled creepers and shrubs; and out of this greenery peep bits of broken columns, old tombs, scraps of arches, arched windows and doorways, all in the most picturesque state of ruin. I hope it was not very shocking, but I think all this gave me as much pleasure, at least, as the glories of the wondrous Kootub. Mr. Smith and my husband went into learned disquisitions over dates and dynasties; and our charming friend Mrs. Brandis, who accompanied us, sat and sketched, while I retired within a maze of natural loveliness, full of enchanting effects, and fed my eye and my heart too, and took in so much enjoyment, that my day at the Kootub will be one long to be remembered.

One of the most curious things near the Kootub is an ancient quadrangular court, with a gallery all round, supported on quaint old pillars, completely covered with carving and sculpture. These date long before the Mohammadans. Mr. Smith says they are of Jain workmanship. The usual figure seated in meditation is to be seen on some of them, though much mutilated by the Mohammadans. On the monuments of Mohammadan times you see no representation of any living form—nothing human, whether of man, or bird, or beast; and they have shown their abhorrence of image-worship by mutilating whatever is distinctively Hindu, Buddhist, or Jain.

Mr. Smith is a zealous and much-respected Baptist missionary. He and his wife welcomed us with the greatest cordiality, and we have been much with them since our arrival. Mr. Smith is our "guide, philosopher, and friend." He takes us about with unwearied kindness, and I suppose no one knows Delhi so well as he does.

The two most striking buildings inside Delhi are the Great Mosque (the Jumma-Musjid, as it is called), and the Palace.

The mosque is grandly imposing. It stands on an elevated area of great expanse, paved with marble, approached by noble flights of steps, and having three handsome entrance-gates. In the court, which would contain about twelve thousand people, there are always crowds of white-robed worshippers kneeling on the pavement. One of the most singular sights I ever beheld, was to witness at sunset fully two hundred worshippers ranged in two lines in front of the mosque, and, as if moved by one impulse, performing simultaneously the same precise prostrations, and repeating the same prayer. As we went in, we noticed a fakir outside the musjid standing on one foot, with his finger pointing to heaven. He had a wild excited look. When we returned long after, he was in the same attitude on the same spot. In a small receptacle in one corner of the great court there are some highly valued relics. I must resist the desire I feel to moralize on the strong tendency existing in many systems to treasure and venerate such things.

The palace covers an immense space, and, as usual, its entrance-gate is a magnificent structure. Another gate leads on to the Diwān-i-Khās, the Hall of Audience, of which all the world has heard. I suppose it is the most beautiful room in the world.

> "Round thee the polished alabaster sheds
> A more than earthly brightness; the white floor
> Shows like a sea of milk; the pillars stand
> Alike embossed, alike with quaint device
> Endlessly blazoned."

The famous Persian inscription is still to be seen, which means,—"If there is a paradise on earth, it is this—it is this;" and if pure grace, and perfect beauty in construction and effect, could make a paradise, it might indeed be here. The celebrated "peacock throne" once stood in this room; but it is gone, with all the glory and splendour which once filled these halls and palaces and zenanas, where there are now only emptiness and the silence of the dead.

We have visited some tombs of wonderful beauty and massive grandeur, some having interesting traditions connected with them, which I wish I had time to relate. I think the handsomest is Humayoon's tomb, the father of Akbar the Great. It was erected by Akbar, and is almost as grand as his own at Secundra. It was in this tomb that the last of the Moguls—the wicked old emperor—took refuge from the British troops after the siege in 1857. Nizam-ud-deen's tomb is also most lovely. He was a Pīr, or holy man. But it would take volumes to describe all the wonders of Delhi. The number of these grand mausoleums is marvellous. I must say I find "meditations among the tombs" a very oppressive exercise in this wilderness of ruin. It is so melancholy to see these marbles, and mosaics, and beautiful structures, surrounded by rubbish-heaps, infested by squalid beggars, and "Ichabod" written on everything around.

Inhabited Delhi, however, is very pleasing and pretty. The

bazaars are wonderfully clean, and filled with a most picturesque population, gathered chiefly from the far north and west, and the plains of Central India. Some of these men are quite statuesque,—white-robed stately figures, who tread the streets with slow and lofty dignity. I could not help shuddering when I thought how easy it would be for the spirit of fanaticism to awaken in Delhi, and for fiery crowds to rush upon the infidel with their terrible war-cry of *Deen!—deen!* I have not seen in India such fine men, and with such handsome faces, as you see in the Chandnee-Chouk of Delhi. Sikhs, too, and Affghans abound; and here and there, perhaps, a Parsee; but comparatively few Hindus proper.

The Chandnee-Chouk is the chief bazaar in Delhi, and it is a very handsome street, with good shops and houses. It is a mile long, very wide for India, and down the centre has rather an unusual, but effective embellishment, in a stream of water, skirted by pretty trees.

Mission work here is exceedingly interesting and hopeful. Mr. Smith has introduced us to all his work; and we have seen and talked with many native Christians, among them Wilayat Ali's wife and daughter. You know he was one of the martyrs in the Mutiny.

Dr. M. preached twice in Mr. Smith's church on Sunday. There is a Highland regiment, or wing of a regiment, here; and, at the request of Government, Mr. Smith acts as their chaplain, as far as his prior duty to the mission allows. Our hearts, of course, "warm to the tartan." Dr. M. says he thinks he never preached with more pleasure to himself than when addressing these gallant fellows. We also attended Mr. Smith's service in the Urdu language. Mrs. S. played the organ, but all the tunes were native. There was a large congregation of natives, all Christian, and some of them very nice-looking people. Mrs. Smith does a great deal in zenana work, and has access to several Mohammadan families of rank. I have been surprised to find, as we travel towards the Punjab, that the zenanas of the Hindus become rather less accessible, and those of the Musulmans more so. The ladies receive Mrs. S. with great warmth and demonstrations of affection. On the whole, the openings there are everywhere for this blessed zenana work are most wonderful. Oh! for whole armies of our countrywomen to go in and occupy!

But I have said nothing of what we visited the first thing, the first day—namely, the ever-memorable ridge outside the city walls, where the destiny of India was decided, through the blessing of God, in '57. I find that I cannot say much of that dire Mutiny time, still so fresh to memory, so present always. It seems to fill one's heart continually here, whatever else you are seeing or doing.

The chief points of interest are the wonderful natural ridge,—where such deeds of heroism were done, with its different points of defence; and the Cashmere Gate, where the siege was really won, but, alas! where the heroic Nicholson fell, and where many other gallant brave men yielded their lives for their country. There is no tale told of all the Mutiny more thrilling than the gallant exploit which ended in the blowing up of this gate. A chasm by the side still shows where the tremendous explosion made a way for our troops to rush into the city.

People here do not talk much of this Mutiny,—they cannot; it is still too recent and too terrible. Doubtless they often think of it, and of the truth which the old Sikh soldier well expressed at the time,—"It was not man, but God, who led the British soldiers across that ditch and up that wall!"

XXVII.

The Punjab, &c.

SEHARUNPORE, *April 16.*

BEFORE I begin the short account of our proceedings during the past fortnight—which is all I can give you—I must tell you a little tale of Indian kindness and hospitality.

We had reached Roorkee *en route* for Hurdwar. This is a great place of pilgrimage, about twenty miles to the north. The most important melā, or fair, of the year was about to take place, and Dr. M. had arranged to accompany some missionary friends who were going to it. We had taken up our quarters at the dāk bungalow; but, alas, here I fairly broke down, and had to succumb to one of my bad sore throats. What was to be done? Dr. M. was anxious not to lose so good an opportunity of seeing this famous festival. Our friends had joined us, our plans were made, and the time had come to start. He did not like to leave me, disconsolate and sick, to the amenities of the travellers' bungalow; and I did not like that he should lose the melā, and the opportunity of doing some missionary work among the pilgrims. However, succour soon arrived. Mr. and Mrs. Morrison, the Scotch chaplain and his wife, heard of our dilemma. She came at once, bundled me well up, carried me off in her carriage, and deposited me on her own bed. There was no spare room in their house, so Mr. Morrison turned out into a tent. A small cot was established beside me for Mrs. M., and here I was welcomed, nursed, and cared for, until, by God's blessing, I got well.

Now, a sore throat, which may turn to anything, is not what many would care to admit to their house, not to say to their room; besides that the owner of the throat was a perfect stranger, and was sure to cause a great deal of trouble. Yet this was what these kind Christian people did. They opened their house and heart to us, and received us into them without reserve. You will agree with me, after this, that the injunction to use hospitality, and "without grudging," is thoroughly understood and obeyed in India.

Roorkee is a beautiful station, though I did not see very much of it except in entering and leaving. I saw, however, what I shall never forget—namely, the grand Ganges Canal. This wonderful work is nearly a thousand miles in length, and irrigates vast tracts of the country. What at any time might be a barren wilderness is transformed by these waters into a smiling garden. Why should not all the mighty rivers of this land be thus utilized?

Notwithstanding my illness, I greatly enjoyed my sojourn with the M.'s. My husband returned in a week; and then last evening, when the heat, which now gets worse daily, had somewhat abated, we started on our return. Our kind friends insisted on driving us out some eight or ten miles, which greatly shortened our journey; and then we bade them a most grateful good-bye, hoping that we shall meet again, perhaps at home, as the regiment will soon have served its time in India.

The whole road from Roorkee onward was crowded with

people returning from the great melā at Hurdwar, where there had been a gathering of thousands and thousands of pilgrims. Hurdwar, as it is usually pronounced, means the gate of *Hur*, or Shiva.* This being the point where the Ganges leaves the mountains and flows out into the plains, the spot is peculiarly sacred, and is the scene of this annual festival. Dr. M., with the other missionaries, preached for hours morning and evening, gave tracts, and spoke to the people; and they met with very little opposition. Lord Mayo, who had gone to see the fair, stood in the sun literally for hours watching the bathers, as the people went down into the stream, washed themselves and their clothes, repeating their prayers all the time, and believing that this sacred water could cleanse away their sin. His Lordship said he never witnessed anything so strikingly characteristic of Hinduism as that wonderful sight. He and several of his staff attended a simple Presbyterian service conducted by Dr. M. the day following, which was Sunday.

We were much interested, as we came along last evening, to see the pilgrims, and conversed with many of them. Most were on foot, some rode on ponies, and some were in carts which were drawn by fine large oxen covered with tinkling bells. Now and then there was a solitary pilgrim wending his weary way with staff in hand, and burden on his back. This pilgrim-staff is almost as tall as its owner, like an alpenstock. Among the little groups many were women, and mostly poor, old, withered, bent creatures, who seemed tottering on the brink of the grave. I have no doubt that these poor things had gone to the so-called sacred water, knowing that their day was done, and the dark, hopeless night at hand, with an instinctive feel-

* The name, however, is more correctly written Hari-dwār, or the gate of Vishnu—*i.e.*, Vishnu's gate to heaven.—*Edit.*

ing of need for something, they knew not what. Oh, to tell them of the true fountain, where all who wash are made "white as snow"! Many of the men carried little brass vessels slung on bamboos across their shoulders, filled with water from the sacred spot. It was most interesting to talk to them.

As the sun was setting we got into our doolies, and at midnight were set down here in the verandah of the American Mission-house—our friend Mr. Calderwood's dwelling—very thankful to be at our journey's end, and to have a *still* bed to lie upon, after the terrible jolting and jerking of the doolie-bearers.

Eschewing fatigue and sun, we went out this morning to see Mr. Calderwood's schools. There is a large boys' school, where English is taught; but what chiefly delighted me was a charming school for Mohammadan girls. There were thirty-five nice, bright, intelligent little creatures, belonging to respectable families. This is the first time I have seen a female school on this side of India, wholly composed of Mohammadans.

How fierce the heat is becoming! The sun seems to rage without like a beleaguering enemy, and the wind is fiery hot, shrivelling one to a cinder. Yet they say it is nothing to what it will be by-and-by. We barricade ourselves within doors, and close every crevice. Some of the up-country houses are beautifully adapted to exclude the heat—for instance, that of the Morrisons at Roorkee. The walls are thick, the ceilings lofty, the doors and windows narrow, and the ventilation from the roof.

Mr. Morrison told me some of the feats of the hardy little Goorkhas, who did us such good service in the Mutiny. They are small men, but very plucky; carry short swords, hardly more than knives; but this is a very formidable weapon, and it made them quite a terror to the enemy. They wear this knife in their belt, in addition to their other arms, and use it with such precision that they strike a man's head off at a stroke. If any one showed himself over the breastwork, his head was gone in a second, as if by magic! No wonder they were a terror. And they did this bloody work as if it were all a good joke, following the beheading with a laugh. In consideration of their services, the Queen sent the regiment which had particularly distinguished itself at Lucknow, a very handsome silver mace, as thick as a man's arm. The men were so delighted with their gift, that they at once set it up and worshipped it!

April 18.

Left Saharanpore yesterday. The Calderwoods have been exceedingly kind. And who is not kind? We found the station crowded with pilgrims, as thick as sheep in a pen. There was hardly moving room. Our train, of course, was late; so we spoke to many of them. Oh, poor things! One woman especially attracted me, with such a sweet, patient, *good* face; an old creature, with lines of sorrow deeply traced, and such travel-stained, scanty garments! I spoke to her, but her language was Panjabi, not Hindi, and I did not comprehend much; nor did I care to call in the aid of the numerous interpreters, who proffered their services with the usual gushingness of natives. She had come from beyond the Sutlej, and had taken this weary journey, like many hundreds besides, that her *dil*, or heart, might be made pure, she said. How I wished for time and power to tell her the whole blessed truth! But I could only say, that if she wished her *dil* to be made pure, God could do it, and would; for He was her Father, and He loved her, and had given His Son to die, to prove His love and His willingness to save His creatures.

Presently the Rajah of Kuppurthulla came on to the platform, with two sons and a numerous retinue. He is a large man, with good features, but a rather sensual expression. He is a professing Christian, but unbaptized. He spoke good English, and introduced his sons to us.

LOODIANA, *April 20.*

We are in the Punjab, the region of the "five rivers," though the aspect of the country is such that the description might rather be "a dry and thirsty land where no water is." The plains look a waste of sand, terribly brown and burnt-up, and the hot dust seems to stifle one.

We had to change our mode of travel to get here (as the railway is not yet open all the way), and take to the old dāk gharree, which soon will be as rare in the land as our mail-coaches are at home.

We had a most amusing and characteristic start from Umballa, where we were again most kindly entertained by Mr. and Mrs. H. We had ordered our gharree for ten at night, in order to travel while it was comparatively cool; but eleven, and twelve, came before it appeared. At length, however, we got ourselves and possessions stowed away inside and out; we spread our quilts and pillows on the seats, which were metamorphosed into a sort of couch by the ingenious introduction of a bit of board between, settled ourselves comfortably, and fondly hoped we had started. But, lo! the wheel would not turn. We worked, and mended, and hammered, and strove; but no! it would not move. There was nothing for it but to send for another gharree: and so all the packing, and stowing, and arranging had to be done over again; and the worst of it was that the poor horses had to make up for lost time. After a few preliminary kicks from the half-asleep syces, they started off at full gallop,—a pace which had to be maintained the whole stage, for if there was the slightest relaxation they stopped, and plunged, and refused to go at all.

We sped along in this fashion all night; the road was excellent; and at nine o'clock, before it was very hot, we drove into the American Mission compound, and were received, literally with open arms, by dear Mr. and Mrs. Rudolph and the other missionaries.

We have enjoyed our visit here exceedingly. There are several mission-houses in the compound. Opposite to this one Mr. and Mrs. Myers live. We always dine with them, so we seem the guests of all; and they are so kind, and such a loving Christian atmosphere pervades the whole mission, that it is quite refreshing to be here. Mrs. Myers takes charge of the Female Orphanage, which is a most flourishing institution, and largely attended. Miss Jerrom, who is working hard in the zenanas of Loodiana, and making new way constantly, lives in a third house, a little further off, though in the same compound. She has taken me with her in the early mornings, while on her usual rounds among her pupils, and I have enjoyed these visits immensely. One of our most delightful visits was to a lady of high rank, a Begum, who interested me profoundly.* Another morning we went to the zenana of a devoted follower of General Colin Mackenzie, who is now dead. The Beebees received me enthusiastically, as a friend of their friends, and entertained us with tea and all manner of sweets and fruit. I tried to find out our own dear old "Beebee Saheb," the wife of Aga Mohammad

* This lady has since then asked to be baptized.

Khan, who lived so long with us in Bombay, and who became a Christian, and was baptized by Dr. M.; but, alas! she had left Loodiana.

The native houses here are very peculiar, but I should think well adapted for the intense heat of the climate in the hot season. They look like mud heaps; and they are really built of mud, one-storied, flat-roofed, and have no windows that I can see.

LAHORE, *April 21.*

We left Loodiana on Monday at five in the afternoon. The heat was terrific. I felt baked alive as we crossed the curious bridge of boats over the grand Sutlej. Mr. Rudolph accompanied us, his health requiring a change. We joined the railway at the Beas river in the middle of the night, where there is no sort of waiting-room. Weary indescribably, I crept into an empty carriage and lay down; but it was stuffy, hard, and unbearably hot, so I crept out again. Then came a hurricane—differing, however, from other hurricanes we have been used to, in that it poured sand, not water. It was a dust-storm, exceedingly murky and disagreeable, except that it undoubtedly cooled the air. Finally, our difficulties came to a climax after we had started, when the quilt on which my husband was sleeping took fire; a live piece of coke from the engine came in on us very unceremoniously; after which we had to keep awake by turns, to watch lest we or our effects should be consumed.

And now we are at Lahore—

"Lahor of Great Mogul,"

as Milton calls it; though doubtless, in your minds, it is more associated with the name of Runjit Singh—the Lion of the Punjab, the warrior-king of the Sikhs—than with either Milton or the Great Mogul.

We have now the great privilege and pleasure of being the guests of Sir Donald M'Leod, the truly excellent and distinguished Lieutenant-Governor of the Punjab.......When we arrived at the station in the early morning, we found a carriage waiting for us, drawn by four camels—or dromedaries, rather—each one surmounted by his driver, gorgeous in scarlet and gold. I was so charmed with this novel state, and with the gentle, huge creatures who carried their heads so proudly and trotted away so nimbly and smoothly, that now the camel carriage is most kindly put at my service whenever I want to go out. When we entered the beautiful garden, and drew up at Government House, Sir Donald himself descended to receive and welcome us, which seemed to me an act of great kindness and courtesy. He conducted us through the beautiful house, which seemed so deliciously shady and cool after the heat and sand and glare without; introduced us to his niece, Miss Innes; raised the heavy folds of a huge dark curtain which hung over a narrow door opening from a circular chamber—once part of a tomb, he said—and showed us into the pleasant quarters allotted to us.

[This admirable man, alas! has passed away; and now it is impossible to recall his great kindness to ourselves, and our delightful visit to Lahore, without the deepest feeling. I cannot pretend to speak of the varied public career of this distinguished civilian, nor of what he has done for India; but I may be allowed to record our own affection for him personally, and our high admiration of the many excellences of his beautiful character.

Sir Donald possessed many of the qualities which natives respect the most in our countrymen—unswerving truth and justice, mingled with kindness, benevolence, and courtesy. Our dear friend, Behari Lal Singh, thus speaks of the influence Sir D. M'Leod exercised over his own life: "It was the pious example of this gentleman—his integrity, his honesty, his disinterestedness, and his active benevolence—that made me think Christianity was something living, and that there was a living power in Christ. Here was a man with some three or four thousand rupees a month spending little on himself, and giving away the surplus for the good of my countrymen. This was the turning-point in my religious history, which led to my conversion."

This great and good man was full of active labour to the last, especially for India, and many days of active usefulness seemed still to lie before him; but the awfully sudden call came, and now he is not, "for God took him."]

Progress in the Punjab has been as wonderful at least as in other parts of India. The change indeed is great since old Runjit's body was laid on the funeral-pile along with eleven of his living wives! Not only that his son, the Maharajah Dhuleep Singh, lives the life of an English and Christian nobleman in Britain, but that his country has made such a wonderful stride both in mental and material progress.

A meeting was extemporized one evening for Dr. M. in connection with a literary and scientific society, which owes much to the zeal of Dr. Leitner. There were over two hundred young men present who perfectly understood English, and several spoke in English when Dr. M. had concluded. The American missions have done much for the Punjab, as for many other places in India. We had delightful intercourse with all the members of the mission in Lahore. Dr. M. was also greatly interested in the plans of two excellent missionaries of the

Church Missionary Society—Messrs. French and Knott. They are preparing to establish a training-college for native preachers, the teaching to be conducted wholly in the native languages. We found that the head-master of the American Mission school was one of the *alumni* of our own college in Calcutta, the Rev. Guru Das Moitra.* He and his wife got up a delightful little entertainment for us. They invited all the native Christians in Lahore to meet us at breakfast, and it was one of the pleasantest mornings in all our visit.

One marked religious feature of the Punjab is, of course, Sikhism; and this we had an opportunity of seeing in perfection in the holy city of the Sikhs, Umritsur, as we returned to Umballa. We spent a most pleasant day there with our kind friends the Rev. Mr. and Mrs. Keene of the Church Missionary Society. Mr. K. took us to see the far-famed golden temple, which is one of the most striking sights I have seen in India. The dome is really of gold, curiously carved, and with four doors, also of gold. The temple altogether is very beautiful, standing on an elevation surrounded by a very fine tank of water, which is considered holy. In crossing to the temple, the attendant priests, in the politest way, out of a store which they had in readiness, slipped something on to our feet, lest our shoes should pollute the sacred floor.

In this temple the *Grunth*, or holy book of the Sikhs, is chanted almost without intermission to listening multitudes, while all around hang the swords of the line of warrior-gurus. These swords are worshipped. We saw great numbers of them in different parts of the temple; but the most striking part of the exhibition was the chanting of the *Grunth*. A great number of people sat in a circle under the great dome, with the

* Now pastor of the Bengali Church in Calcutta.

holy book under a golden canopy in the midst; these men swayed themselves to and fro, now and then touching the ground with their foreheads—though their religious fervour seemed rather forced—and continued the chant in monotonous but not at all inharmonious voices, while many people streamed in and out, and stood for a while to listen. I was exceedingly struck with the fierce, keen eye of some of these Sikh devotees, especially of those called *Akālis,* whose look denoted wild fanaticism; and it seemed as if it would not take very much to make the old spirit flame out afresh.

XXVIII.

Lucknow.

WE must now make a bound over time and space. The months which intervened between our up-country and down-country journey contained far too much in new experiences and new pleasures, in new work and new and supreme beauty, among the glorious Himalaya, for the record to be epitomized so as to find a place within the limits of this little book.

We left Simla in the beginning of November, and a week thereafter found ourselves at Lucknow.]

LUCKNOW, *November 7.*

We have made a detour in our downward journey to see this place, so full of deathless memories; so lovely, too, in itself, and, thank God, so quiet and peaceful now.

We left the main line at Cawnpore, whence a branch railway strikes cross-country to this. In getting to the Cawnpore station in the early morning, we crossed the magnificent Ganges—our old friend—by a bridge of boats. It looked grander than ever in its sea-like expanse, with the shadows from wood and building on its banks reflected deep in its golden waters. The station put me in mind of an Egyptian one in the Desert—rude, rough, dusty, dilapidated, and full of the most unaccountable delays. Happily, we are always amused by the scene at a station; it is so droll to watch the natives, and to see the fuss they make about taking their seats. The grouping, too, is extremely picturesque; for they generally travel, not singly, but in little companies. It is always a pleasure to us to talk to them. We chose out a man to have a chat with; not for the gaiety of his attire—of which I took particular note, however—but for his frank, open, intelligent face and brilliant eye. He wore a bright blue cloth coat, piped with red satin and broadly bordered with gold. His trousers were pink, *gathered* so tightly on to his slender calf that they looked as if he had "growed" in them: they put me in mind of the quilling process our grandmother's caps used to undergo when we were children. On his head he had a green cap edged with purple, and a gold band. Strings of beads, ear-rings, and red shoes embroidered with gold, completed his toilet. I hope you do not think I exaggerate: I took it all down on the spot. The natives deck themselves like a bed of flowers, and blend all colours together. But does not Nature do the same?

Oh, the shouting and gesticulation, and roar and din there was! The noise of the train when we started, seemed a calm after those shrill voices.

Oude is a garden. The whole country is well wooded and watered, and covered with fields of the most luxuriant crops. It is the richest country I have seen in India; more like the Carse of Gowrie than anything else;—only there is here no background of hills,—it is flat, flat to the horizon. Indeed, the whole country from Delhi has been exceedingly beautiful, presenting a striking contrast to the sun-burnt plains we saw as we went up before the rains. The crops are magnificent, and of marvellous variety: *jowari*, *bajari*, and all the grains of the country;

rice, mustard, sugar-cane, flax, hemp, cotton, and wheat sown at the end of the monsoon, which now covers the fields with delicate green. Then the woods also are lovely in their fresh green. We have the abounding neem-tree, with its dark, thick foliage, the peepul, tamarind, mango, the graceful acacia, with its yellow blossoms, and many others, charming specimens of tropical growth. What is wild and spontaneous is just as luxuriant; the tall grasses wave like nodding plumes, and the whole line is skirted by beds of the most lovely water-lilies. I tried to preserve some of the grasses; but they were too ripe, and vanished in down.

Lucknow itself is full of natural beauty. I think it is the prettiest station I have yet seen; not at all distinctively Eastern, but rich and park-like, with green grass, and fine trees, and splendid buildings. Only, on closer inspection the buildings disappoint you terribly. The Imambarra, which is now turned into an arsenal, is a room of magnificent proportions; but you find it is made up of plaster and stucco, the entrance-gate being flanked by two odious plaster sphinxes. The palace of the Kaiser-bagh looks exceedingly grand and imposing at a distance; but its architecture is of the same false character. Ruskin would go out of his wits in Lucknow. We should certainly have come here before we saw the pure, lovely erections of Agra and Delhi; but the natural beauties quite make up. An area of many miles is covered with garden and park, and long, beautiful, wide avenues, skirted by noble trees. The houses and bungalows are tastefully embowered with evergreens and creepers, lycopodiums and orchids, among which the brilliant bougainvillia shows its lovely blossoms. We found a friend here whose acquaintance we made at Simla; and she and her husband, Captain N., have driven us about everywhere. Unfortunate as I too often am! I caught fever from a rash visit I paid to a *very* dirty hill habitation, near Simla, and was in bed when our friends took Dr. M. to see the Alumbagh, with its precious possession, the grave of Havelock. Happily before the fever came on I had visited the "Residency," the "Bailey-Guard," Dr. Fayrer's house, and the other places which the thrilling events which occurred during the famous siege of 1857 have made so memorable. It is, of course, round these scenes, where the struggles, and the fightings, and the enduring, and the victory occurred at that terrible time, that every interest in this place must now cluster.

The Residency is very much a ruin; except the chambers, or rather cellars below, and a few other places which have been partially restored, where the beleaguered company of our countrymen and countrywomen endured that "great fight of afflictions" during the long months from June to November before deliverance came.

I wandered about these places, picturing the scenes which must have occurred when weak women, and poor little children, and stricken men, had to endure the nameless horrors of that protracted siege,—in wounds, disease, privation of every sort, and death itself. One seems to hear the ceaseless roar of the artillery, and the explosion of the bursting shells!

But, thank God, there is another side to the picture here. It is not like Cawnpore! There is something else one seems to hear—namely, that thrilling cheer which rose from the depths of those poor tried hearts, where patience had had her perfect work, when our own true-hearted, gallant Highlanders fought their way through the streets, and brought the "relief!" Cannot you see them shaking hands with the poor ladies, and tossing the little children, and bidding "God bless you" to all

—congratulating each other, too, I do not doubt, that they had been selected for this high service for their country, and their Queen, and their God?

What a moment, never to be forgotten, must this have been for the brave leaders, Outram and Havelock! Great is the joy of being saved; but the joy of *saving* seems so much the greater!

And yet it must have been a tempered joy; so many were beyond the reach of their help. The great and the good Sir Henry Lawrence was gone,—a loss never to be repaired. Many another brave heart was silenced, and many a comrade laid low.

What makes Dr. Fayrer's house the hallowed spot it must for ever be, is that here, in the verandah where we stand, Sir Henry Lawrence breathed his last. He had finished his work, he had "done his duty," as the humble hero said of himself; and now at his Lord's summons he was ready to yield his spirit to his Father. Amidst the tears of all who had gathered round to see their honoured and beloved chief to the last, and the sobs of rough men who had surely been inured to much, one of the greatest and best of Britain's sons passed away to his reward.

On his tomb is written the simple and most beautiful epitaph he himself prescribed:—

Here lies Henry Lawrence, who tried to do his duty.
May God have mercy upon him!

One of the most touching places you visit is the cemetery, where Lawrence's simple monument stands; and where General Neill, and many, many others lie, now quietly taking their rest.

The burying-grounds in India everywhere are to me peculiarly sad and impressive. There precious dust sleeps far from beloved kindred and beloved home. One can only hope that a joyful reunion awaits these severed ones, when the eternal day has broken, and the shadows of earth have for ever fled away. And meanwhile, does it not seem as if these hallowed graves have taken possession and occupy the land for Him who is the resurrection and the life, giving promise that "the time to favour India, yea, the set time," will come, and that He shall yet reign over it with fulness of blessing?

XXIX.

The Marble Rocks of the Nerbudda.

JUBBULPORE, *November 13.*

AFTER two very pleasant days of much-needed rest with our kind friends the J.'s at Allahabad, we came on here, which at present is the terminus of the railway to Bombay. There is a gap between this and Bhosawul, which will very speedily be filled up, and then the line from Calcutta to Bombay will be complete.

We are lodged in what by courtesy is called a hotel, though this appellation would hardly summon up to your minds a true picture of our surroundings, which are wonderfully primitive. The room contains a cot, two chairs, a good big comfortable table, some dirty matting on the floor, with the indispensable bath-room beyond, and its rows of chatties full of water. The cot stands in the middle of the floor, and is the chief feature. It looks a rude enough article, fashioned from a rough framework of wood, supported on four sturdy legs, with a quantity of broad country tape wound over it to form the bottom. On this our quilts and pillows are spread; and I am sure no one ever reposed on bed of down with more satisfaction than we rested our weary selves on this simple but elastic, pleasant couch, when we got in last night, and so took our ease in our inn.

"Man wants but little here below;" far less, indeed, than one is apt to think.

Mine host is a huge Madrassee,—the biggest native, I think, I ever saw. He has a very dark complexion, and only one eye; which, however, has enough of shrewdness in it for two. He wears a motley garb, the top garment being made of Rob Roy tartan; and altogether he has rather an equivocal look, though he is a most kind and attentive host. There was a peculiar noise last night; and this morning Ramasawmi (our host) having failed to make his appearance, I inquired about him, when his major-domo whispered confidentially, "Mem Saheb, him tipsy." *Apropos* of which, a lady told me, that once on a former visit all her servants had got tipsy in company, and when she remonstrated, this gentleman told her unblushingly, "Mem Saheb know very well that at Easter-time all good Christians get drunk!" He is a Christian himself—by descent.

November 15.

We are very fortunate people. Being at Jubbulpore, we, of course, wanted to see the famous marble rocks on the Nerbudda. Happening to mention our desire to a pleasant, intelligent man who sat next us at the *table d'hôte*, he most kindly offered to send us part of the way by the railway on a lorry, instead of driving, as we intended. This gentleman, we found, was a sort of railway chief. He knew our dear friend C. B. Ker, and seemed to know us too.

Another gentleman, Major Roberts, who is stationed here, soon found us out, and has been most kind and friendly. He is a perfect type of the true Christian gentleman you so often meet in India. He offered to accompany us on our expedition; and also most kindly sent an elephant out, to take us on from the point where the lorry must set us down. We started at seven o'clock, accompanied, also, by a nice young engineer our railway friend sent to take care of us, and see that the lorry did its duty. This small machine—a tiny square platform on wheels—just held our four chairs and a good big picnic basket our host had filled most amply for us. We were pushed along at a great rate by four men, who ran in the nimblest way on the rails, never touching the ground, nor making a slip. We enjoyed the fresh morning air, and the views of the pretty country exceedingly, though I did feel a little rickety, and as if I must topple off. The country round the Nerbudda is rich and beautiful, diversified with hills, and trees, and luxuriant crops. The hills, which mostly are green and prettily wooded, were never out of sight. The birds were unusually numerous and blithe, twittering and making a great ado, and showing off their brilliant plumage in the early sunlight among the boughs.

Jubbulpore itself is a beautiful station; its chief feature being that in every direction there are clumps of the feathery bamboo, with its rich green foliage in long pointed fronds. It is one of the most graceful trees we have.

After a ten miles' delightful ride we came to our elephant, which was standing in quiet dignity waiting to receive us. On her capacious back (her name was *Maggie*) there was a machine very much like an outside Irish car; and overtopping her long loose ears, sat a lad with an iron spike in his hand. The huge creature knelt, cushions having been daintily placed for her knees; we scrambled up a ladder, and took our seats—two and two, "to make the balance true;" placed the important basket between us; the mountain slowly heaved, and we were off. Maggie was delightful. She took her way direct cross-country through the tangled jungle, picking her way with a wonderfully nimble tread over the low thorny bushes, and putting aside with her trunk every larger obstacle. She carefully avoided taking us below any trees where the branches could interfere with our heads, and altogether behaved in the most discreet and sensible way. We found she had been long in the service, and was a practised hand when shikar parties were abroad.

Another ten miles' ride brought us to the travellers' bungalow, which is most beautifully situated on an elevation commanding the river, and the entrance to the cliffs. We rested a little, had our lunch, and then set out in a boat to explore.

The scene from the river is exceedingly striking, and quite unique, from the wonderful white marble rocks which rise sheer from the water some two hundred feet. There is a kind of chasm a mile and a half long, which winds and twists, presenting new views of loveliness at every turn. The water is pure, of a dark green shade, and very deep, and reflects the picturesque forms of the towering rocks overhead in the most striking way. In some places the channel narrows until you see nothing but the wall-like cliffs, and the deep blue heavens over your head; and then again it widens, showing lovely bits of country, with trees and shrubs fringing the outer margin of the rock-bound river, while now and then a little island-rock of fantastic form rears itself from the deep green water, direct in your path. Some higher portions of the marble masses look weather-beaten and soiled; but others are polished and pure, and lie in billowy whiteness, like wreaths of fresh-fallen snow. It is altogether one of the most lovely and romantic scenes you can picture. The natives have a legend that "Indra" forced this channel open for the pent-up waters of the Nerbudda to flow out; and they say the footprints of Indra's elephant are to be seen on the rocks; but I fancy only by the initiated, for I cannot say we found them out. There is one place they call "the Monkeys'

Leap," which is not very wide, but I think it would take all the agility of the chattering, grinning, impudent little things we saw around in myriads to clear it. As we rowed back to the bungalow, we saw a small crocodile enjoying himself on a cool, polished marble slab; he tumbled lazily into the water, as we ventured to intrude on his privacy by rowing a little closer. On the summit of a conical little hill, beautifully wooded, which rises close to the river, there is a small Hindu temple, which we visited. It commands magnificent views; and we sat here enjoying the beauty, in a cool bit of shade we discovered, until it was time to summon our friend Maggie again, and the sun was low enough for our return. We found the lorry and the men where we had left them; and having said adieu to Maggie, we sped back to the hotel, which we reached about nine.

There is an interesting mission of the Church of England here, presided over by Mr. and Mrs. Stewart. Mr. Champion is absent. We called at the mission-house at once, and were most warmly received, although the family are in great sorrow.

There is no chaplain at present. A nice young clergyman who came out with us came here; but he has been early called from his earthly work to the service of the upper sanctuary. We liked him very much. He was not High Church, as so many of the chaplains are now, and used to alternate with Dr. M. in holding the little service in the saloon every forenoon. Mr. Stewart does all the chaplain's work along with his own. Dr. M. preached on Sunday to the soldiers, and had two meetings besides in the cantonments—one at six in the morning, and another in the cool of the evening; and it was delightful to see them crowded with soldiers. Major R., who works much among the men, organized all these meetings.

The mission schools aré most interesting. Mr. Stewart gathered in more than a thousand poor starving children during the famine: but many were too far gone to be saved; and others, when they got food, were seized with cholera and other diseases, and were carried off in scores. These are some of the scenes which break a missionary's heart.

There is a famous jail here, which is also a school of industry, where a great many of the captured Thugs are confined. We have gone all over it with its most intelligent and kind superintendent. I had never seen Thugs before, and was surprised to find them rather exceptionally mild and meek, instead of the monsters of depravity one would naturally expect. I questioned a fine old Thug, with a most benevolent countenance, how he used to do the strangling; and, to my horror, he seized the throat of a youngster sitting by, and proceeded to show off his sleight of hand at his particular art. The poor boy looked awfully frightened; and it gave me such a shock I hardly recovered it all day. It is done in a moment; and in giving the specimen twist to the poor lad, the old Thug stopped just in time.

SEONEE, *November 16.*

We left our quarters at Jubbulpore early this morning, and are now fairly *en route* for Chindwara, which lies rather to the west, and quite off the beaten track of travellers. Our object is to visit Mr. and Mrs. Dawson, who have settled at this station, and commenced the first mission of our Church to the Gonds, one of the aboriginal tribes of India.

We have come eighty miles to-day, and have made a most charming journey in an old friend—a dāk gharree. Our start was, as usual, amusing enough. In half an hour from Jubbulpore we came to the Nerbudda, here a good broad stream.

The banks presented a busy scene. On both sides there were long strings of bullock-carts loaded with cotton-sacks and all sorts of merchandise, waiting to be ferried across on a flat, which was doing its part diligently; but it would have taken twenty flats to convey across all the vehicles and people who were patiently waiting their turn. There seemed to be enormous traffic,—which will be absorbed by the railway when it is fully opened. I ardently wished we had waited for that happy event, for the delays were inconceivable—first, for the flat; and next for bullocks strong enough to drag our heavy machine through the deep sand on the shore, and up the steep acclivity; for to this work our poor little horses were quite unequal. At length they came, and they were buffaloes!—great, clumsy, good creatures, which rescued us at once. There were large herds of buffaloes enjoying a bath in the river, with only the tips of their noses showing above the water.

After this, we got on delightfully. Our kind friend Mr. Monteath, the Director-General of the Post-Offices, had written to some of his people on the line to look after our comfort. So we had excellent horses, and every sort of civility from the officials.

As we approached the travellers' bungalow at Seonee—one of the most comfortable and best appointed we have been in—a long row of lighted apartments, opening off the wide verandah, showed occupation. It is marvellous how many travellers there seem to be on this road. But clearly Bombay is to be the port for all India; it is so much the nearest to England.

A bullock gharree in process of packing stood in front of the bungalow as we drew up, which announced the agreeable fact that somebody was starting, and that a room, consequently, would soon be vacant. I therefore made a dart at the door of that whence the boxes were issuing; asked two ladies within if I might enter and wait; they politely acquiesced; and not five minutes after, another party arrived. But possession is every point here; and I am sorry to say the new arrivals had to spend the night in the verandah—though, as they were gentlemen, it did not so much matter.

My tired husband had to start for the village at once, in search of means by which we could continue our journey to Chindwara. In an hour he returned, having been partially successful; and then we had our dinner, which we did full justice to, after our twelve hours' drive.

XXX.

The Gonds.

MISSION-HOUSE, CHINDWARA, *November 19.*

HERE we are, with our kind friends Mr. and Mrs. Dawson, quite settled, and tolerably rested, after a rather adventurous journey of more than thirty hours' duration.

We have certainly had varied experiences in modes of travel. Dr. M. returned to the bungalow at Seonee, believing that all was satisfactorily arranged with the head-man of the village for our transit to this place. He said there was no such thing as a palki to be had; but he made fair promises as to doolies, and engaged that a sufficient number of bearers should be forthcoming, and ready to start in the early morning. As there were absolutely no roads, and no horses to be had, this was the only mode of conveyance possible. Mr. Dawson, however, had kindly promised to send his horse half-way to meet us. Dr. M. set off at daylight to see what progress had been made as to the constructing of doolies and collecting the men; but it was past ten o'clock before we actually started. A palki belonging to an old Brahman, gaily painted with gods and goddesses, but with a very rickety bottom, was at last brought for me, for which we paid a fancy price. A dooli of very simple construction was extemporized for Dr. M. This was a common native charpoy, or cot, with the feet up, slung from a stout bamboo, and carried on the shoulders of the men. It had the advantage over my conveyance, however, of being strong. I had no sooner got in than the cane bottom began to crack ominously, and I had the pleasant sensation that at any moment I might drop through,—a catastrophe which seemed so imminent before we had proceeded a mile, that we had to call a halt, and send back to the village for some strong rope. Of course, there were more of those exasperating delays, and more noise from the babel voices of our twenty-four men; but at length I was well tied in, the frail concern was bound up and bandaged in every direction, and we did actually start.

It was no wonder, after all this, that the shadows were beginning to lengthen over the solitary wastes which we had traversed all day, and the sun was near his setting, when we arrived at the half-way house, where Mr. Dawson's horse and man were waiting. All were dreadfully hungry. The men said they must have two hours to cook and rest—no unreasonable request after such hard work. We had come twenty-two miles; but there were twenty-four ahead, and it was rapidly getting dark. The country was very rough, and abounded in nullahs, and there were certainly possibilities as to wild animals in such a thorough jungle. But here was only a very miserable little village. That most useful refuge for the poor wayfarer, which a parental Government so kindly provides—a travellers' bungalow—was not to be found in those remote regions. What was to be done? My husband decreed that we must stay where we were all night. It seemed to me a dreadful look-out, and I am afraid I rather murmured; but, as usual, he was right. There was a police-station, and, most happily, there was a schoolroom, though it was only a rough sort of shed. Into this asylum our doolies were carried. But it did look an eerie place to sleep in. The walls went up only half-way to the black rafters, which, I saw at a glance, were the abode of my special horror—bats and rats; and the wind *soughed* in, mournful and chill, at the openings. You will be surprised, then, to hear that we spent rather a pleasant evening. Indian travellers are always prepared for emergencies. A certain tin box, which fitted in nicely at my feet in the palki, was produced; and therefrom came stores of tea, sugar, bread, a tin of hunter's meat, and, though last, not least, candles, and a tiny travelling candlestick. We bought a small brown chatty; for to borrow one would have simply been to pollute it, and so unfit it for the owner's use. This was soon filled with water, and set to boil on a fire of sticks in the yard. A most polite chowkeedar, or policeman, helped us greatly. He gathered the sticks, made the fire, and brought us some delicious milk. The top of my palki made a famous table, covered with a clean napkin; and I do not think the daintiest repast was ever more highly relished.

The moon had risen gloriously, and shone brightly in, destroying the horrid gloom of the place. There was a small verandah without, which soon filled with village people, when they found their visitor was a padre saheb, and that he wished for an audience. As I performed my little operations within, I heard a most animated talk going on; and very soon an old familiar sound reached my ears, which seemed to bring with it a dream of other days. They were talking in Marathi! The rough Marathi sounded as sweet as the accents of one's mother tongue. There were two Poona Brahmans, intelligent and very loquacious; the schoolmaster, also, a venerable man, with a clean shaved face and large red turban; his young assistant; a few villagers; and some bright young boys;—while our small army of bearers encamped round the fire in the yard, listening most attentively as the missionary seized the opportunity of telling them the glad tidings of salvation, which some of them said they had never heard before. Thus, the evening passed rapidly away. Our men stretched themselves in a ring round the fire, wrapped in their dark blankets. I crept into my little sanctuary (the palki), barricaded it thoroughly, and armed myself against contingencies with my husband's walking-stick. Very soon there was a sharp, scraping sound at the foot of my bed, where the tin of meat had been; and using the stick with effect, I soon saw a huge black creature hop nimbly across the sleeping form close by; but as there was no interruption of the quiet breathing, I thought it best to take no further notice. There was plenty of other company besides the rats, which kept dropping upon us from the roof. Speak of mosquitoes and such minor plagues!

Before dawn the tea process was repeated, accompanied by some very good chowpatties, or *scones*, which our friend the chowkeedar had made for us unasked. He and the good old schoolmaster turned out to see us start; and after many salaams from the kind village people, we were once more *en route.*

How lovely is the Indian dawn! The light seems to come much more gradually than it departs, when "at one stride comes the dark." The tender lines of light steal up softly along the horizon. First a pale pinkish gray; then a delicate lilac, which fast deepens to a darker pink; and then the rosy flush mounts and rapidly spreads itself, until the heavens and the earth are filled with the glory of the rising and rejoicing sun. It was well worth having endured the disagreeables of the night, to enjoy the perfect peacefulness and beauty of the morning.

The country was hardly pretty—yet not unpleasing, from the green of the overspreading jungle. Travelling in this way, one sometimes wonders where the millions of India hide themselves; the population seems to be so scattered, the villages so few and far between, and the face of the country so given over to jungle. Cattle seem almost more plentiful than people. What villages we passed were pretty and clean; the huts fairly embedded in the trailers of the gourd and pumpkin plants, which freely clambered over the thatched roofs. This would account, I dare say, for the few villages which were visible, the houses being hidden away in the heart of this abundant greenery.

As it grew towards the afternoon, we came into regions where there was more cultivation. We soon noticed some clumps and lines of fine forest-trees ahead; and then, here and there, a white bungalow gleamed out from the green. Presently there were roads, and other indications that we had got within reach of civilization; in short, we had arrived at Chindwāra. Our poor men rejoiced, for they were very tired; but I knew a kid to make merry with when we arrived would put it all right.

My husband cantered on, and I soon got into the wide streets of a flourishing, pretty, little native town. It is a good deal more than a village, and is beautifully clean and tidy, the houses being quite dazzling with whitewash. All the people rushed to their doors to gaze at the mem saheb, and the palki so gaily embellished with the god Gunputi's twisted nose. The first thing I noticed was that the houses opened to the street, and the women went out and in with natural freedom, and that they looked bright and happy, as villagers do in our own land. Some of them made a most polite salaam to me as I passed; the children clapped their hands and shouted; the dogs barked; when suddenly we turned into a large compound, and a friendly hand seized mine, and kind voices called out, "Welcome to Chindwära!"

"Where is Chindwāra, and what do you there?" I have no doubt you will ask.

Well, Chindwāra is in the Central Provinces, and stands on an elevated plateau, surrounded by mountains a little distance away. The country about is pretty and well-wooded, especially close by the station; and the climate seems delicious. The place stands so high that it affords a delightful change from the plains, and forms a kind of sanitarium for Nagpore and the districts round, whence people come in search of health, or it may be of rest and recreation.

This pleasant station lies in Gondwana—the country of the Gonds, one of the aboriginal tribes of India; and it has been chosen as a good position for a mission to these people. This is now established in connection with the Free Church Mission in Central India; and is presided over by the Rev. Mr. and Mrs. Dawson. Our object, then, is to see this interesting race, and the mission established for their benefit; to judge of the prospect of success among them; and also to bring friendly greeting to the missionaries, and assurances of sympathy from the Church at home. Mr. Dawson seems overjoyed to meet my husband, he being the first missionary brother that has as yet been able to pay him and his work a visit.

There is an excellent catechist associated with Mr. Dawson in the mission—Mr. Samuel Hardie, who is devoted to his "beloved Gonds," as he calls them. He is a native of Madras, and of Tamil extraction—a simple-hearted, good man.

It is not yet three years since the mission was begun; and what has been accomplished is as yet little more than breaking up the fallow ground. Mr. Dawson has had to be his own pioneer. In the first place, the Gondi language had to be mastered without the help of grammar or dictionary; for this jungle tongue is still almost an unwritten language, except that the Rev. Mr. Hislop of Nagpore was able to take down from the lips of a minstrel a long legendary Gondi poem, which after his death was published by Sir Richard Temple. The two labourers have had to pick it up word by word patiently, by converse with the people; and in this they have both made great progress, for they now preach in it. Mr. Dawson has begun to compile a Gondi grammar, and is now translating the Gospel of St. John.

While this process of learning the language was going on, they preached in Hindi; but Mr. Dawson says that when he began to address the people in their own tongue, they became much more friendly, and more ready to listen to his message.

Very few Gonds reside in the native town; but their villages lie thickly scattered in all the country round Chindwāra. In a radius of six miles there are seventy Gond villages, containing a population of five thousand. This Mr. Dawson calls "his parish"—a pretty extensive one. He and Samuel spend four mornings of every week in visiting these villages in succession. Their inhabitants, however, are not wholly Gonds: there is a considerable mixture of Hindus, and these of low caste generally; and Hindi, or, farther south, Marathi, is understood by the Gonds nearly as well as their own tongue.

The whole Gond people number a million and a half; and the districts over which they are scattered would nearly equal in extent Great Britain and Ireland. They are a very ancient people, comprehending several tribes, and seem to have been the most important and powerful of all the aboriginal races. They alone of these races seem to have had a political history. They founded dynasties, and had what may be called kingdoms of their own. There were, from first to last, four Gond kingdoms; and there is still a Rajah, acknowledged as head by the tribe, who lives in Nagpore, and is a descendant of the Rajah of Deoghur, who was one of their greatest men. He is, however, a Mohammadan in religion.*

Some rather remarkable architectural remains, chiefly of ruined forts, are still to be seen, and attest their former greatness. Ancient Gondwana covered a vast extent of territory, and included most of the country which is now comprised in the Central Provinces. The final fall of their power took place under the Marathas, more than a century ago. Now the people are thinly scattered: they often live intermixed with Hindus. It is remarkable, however, that religiously they have not been more powerfully affected by Hinduism and Mohammadanism. Their religion is a kind of demon-worship. They are exceedingly ignorant and superstitious; and being afraid of the bhoots, or spirits, which they believe to be powerful and malevolent, they propitiate them by sacrificial offerings of animals. One of the most important of their festivals is held just before the monsoon sets in, when they sow their crops; and it must be celebrated in the jungles, quite out of sight of their dwellings. They set up stones to be worshipped, and even daub them with red paint like the Hindus, though rightly they have no idol-worship and no temples. They do set up these stones, however, both at the entrance to their villages and in the groves where

* The entire number of Gonds may, according to Colonel Dalton, amount perhaps to three millions; of whom about a million and a half are in the Central Provinces. Many Gonds, in Bengal especially, have become Hindus in religion; others have become Musulmans; others cling to their ancestral demon-worship; while others intermingle this with more or less of Hinduism.—*Edit.*

the festivals take place; the biggest stone being understood to represent the *burra deo*, or great god. The sāg-tree is considered sacred; also the mohwa, from which an intoxicating liquor is made: and their sacrificial rites and chief festivals are conducted where these abound. Another of their great festivals occurs after their crops are gathered in, and is a kind of "harvest home." They do not seem to have proper priests; but there is a tribe which furnishes religious teachers, who preside at ceremonies and festivals, and offer the sacrifices.

There are no infant marriages among the Gonds. When a young couple have agreed to unite their fate, the young man serves his desired father-in-law for his wife, as Jacob served Laban for Rachel; only in this case it is for a shorter period. This is considered as betrothal; and at the end of the stipulated time of service, which may be from one to three years, the wedding takes place, accompanied by ceremonies a great deal too numerous and elaborate for me to describe or remember. The day is fixed by the elders of the village, after a due consideration, of course, of lucky seasons and good omens; a bower or canopy is erected, under which the happy pair stand, and here the nuptial ceremonies are performed. Instead of the bridegroom going to the house of the bride, however, it is etiquette that she goes to him; and, moreover, it is she who promises to "support, cherish, and protect!" The chief part of the ceremony is when the officiating priest ties part of the garments of each together (as we join hands), which symbolizes the union which now exists between them as a married pair. The whole finishes off with feasting, dancing, and revelry.

They have also numerous funeral ceremonies, along with feasting and sacrificing. They offer to the corpse a fowl or goat; which then is cooked with rice, and eaten by the relations assembled to mourn for the dead. The ghost of the dead is afterwards propitiated, and has offerings made to it for one year.

November 23.

We have just returned from one of the Gond villages, and have had a wonderfully interesting excursion. Long before daybreak, Mrs. D. had a comfortable cup of tea ready for us, and we started,—the gentlemen on ponies, and I in a dooli. I should have ridden also, had there been a third horse, for this is the true way to speed over these broken jungly plains. Our friend Samuel had preceded us on his little tattoo (pony), to collect the village people together. We passed over the same sort of country we had come through in getting here—not pretty, and yet rather pleasing from the clumps of trees and the numerous little fields full of ripening crops. The six miles were soon accomplished, and we entered a large village consisting of a good wide regular street, with trees here and there, affording a pleasant shade. The houses looked clean and neat, with small verandahs or courts in front of the better ones; and altogether it was a very well-to-do looking place.

This is, then, a Gond village; and almost exclusively so, for there are only a few Hindu families in it, and these very low-caste—dealers in oil. It forms a great contrast to all Hindu villages I have ever seen, where the houses are always set down anyhow. This straight wide street differs also very much from the arrangement of a Santal or a Kole village.

The Santal villages which lie round Pachumba, the headquarters of our Mission to the Santals of Bengal, are composed of a series of small enclosures arranged very oddly, each one containing four or five mud-built huts, which face inward to the court. These are surrounded by a tall fence made of bamboo posts, firmly and thickly interlaced with branches of trees, on which the leaves still hang, brown and crumpling. These enclosures generally swarm with women and children, chickens, and often litters of pigs. I was the first European woman who had been seen in one of the villages we visited; the women were exceedingly astonished at me, and asked if this was another sort of man. I dare say I looked gigantic in my white morning robe. They were also exceedingly amused at my light-coloured hair. One bright merry damsel pointed it out to another; and then they clapped their hands and laughed immoderately, and I laughed in company. They entreated that I would pull it down, that they might see it better. My watch is always a source of wonderment. The Gond women this morning looked at it in great astonishment. One was so awe-struck at the mysterious sound and motion, that she put her hands together, looked up to heaven, and exclaimed, "God is great!" The Santal women are decidedly less civilized than the Gond women; many are tattooed liberally, in most elaborate patterns, and all wear an extraordinary amount of ornaments. I counted eleven thick bangles of brass and zinc on one arm, nearly as many on the other, and two thick anklets on each foot. Fortunately the wearer was a large strong woman, or she could scarcely have carried such a weight. Hardly a ray of light has yet penetrated the minds of these village women, whether Gond or Santal; but they are open to receive it,—*empty*, so to speak. They are not filled with prejudice and error; they believe in bad spirits and *bhoots;* they have a sort of idea of the Supreme, but none of a Saviour, and hardly any of the need of salvation.

But, to return to the congregation we found waiting to receive us this morning. The Gonds are employed chiefly in cultivation; but here about sixty had assembled, having left their fields when they heard of the padre saheb's visit. The two head-men of the village, both Gonds, were present, and a great many women; indeed, the women were the decided majority; and the number of children was truly marvellous, who owed to nature all the garb they wore. Each child had a string tied tightly round the stomach—with what object I could not discover; beads, also, and charms to avert the evil-eye in abundance,—but this was all. It is quite easy to distinguish the Gond from the Hindu women, the clothes and features are so different. The latter wear coloured *sarees*—a sort of sheet-like garment. The former dress much like the men: a piece of cloth is wound round the waist, caught up between the legs; and another piece, like a small sheet, envelops the upper part of the person. As usual, the women are fond of ornaments, and wear bangles, armlets, anklets, and necklaces made of brass, zinc, and glass.

The Gonds, in appearance, are pretty much like the other wild tribes we have seen; stalwart, well-knit figures, dark-complexioned, with broad features and thick lips. They are *not* handsome, yet certainly not ugly. In character they are, like other aboriginal people, truthful and honest, but are not quite so merry and light-hearted as the Santals and Koles. They are industrious, and also very manly, being capital *shikarees*, or hunters; but, unhappily, the vice which clings to all other wild people is very prevalent among them,—they are exceedingly fond of drink.

Our visits to the villages have been repeated nearly every morning, and it would be impossible to tell how deeply interested and moved I get over these simple Gond people. They know very little; but they seem so willing to be taught! The truth must be broken up for them into fragments; literally "line upon line, precept on precept." Samuel does it admirably, with the most expressive gesticulation. What they comprehend best are simple illustrations taken from everyday life; like that of sowing the seed, taking medicine to make you well, and such like.

When the gentlemen have finished preaching, I usually gather the women about me; and it is wonderful how well I make myself understood in Hindi. They seem eager to hear; and generally, when an idea fixes itself in their minds, they look up with much brightness, and repeat it over and over. One poor woman on the outskirts of the group I noticed to-day particularly. She spoke little, but drew her *chudder* (sheet) over her head, clasped her hands together, and put them up to her forehead, and now and then cast an appealing look upward to the sky, as if she realized the unseen presence of the Father. When I at length spoke to her directly, a tear rolled down her face, and she said she did not know much about being a sinner, but she knew about being sorrowful, and she needed a Father's love and care. The *bhoots* only hurt them, and are cruel; but if Jesus had come down from His home in heaven for the sake of poor creatures such as she, He must be good and kind, and would help them. The *love* of God is what touches and opens these poor hearts; and this thought is familiar among the people of these villages already, as well as the name of Christ. Dr. M. has already taught some of them to repeat a short, simple prayer, by making them repeat it word by word after him; and they have promised in this village to meet every Sunday morning and repeat this prayer together.

In worldly circumstances they seem rather prosperous and comfortable. The women carried me off in triumph to see their houses; and having entered one, I was obliged to go into all, or the poor things would have been vexed. The dwellings are all alike, with two rooms divided by a most peculiar arrangement of mud erections, like presses without doors, where the grain is kept dry and safe from vermin. The rooms were wonderfully clean, well whitewashed, but with hardly any furniture, except some brilliant brass platters and drinking-cups, burnished like gold. Life seems to be a very simple matter among these poor people. In one house an old woman, with silvery hair, and absolutely toothless, welcomed us with great dignity; and then fairly broke down and sobbed, crying out, "Oh, my husband—my old man!" And going into the court, we found the patriarch of the family, a very aged man, lying in the sun, that he might be warm. He was a remarkably powerful man, but the sands of life were low, and he had evidently lain down to die. The grief of his wife was most touching to see. Alas! they are of those who "sorrow without hope." Their ideas as to a future state are altogether dark and cheerless.

We bade adieu to our kind friends Mr. and Mrs. D., and my little friend Tom, the child of the house, on the 29th; and I am quite sure I shall never forget our delightful visit to the mission-house at Chindwāra. Mr. D. and Samuel gave us a kindly convoy to our first halting-place; Samuel continuing with us another stage or two, until his brother Joseph arrived, kindly sent to meet us with their bullock gharree by Mr. and Mrs. Cooper of Nagpore; for now we were bound for this advanced post on our route to Bombay.

We first made the very adventurous descent of a ghaut, where the road, or track rather, was full of breaks and landslips, and overhung alarming precipices, which it made one dizzy at least to look over. But our brave little bullocks behaved admirably, picking their steps with great circumspection. The beauty of the jungle-clothed steeps was wonderful, and the views very grand of the distant hills, covered with forest and low shrubbery in all the lovely colouring of the early autumn. We passed many groves of the sāg-tree, which the Gonds worship. It is a kind of teak, and has long, pointed, pretty leaves. Also the mohwa-tree, which is popularly said to intoxicate if you even lie under it. At the foot of this descent we got into better roads, and for the next three days wended our leisurely way through the plains, which looked rather bare and brown when compared with the rich green of the valley of the Ganges. We halted at night at the travellers' bungalows, which are placed at convenient distances apart. A keen sense of gratitude is always associated in my mind with these bungalows and their modest appliances. It is so pleasant, after a long day's march, to arrive in the cool of the evening, and find rest and food and a night's shelter. We looked out for "king cotton" as we came along; and though we did not traverse what are actually the cotton districts, yet we passed by many fields, and plucked some branches of the tall shrub with its ivy-shaped leaves and bursting pods of soft, downy white. The condition of the people has much improved since the rise in the price of this export. The cultivator has become rich; he has better food and clothing; and his wife, instead of zinc and brass, now wears silver and gold ornaments. This state of matters is of course resented by the Brahmans, who say, "Every cooly now takes to dressing like a Brahman." One is thankful for everything which tends to equalize the classes and interfere with caste, and also for whatever helps to lower the pride and arrogance of these pretentious "gods of the earth."

NAGPORE.

We have spent one of the most delightful weeks I can remember with our dear friends Mr. and Mrs. Cooper of the

Free Church Mission here. Mr. and Mrs. Whitton are also in the mission-house; so we are a considerable party. But to this Mrs. Cooper seems accustomed. One evening some American missionaries arrived; the next a German came in; but though all may be perfect strangers they are cheerfully and hospitably received, and when bedrooms fail tents are pitched *ad libitum* in the compound.

We have been wholly engrossed in seeing the admirable mission-work conducted by our friends, and have not done much sight-seeing outside.

We have been greatly interested in the Institution,—which is a first-rate school, where high-class Christian education in English is given,—also in the vernacular schools, and the native church; but what I have chiefly enjoyed seeing is the female boarding-school under Mrs. Cooper's charge. On the day we arrived I noticed a good substantial whitewashed building standing in the compound, close to the mission-house; this, on inquiry, I found to be the girls' schoolroom; and a most pleasant room it is, large, airy, and cool. I soon made acquaintance with the children, of whom there are about fifty, of all ages; and what is peculiarly interesting to us is, that the head-mistress and her assistant, who is also her sister, are old protegées and pupils of our own, whom we trained in a similar institution in Poona. It is so cheering to see them now, so usefully employed, and so thoroughly respected. I am much struck with the happy looks of the children, they are so bright, and merry, and intelligent. The whole family from the mission-house, the orphan children, and, indeed, the whole compound, meet in the schoolroom for morning and evening prayers; and the sight then is a beautiful one. Three very small children first sing together a simple hymn, "Suffer little children to come unto Me," which we picked out of an American hymn-book years ago at Poona; then little Jamie, a wee boy, comes to his perch on Mr. Cooper's knee—which is his by right, he being the youngest child in the school. It is very droll to see how steadily and sedately he comes and scrambles up at the appointed moment, as if afraid he should be superseded. Tommy is another foundling boy, and all the rest are girls. It is quite beautiful to see Mr. C.'s love to the children, and their complete trust in him. One expects this love in a woman, but it is peculiarly nice in a man; and Mr. C. is thoroughly the father and friend of the whole Mission, while Mrs. C. is indeed the mother. One of the girls is a Gond; of the *Raj*-Gonds, as she told me herself, or the kingly tribe. She is as bright and intelligent, Mrs. C. says, as any girl in the school. There are two Gond lads, too, in the compound.

This Nagpore Mission owes its origin very much to Sir William Hill, who most generously gave upwards of £2600 to help to found it. Its first missionary was the late much lamented Mr. Hislop, an accomplished naturalist as well as a zealous missionary. My husband accompanied him and Mrs. H. when they came here in 1846 to commence the Mission. Travelling was a very different matter in those days from what it is now; and it took the party six weeks to get here from Bombay.

Mr. Hislop did signal service to the Government in the Mutiny time, when matters looked so threatening for Nagpore and all the Deccan. A Mohammadan who knew of the designs and movements of the mutineers, had a son in the mission-school. This man and his son, anxious about the fate of their friend and teacher, stole out of the city at night, came to Mr. Hislop, and informed him of the plan to massacre all the

Europeans on a certain day. Mr. H. at once communicated with the authorities, who immediately took the needful precautions; and thus, under God, the missionary was the means of saving all this part of India. We saw the fort at Sitabuldi, where the Europeans took refuge at that terrible time. We also visited Kampti, the large military station about ten miles away.

Our charming visit came too soon to a close. On the last morning we met at seven for breakfast, and then had the usual delightful little service in the schoolroom, and heard for the last time the three little lambs sing their sweet, "Suffer little children to come unto Me." Then dear Viramā and Maggie (our old Poona friends), and the girls, and the dear little ones, even the servants, all gathered round to see us depart; a number of the native Christians also came to say good-bye; and soon we were speeding away towards the western coast.

We got to the Thull Ghaut in the early morning, and took about an hour and a half to make the descent. This incline is indeed a marvellous work of engineering skill. We shall see the Bhore Ghaut, which is still more wonderful, when we go to Poona.

What a vision of loveliness the ghauts were! A thin blue veil of mist hung over the more distant ranges; nearer, the giant forms arose, some pointed, fantastic, and jagged, while others lay in beautiful billowy undulations, and green table-land; and then, as we got farther down, the slopes grew lovely with wood and low jungle, and broke into dells and gorges and deep ravines, at the bottom of which, far down, pretty little streams showed like silver threads, which, in the monsoon, would be turbulent torrents, noisy and brawling enough.

Thus we creep along the wonderful incline, skirting precipices, over which we seem to hang in mid-air, and gazing down into depths which are lost in jungle. And so we descend toward the beautiful sea. The low, rough plain of the Konkan stretches before us, waving with its groves of countless palms. We speed on, and *there* are the palm-crowned heights of the island of Salsette, with the deep blue ocean beyond going away to the horizon; then there is the picturesque little hill with the white bungalow on the top—all that remains of "Sion Fort;" then there is the long stretch which carries us over low flats formerly redeemed from the sea; and then the temple of Mahaluxmi, at the entrance of the long shore-drive by "the breach;" and then there is Malabar Hill, stretching away in its beautiful point far into the sea, crowned with white bungalows, which gleam out from stately palms and other trees of tropical growth; and the long strip of land called Colaba, going away to the rocks. And here, on the left, is the glorious harbour, with its picturesque islands—Elephanta and the rest—the shipping, and the white sails of the fishing-boats, and the blue, blue sea. The familiar, beautiful scene,—awakening so many fond memories!

And now the station is reached; and here, on the platform, waiting to greet us, is our beloved friend, Dr. Wilson, without whose presence Bombay would not be itself. It is not a dream. We are arrived once more in Bombay!

When the last page of this little work is leaving the press we hear of the death of this venerable man. Dr. Wilson of Bombay has passed to his rest!

He had early and heartily devoted himself to a missionary life, and left Scotland for the East in 1828. He has occupied a most conspicuous place in India for the long space of forty-seven years.

Dr. Wilson's mind was marked by great comprehensiveness and energy.

He read much, and seemed to recollect all he read; so that he had accumulated a wonderful mass of knowledge. Few men knew more about India as it was; and perhaps no man knew so much about India as it is. In studying the great heathen systems of religion with which he was chiefly brought in contact—Hinduism and Parsiism—he had consulted the original authorities in Sanskrit and Zend. His work on "The Parsi Religion," published in 1842—at a time when the critical study of Zend had just commenced under the great French scholar Burnouf—gives evidence of careful and conscientious research; although no doubt the investigation of the Zendavesta has been greatly advanced during the last thirty-three years by such Continental scholars as Westergaard, Spiegel, and Haug.

Nor was he by any means a mere student; he was also a man of much practical sagacity. We need not wonder, then, that on Indian questions his opinion had very great weight both with Government and the public.

What is yet more remarkable, no man was ever more popular with the native community. Though he was ever anxious to press on all his native friends the claims and offers of the gospel of salvation, yet he enjoyed the profound respect of all classes of Orientals,—Hindus, Parsis, and Mohammadans. To all of them, as much as to Europeans, he was ever most kindly, accessible, and obliging.

Long will the well-remembered form of Dr. Wilson continue to be missed by the inhabitants of Bombay.

Quis desiderio sit pudor aut modus
Tam cari capitis?—*Edit.*

XXXI.

A Few Parting Words.

THERE are many recollections of our last residence in India which I should like much to have added, had it been possible to do so.

It would be delightful to speak of our sojourn in beautiful Simla—which extended over full six months—and of our work and pleasant life there; but the record of this would take a book to itself. At all events, this visit, and a subsequent one we paid to the hills at the invitation of our dear friends Mr. and Mrs. Aitchison, have furnished us with a lasting store of the most happy and delightful memories.

I should like also to tell of our pleasant connection with the "Simla Union Church," which my husband was able to organize, and which it was his great privilege to minister to for a season, and then to hand over to our dear friend Mr. Fordyce, its present excellent pastor.

Most pleasant, indeed, is the memory of the Christian intercourse we had with many dear friends at Simla. The friendships which we were privileged to form there, are many of them deathless.

There are other things, too, one would delight to speak of; the hill people, for instance, who interested me much. Those who live in the neighbourhood of Simla certainly took me by surprise, from their Hindu, or what is called "Aryan," look. They have not the features of the wilder tribes. They are fair in complexion, intelligent, and bright in expression, and seem to be light-hearted and merry. Unhappily, they are rather dirty in their habits and persons; though not nearly so much so as the people who live further in the interior, and who have a Mongolian aspect. The women are altogether interesting and picturesque: they are exceedingly handsome, wonderfully fair, open, frank and natural in manner, and yet perfectly modest.

And then, in recalling this glorious region, who would not like to speak of all the surpassing wonders and beauties of the natural world? The giant mountains, crowned with their perpetual snows; the dark depths of stupendous precipices; the rocks and clefts, and dizzy steeps, and towering peaks; the little knolls, also, and slopes carpeted with beauty; and the distant terraced little fields, glowing in the gold and crimson colour of new and strange cultivation. Then the forests of gigantic pines, or deodars, in their light, wavy green, or dark cedars and "excelsior" fir; or the gorgeous tree-rhododendron, with its masses of brilliant blossom. Then the whole family of trailing, interlacing, many-shaded green things which delight to climb, with their lovely flowers in crimson, canary colour, and every hue of the rainbow; and the wealth of the fern-world, from the tall bracken to the lowly, delicate lycopodium, which clothes every rock, and bank, and old tree-trunk with loveliness; and the inexhaustible treasures in wild-flowers, and garden-flowers which grow wild—gloxinias, bigonias, and dahlias, in the wildest profusion, which spread all over the hills as soon as the mists gather, and the rains come. Then the no less wonderful cloud-world, which gives abundant occupation to any one who cares to study it and note its ever-changeful moods, until it settles to its cold-weather serene expanse, with hardly a cloud like a man's hand to break it, of deep, intensest blue. All this one would like to expatiate upon; but who could picture the Himalaya in a page? No; "the abode of snow," and the abode of so much else that is supremely grand and beautiful, must be passed by,—at all events, for the present.

I must also leave our return to Calcutta, with our busy life and absorbing work during a three years' sojourn in the mission-house in Cornwallis Square, while we watched the developing of different schemes for the advancement of the Mission.

Pre-eminent among these was the successful establishing of the new mission to the Santals at Pachumba, under our friend Dr. Templeton. This has been marked by steady and most encouraging progress, until it promises speedily to become one of the most important branches of the Free Church Mission in India. But it is not necessary to say more of it, or of the progress of the gospel generally among the Santals, as this has been done lately by our friend Dr. Graham, in his valuable little book.*

I may also refer to what is perhaps the crowning joy to me in the recollections of our last sojourn in India—namely, the planning and commencement of a new building, to be the centre of all our work among the females in Calcutta. Happily this building is now not only completed, but occupied. There is accommodation in it for additional lady-teachers, and a "Home" ready for their reception.

When the Lieutenant-Governor of Bengal (Sir George Campbell) did us the honour to lay the foundation-stone of this build-

* "The Gospel in Santhalistan."

ing,* he gave strong expression to the sentiment that purely secular education is quite unsuited to the women of India,—surely a weighty declaration, as coming from a high official, and an enthusiastic friend of popular education. But the education which Government gives, and is pledged to give, is purely secular. It follows, therefore, that this momentous work ought to be prosecuted with double, ay, tenfold energy, by missionary Churches and Societies.

Of the out-stations occupied by the Bengal Mission of the Free Church I saw two, Chinsurah and Mahanād.

We paid a charming visit to the former, when it was under the supervision of the Rev. Mr. and Mrs. Beaumont, now at Poona. Some of the names of our most honoured missionaries have been connected with Chinsurah; and this gave additional interest to our visit. It is a beautiful station, lying about twenty-five miles north of Calcutta, on the right bank of the Hooghly. It was formerly a Dutch settlement, and a place of some pretension.

We were greatly interested and pleased with all we saw of the mission-work, especially the Institution, which was examined by Dr. M., assisted by our friend Mr. Mowat,† who had accompanied us on our expedition. The lads did admirably. There were upwards of five hundred on the roll.

Our friends took us to see Bandel, an interesting place in the neighbourhood, where there is a Portuguese church—the oldest Christian place of worship in Bengal. It was built in 1599. When we arrived, we found a grand fête going on in honour of a certain St. Catherine, who had performed some wonderful

* The Bengal Government kindly contributed, as a grant-in-aid to this building, the sum of £1500.

† Professor in the Free Church College, Calcutta.

miracle in behalf of the church. Some rockets were shooting high into the air; and the kind old padre invited us to come into his verandah, that we might have a better view of what he doubtless thought was a very grand display.

The little church seemed in good preservation, and was filled with kneeling worshippers and robed priests, with candles, and incense, and tinsel, and all the usual paraphernalia. This sort of worship always appears to me doubly saddening in India; it seems so perilous in an idolatrous land.

The Mission at Chinsura is now under the care of the Rev. Prosunno K. Chatterjee, with Mr. Kedernath De as head-master of the Institution; Mahanād is under another Bengali pastor, the Rev. J. Bhattacharjya,—names which must be familiar to many of my readers.

I visited Mahanād two or three times, and always with new pleasure. I do not know anything I enjoyed more than a day spent in that pleasant Mission-house, so simply yet so neatly fitted, in the midst of its interesting and, I might almost say, model Christian family-circle.

I delight to dwell on all these memories, and to recall the kind and warm-hearted native Christian families connected with the Mission who are scattered through Bengal; though their touching farewells, and the beautiful tokens of regard they presented us with as we were leaving, are things, perhaps, not to speak of so much as to remember always.

One of the most gladdening thoughts to me, as I look back, is this,—that there are so many Bengali Christians who already are occupying positions of respectability and influence in society. Some are in Government service; others are in the Church's service; while there are others who have struck out a line of independent action for themselves. Foremost among these last is my dear and valued friend, Mr. Mookerjee, a merchant of position and standing in Calcutta, whose kindness to me personally, and active help in many schemes which I had set my heart upon, I shall never forget.

I regret very much that it is impossible to speak of the delightful visits we paid when *en route* for home after our final adieu to Calcutta. For example, Madras, where we spent a week of the deepest interest and enjoyment. Nothing could be more delightful than the female schools there, which have been carried to a very high point of excellence, and which interested me particularly; the noble Institution, also; and, indeed, all the work conducted by Mr. Miller, Mr. Stevenson, and their able associates. The happy intercourse, I would add, with many kind friends, both European and native, and the kindness received,—these live very fresh in our memories. From Madras we proceeded by railway to Poona, and thence to Bombay. In both places we saw many dear old friends, and revived many old associations. Then we saw the Rural Mission, under our admirable friend, Mr. Narayan Sheshadri, whose visit to this country and America will long be warmly remembered by multitudes.

Each and all of these visits it would be a delight to dwell on; but I am compelled to stop. If I have succeeded, in any degree, in awakening a deeper interest in that great Eastern land, especially in the sorrowful inmates of its zenanas, I shall feel, with deep gratitude to God, that my object in writing these simple sketches has been fully gained.

NOTES.

CONDITION OF WOMEN IN INDIA.

I MAY still add one testimony to what has been said on this deeply important subject.

A very interesting collection of female compositions in Bengali prose and verse was published in 1872 by the Hare Prize Fund in Calcutta. The collection extends to 267 pages. Many of the pieces are said to be most creditable to the writers. One of them has seemed to me most touching. The little poem may be called "The Lady and the Dove." Dr. M. rendered it into English verse, and has published the original with a translation in the *Indian Antiquary*. I subjoin a few of the concluding verses. The lady sees her pet bird drooping, and asks what is the matter; tells the dove of its many blessings; then suddenly says, "Oh, I see it is *captivity* that saddens you!" Then she compares the dove's captivity with her own, and dwells on the overwhelming miseries of woman's lot in India.

"Words ungentle vex not thee,
Nor great load of slavery;
Every want at once supplied,—
Why art thou not satisfied?

"But the heart will die, before
Half our trials it count o'er;
Oh were I a dove, like thee,
Then, methinks, I'd blessed be!

"Shall I speak to God on high?
But I tremble as I try!

We are not THY daughters, sure,
Who must woes like these endure!

"All untrained in truth, the soul—
Swayed alone by harsh control—
On, like purchased slaves, we go:
Ah! dost THOU then mean it so?

"Still, although the heart is broken,
Must the pang remain unspoken.
Veil the face, and hide the woe!—
Ah! dost THOU then mean it so?

"Wretched custom's helpless slaves—
Whelmed in superstition's waves—
Thus our precious life doth go:
Ah! dost THOU then mean it so?"

GOVERNMENT EDUCATION IN INDIA.

A VERY earnest discussion is going on in India at present as to the moral results of Government education. It is all but universally admitted that, in the higher schools and colleges, these have been exceedingly unsatisfactory. Many contend that the instructed Hindu is less moral than the uninstructed. A formal petition has been sent in to the Bengal Government by the inhabitants of Dacca, that morality and religion be introduced into the system of Government education.

Waving, however, all other questions as to this proposal, there is the preliminary difficulty, that Government has repeatedly pledged itself to neutrality in the matter of religion.

The simplest solution of the problem is for Government to withdraw from all direct connection with higher English education, and encourage this by a well-considered system of grants-in-aid.

The Universities would maintain their present standard of examination, so that the value of their degrees would remain precisely as it is.

Nor would the extent of education be diminished. Educated natives would set up schools in abundance. Colleges too would soon arise, which they would take a pride in maintaining. And it is certain that morality, at all events, and probably the great truths of Theism, would be taught in such seminaries to a much greater extent than they are taught at present in Government institutions; so that the quality of the training would be decidedly improved.

There could not be a better time to press for this change than when India is under a ruler so thoughtful and deeply conscientious as Lord Northbrook. His Lordship would recognize all the gravity of the question, and would not shirk it.

Government should still carry on professional or technical education,—colleges of medicine, law, and engineering.

Nor should its primary schools be given up. They teach the mere elements of education, and have never been stated to interfere with the religious belief or the moral character of the pupils.—*Edit.*